Noteworthy Recommendations for
Stick-to-it-iveness Succeeds

"Foster Furman has a warm and wonderful way of communicating the importance of teamwork, diligence, and above all, success."—*Franklin Graham, President, Samaritan's Purse, Boone North Carolina*

"Foster Furman is a noteworthy Christian businessman. For several generations, his family has contributed to the quality of life in Pennsylvania, His story sets a fine example for today's youth with its credo of 'stick-to-it-iveness.' Readers will be amply rewarded by investing their time in this saga of success." —*Dick Thornburgh, former Governor of Pennsylvania, former U.S. Attorney General*

"F. Foster Furman, in his book *Stick-to-it-iveness Succeeds*, clearly shows how faith in God is the cornerstone to having a joyful, productive life. Whether in a profit-making company, such as Furman Foods, or a not-for-profit organization such as MAP International, the same qualities—commitment, hard work, unwavering beliefs, and 'stick-to-it-iveness'—are essential qualities for success.

"MAP International, a Christian global health and relief organization, is proud to count Furman Foods and F. Foster Furman among our faithful partners. Stick-to-it-iveness DOES lead to success!"—*Larry E. Dixon, President, MAP International, Brunswick, Georgia*

"In our confused society today with its lack of integrity and morality at high levels, it is refreshing to read the life story of a dedicated man who emphasized strict adherence to the highest of principles in the business community as well as in his personal world.

"F. Foster Furman's story reads like a Horatio Alger story of yesterday. Faith, commitment, energy, and discipline each has its own reward, but in the growth of Furman Foods, Inc., one can see how each came together to form a very unique story in modern business.

"This story is a good story, written from the heart by a man who was at the heart of the entire process. It makes for good reading, conveying the disciplined virtues so needed in today's marketplace."—*Donald R. Hubbard, Former Senior Pastor, Boca Raton Community Church*

STICK-TO-IT-IVENESS
SUCCEEDS

F. FOSTER FURMAN

R.R. 2, Box 480
NORTHUMBERLAND, PA 17857
PHONE (717) 473-8008
FAX (717) 473-7367

AUTHOR OF
STICK-TO-IT-IVENESS SUCCEEDS

OCTOBER 1994

Seventy-three years ago, at age 11, Foster Furman carried wood into the kitchen to can the first 360 glass jars of tomatoes on the cook stove. The annual pack today is over 168 million cans.

Foster was C.E.O. of Furman Cannery from 1944 to 1976. During those 32 years, annual sales grew from $200,000 to $10,500,000.

In 1932, he attended Philadelphia College of Bible, and in 1933, attended evening classes at Susquehanna University.

He has been an active Gideon for over 40 years, serving as state chaplain and other state offices. He teaches Sunday school lessons over WKOK radio. For many years, he served on the Council of Trinity Lutheran Church and also taught Sunday school for many years.

Foster has been active in legislative affairs on local, state, and national levels. In 1988, he received the special achievement award from the Central Susquehanna Valley Chamber of Commerce. In 1993, he received the Alumni Award of the Year for outstanding service to the alumni, church and community from the Northumberland High School Alumni Association. In 1994, he received the Life Achievement Award from Philadelphia College of Bible.

He has been married to Hazel Epler for 58 years. They have four children, 13 grandchildren, and four great grandchildren.

His favorite scripture verse is Psalm 127:1, "Except the Lord build the house, they labor in vain that build it. Except the Lord keep the city, the watchman wakes in vain." Foster states that any success he may have achieved, he wants credited to the blessing of the Lord.

STICK-TO-IT-IVENESS SUCCEEDS

By F. FOSTER FURMAN

President of Furman Canning Company 1944–1976

Foster Furman
psdn 37 3-5

STICK-TO-IT-IVENESS SUCCEEDS

By F. FOSTER FURMAN

Scripture taken from the HOLY BIBLE, NEW INTERNA-
TIONAL VERSION. Copyright ©1973, 1978, 1984 by
International Bible Society. Used by permission of Zon-
dervan Publishing House.

Cover: J.W. and George Orlando Furman with wagon
loads for curb market in Shamokin; 1911.
Cover photography by David VanderVeen Photography
of Milwaukee, Wisconsin.

ISBN: 0–89957–076–3

The author would like to hear your comments.
Please write to:
F. Foster Furman
RR. 2, Box 480
Northumberland, PA 17857-0502

Printed in the United States of America

To FATHER and MOTHER

John Wesley Furman   **Emma Eister Furman**

Who took us to Church and Sunday School, instead
of sending us.

TABLE OF CONTENTS

PREFACE

Every businessman starts with a dream. A hard-working family called the Furman family started with a dream and principles that honored God.

In today's world, there is the idea that principles must be compromised, that you cannot tell the truth and succeed.

This book demonstrates that you can tell the truth, you can honor God, and the success that results will amaze you. There is an added advantage with this kind of success. It has a reward that is eternal. It has the satisfaction that you have reached the top of the ladder without having defrauded others. This is success that allows you to sleep in peace, and when you take your final sleep, the waking does not provide a shock, but a reward.

This is the conclusion that you will come to as you read this amazing story of a farm boy who climbed the ladder of success without kicking others off the ladder. The title of the book, *STICK-TO-IT-IVENESS SUCCEEDS*, indeed describes part of the story. The other side of the story is perseverance in that which has eternal values.

As you read this amazing book, you may begin to wonder if you have anything eternal to stick to. May it create a desire in your heart to stick to something that you do not have of yourself, but that Jesus Christ only can give—and that is eternal salvation.

I recommend this book to anyone who craves for such a success.

Dr. Spiros Zodhiates
President, AMG International
Chattanooga, Tennessee

ACKNOWLEDGEMENTS

Special thanks to Joan Zodhiates who took time out of her busy schedule to edit this book. Also special thanks to Dr. Spiros Zodhiates for his help and wise council. Thanks to Marietta Swartz for typing and editing; to Heather and Elisabeth Furman for proofreading. Without Jimmy Kohl's encouragements, I may not have spent parts of four years to write this history of our business instead of hunting and fishing. I am also indebted to each of my family and business associates for giving me very valuable information. Almost everyone mentioned in this book supplied vital information.

Special thanks to the Board members of Furman Foods, Inc. whose support and financial help made this book possible.

I also thank the Lord for good health at the age of eighty-three, making it possible for me to complete this book.

I owe a special thanks to the following people who are examples of success that God gives to those who have dedicated their lives to Him and who also have contributed to this book: Dr. Sherril Babb, Chapter 21; Dr. Frank Severn, Chapter 22; Attorney Robert Diehl, Chapter 23; and Mr. Bill Glass, Chapter 24.

INTRODUCTION
STICK-TO-IT-IVENESS SUCCEEDS
If at First You Don't Succeed, Try, TRY AGAIN.

The above fits J. W. Furman. In 1949, at the age of seventy-three, he completed a book named *STICK-TO-IT-IVE-NESS* that describes some of the many hardships Father and Mother faced. I would venture to say that principle may describe the whole family. J. W. Furman must have inherited the character that led John Firmin to leave England in 1630 to come to Massachusetts with Governor John Winthrop.

We hope this book will show how our family worked together, and trust it may encourage other families faced with difficulties to work together until they succeed.

Today, 1993, the Board consists of seven members of the third generation and one member of the fourth generation. There are three of the second generation (all over seventy) who act as consultants, and there are eight more family members who work in the business. Of course, we have our differences, but most conflicts are resolved when we read the Bible and pray, including before board meetings.

Our family goal was to pay off the mortgage. What a thrill to watch our business grow from 360 glass jars of tomatoes, prepared on the cook stove in our kitchen, to an annual volume of 140 million cans! Today, Furman Foods, Inc. is the largest tomato packer east of Bowling Green, Ohio, and the second largest vegetable cannery in the state of Pennsylvania. Before the Depression in 1928, even if we had sold everything, including our furniture and dishes, we could not have paid even half of our bills. It is amazing how the Lord prospered us, so that today, Furman Foods, Inc. carries a two-to-one current financial ratio. We are told it is one of the best in the entire food processing industry.

It is truly satisfying to see a modern factory on a farm that was said to be so poor when we moved here in 1918, that if a crow was planning to fly over it, he'd better carry his lunch; or that a billy goat would starve there overnight. We hope this book may encourage some hard driving business person to realize that they can be successful, and at the same time, enjoy life as they climb to the top.

We also hope it will encourage some young people who dream of owning their own businesses. May they realize the best way to enjoy life and climb to the top is to run their business according to the rules in the Bible.

Chapter 1
The Way of a Man with a Maid

The heights by great men reached and kept
Were not attained by sudden flight,
But they while their companions slept
Were toiling upward in the night.
—Henry W. Longfellow

The fascinating story of John Wesley Furman and Emma Eister Furman started in the beautiful rolling hills of central Pennsylvania. It began in Stonington, on Route 61 about six miles east of Sunbury, on the road to Shamokin. As the Dutchmen would say, it was about eight fields east of Sunbury. It is in the rich farming district of the Susquehanna Valley. This area was an ideal place to grow vegetables for the fresh market because it was close to both Sunbury and Shamokin.

Sunbury is the town where Thomas Edison installed the first electric lighting system. That generator is in a museum in Fort Myers, Florida.

You might recognize Shamokin as being on the western edge of Pennsylvania's famous hard coal fields. In 1900, when our story begins, Shamokin was one of the fastest growing and richest parts of the state. COAL WAS KING. Anyone who could produce quality fresh vegetables early in the summer had a very lucrative market in Shamokin. The secret to success was to be the first to have fresh vegetables. Remember, these were the days before rapid transportation or refrigeration.

Transportation, communication, travel, sports, finances, and many other things have changed. However, one thing that has not changed is that as young men and women reach their teens and twenties, many of them begin to look for someone with whom they can share their dreams, ambitions, and their lives. The hero and heroine of our story were no different. Mother and Father lived in the same rural community and often went to the same church and Sunday school. In their small community, everyone knew everyone else. Often the whole family was well acquainted with all the families in the community. Thus, they knew a great deal about each other before they started dating.

These were the days before cars and hard surfaced roads. Someone describing the roads said you actually went through them instead of riding on top of them. Sometimes the mud was six to ten inches deep. However, I remember Father telling of groups of young people walking three to five miles to attend a festival or a box social. These box socials were sponsored by a local organization and used for fund raising. The money paid for the box went to the sponsoring organization. For a box social, each girl would fix an attractive snack in a box. At the social, there would be an auction. The highest bidder would get to eat the snack, spend the evening with the girl, and see her home. Usually, the girls would advise their boyfriends on which box to bid. If more than one person knew to whom a box belonged, or the girl was very attractive, the bidding would be rather brisk. If a wealthier young man saw the boyfriend of an attractive girl bidding on a particular box, he would sometimes run the price up so high that her boyfriend could not afford to buy it! To understand this, you must realize that the average wage was less than ten cents per hour.

The distance from Father's home to Mother's home was about a mile across the fields or about two miles by road.

2

Since the main mode of transportation was what one called "shanks mare" (walking), that was the way Father usually went to see Mother. On special occasions, such as a meeting, he would go to see her by horse and buggy. However, getting the horse groomed, putting on the harness, and hitching the horse to the buggy took thirty to forty minutes. In fact, it took longer to get the horse ready and drive over than to merely walk across the fields. When he returned home, he didn't just turn the ignition off. He had to unhitch the horse, water it, take off the harness, and tie the horse in the stall.

In June of 1990, my wife, Hazel; my sister, Mary; my brother, Andrew; and a first cousin, Frank Eister, visited the homestead where Mother lived before she married Father. It was a thrill to visit the farm and visualize Father walking across the fields to see Mother.

For several years, they planned for the future. At the time, most jobs paid ten to twelve cents an hour. Finally, J. W. (my father) found a good paying job at fifteen cents an hour. It was at a powder mill—a very dangerous job—several men had recently been killed in an explosion. Soon after they were married, having saved the huge sum of $300, he quit. (Today, that would be equivalent to about $18,000, but still only a fraction of what was needed to start vegetable farming.)

Father and Mother were to be married December 4, 1900, in St. Luke's Lutheran Church in Sunbury. On that rainy Tuesday evening, Father almost had a tragedy. When moving a five dollar gold piece from one pocket to another, he dropped it on the ground. The five dollars was for the minister, and in today's terms, it represented about $300. (Any ministers reading this probably wish for the good old days.) There were no street lights, cigar lighters, or flash lights. However, because he was a heavy smoker, he had plenty of matches. This was before the invention of safety matches. They were the old-fashioned wooden matches called barn burners because barns were actually set on fire when mice or rats would find one and gnaw on it. The barn burners made a lot more light than safety matches. Using the barn burner, it took Father about ten minutes to find the five dollar gold piece which almost made him late for his wedding.

After a very plain ceremony, Father took the midnight train home and went to work on Wednesday, as usual, and Mother stayed with her older sister in Sunbury. His fellow employees at the powder mill did not know anything about the wedding until they read the Thursday paper. They told Father that, if they had known he was going to get married, they would have helped him with his work on Wednesday so he could get off work early. Saturday night when he went to his wife's home, the community gave them a great serenade, or a belling as it was called. As the custom was, he passed out cigars. At Christmas time, there was a wedding dinner in their honor at her mother's home. As Father was passing out cigars, Mother said, "Wes, please do not smoke." Father said, "All right." He never smoked again even though he lived to be ninety-seven years old. He often remarked that the money he saved by not smoking or drinking made it possible to start the business which today has gross sales of almost fifty million dollars annually.

The newlyweds were now faced with the important decision—where should they go to keep house? Father was the oldest of six children, and Mother was the youngest of ten. About ten years earlier, her father, a very prosperous farmer, had built a nice new house but had only lived about five years to enjoy it. Mother's brothers and sisters wanted them to move in with her mother and a brother to help run the farm. Yet, Mother and Father were afraid of too many bosses. A young couple moving in with in-laws often causes trouble. Her mother said, "Let them take their own way. If they do not make a go of it, they can blame no one but themselves." That was good advice then and still is today.

In the neighborhood was an abandoned farm. Uninhabited for years, it was overgrown with weeds. Both the house and barn were in deplorable condition. Today, most couples would be unwilling to move into the rat infested house. They would probably bulldoze it down and build a new home. Since Mother and Father did not want to pay on a mortgage for twenty years, they decided to repair the house. Many young people today want to start out in as nice a home as their mother and father have after working for twenty or thirty years. Young people could save themselves and their children a lot of financial trouble by buying or building a home they can pay for in a reasonable number of years. Mother's relatives could not understand why she was willing to leave a new house to move into a place where it was unfit to live.

The farm was mostly shale and was well drained. This was ideal for growing "truck crops" as they were called in those days. The origin of the word "truck crops" is uncertain because trucks as we know them did not exist. Today, we would call it "market gardening" or "vegetable farming." The gentle slope of the land toward the east helped to produce early vegetables, and the earliest vegetables brought the best prices. It was also important to find customers early in the season, so that one would have customers later in the summer when the vegetables were plentiful.

The farm contained twenty-one acres and cost $800. Father was able to borrow all of the money he needed with the provision that he only had to pay interest for a few years until the man wanted his money back. While Father was trying to borrow money, something happened that is worth noting. A particular bank he had asked for a loan had told him to come back later. Father was confident that the bank would approve the loan. However, when he returned to get the money, the banker asked, "Was your father's name so and so?" Father said, "Yes." "Was your father ever sold out by the sheriff?" he was asked. Father replied, "Yes, that is true." The banker then said, "I am sorry, but we cannot loan you the money."

For a number of years, my grandfather had been a successful truck farmer. When he had paid off 75 percent of the mortgage, he started drinking. Shamokin was then a boom town because of the coal and had many restaurants and hotels. On days that they had a curb market, the owners would come to the stands and order their produce to be delivered as soon as market hours were over. When Grandfather delivered the vegetables, they would pay him at the bar. He started taking so much of his pay in drink that there was not any money left to pay on the mortgage. Even though he only owed 25 percent of the mortgage, he lost his farm at a sheriff's sale.

Fathers, please take note! Your actions may have a disastrous effect on your children. We thank the Lord that my grandfather later came to the Lord, and God delivered him from his alcoholism. I was sixteen when my grandfather passed away, and I never saw him drink alcohol. Unfortunately, one of my father's brothers followed in my grandfather's footsteps but was never delivered from alcohol. This made a deep impression on my father, for he had always said that, if you never started drinking, you would never have to stop. It also made a deep impression on me. As a sales manager for many years, I attended cocktail parties, but I decided that if I never started drinking, I would never have any trouble stopping.

In fact, at a class reunion, while I was drinking a soda, my wife asked if other people could tell what I was drinking. I said, "No." She said, "To avoid any appearance of evil, perhaps you should not even take a glass in your hand." I thought that was good advice, so when attending cocktail parties, I do not even take a glass of water as I do not think people know if it is water or alcohol.

The Touch of the Master's Hand

'Twas battered and scarred, and the auctioneer
Thought it scarcely worth his while
To waste much time on the old violin
But he held it up with a smile.
"What am I bid, good folks?" he cried,
"Who'll start the bid for me?
A dollar, a dollar—now two, only two—
Two dollars, and who'll make it three?"

"Three dollars once, three dollars twice,
Going for three"—but no!
From the room far back, a gray-haired man
Came forward and picked up the bow;
Then wiping the dust from the old violin,
And tightening up all the strings,
He played a melody pure and sweet,
As sweet as the angels sing.

The music ceased, and the auctioneer,
With a voice that was quiet and low,
Said, "What am I bid for the old violin?"
As he held it up with a bow.
"A thousand dollars—and who'll make it two?
Two thousand—and who'll make it three?
Three thousand once and three thousand twice—
And going and gone!" said he.
The people cheered, but some of them cried,
"We do not quite understand.
What changed its worth?" The man replied,
"THE TOUCH OF THE MASTER'S HAND."
And many a man with life out of tune,
And battered and torn with sin,
Is auctioned cheap to a thoughtless crowd,
Much like the old violin.
A "mess of pottage," a glass of wine,

A game—and he travels on.
He's going once, and going twice,
He's going—and almost gone.

But the Master comes and the foolish crowd,
Never can quite understand,
The worth of the soul and the change that's wrought,
By the touch of the Master's hand.
                                    —Myra Brooks Welch

Chapter 2 tells of the tremendous success of a courageous young couple. About all they had was their love for each other and their faith in God. However, God blessed them as they overcame problems that many considered to be insurmountable.

Chapter 2
Starting a Business with
Three Hundred Dollars

Before Mother and Father could move into the old house, they had to put a new roof on it. The floor of the back porch was rotted so badly that they had to put boards down so they could use the back door. The doors and walls were full of rat holes, and the sides were bulging. The neighbors said it could not be repaired, and that they'd better tear it down. Father decided that, by using long steel rods with threads on the end, the sides could be pulled in to straighten it. Contrary to some builders, it did work. The rod reached all the way through the house. As they turned the nuts on both ends, it pulled it together until the walls were straight. That was considered a great accomplishment in those days. Ninety years later, it is still providing a good home. In the summer of 1990, our family passed by it and remarked how nice it looked.

What a dismal place to take a bride who was used to living in a nice new house! It must have been true love. Money has its place, but starting under those adverse financial conditions may have improved the marriage instead of hindering it. Our affluent society has produced more divorces than any other period in time. Mother and Father were always true to their marriage vows. Because of faith in God and commitment

9

to each other, their marriage lasted seventy-one years and eight months. As the marriage vows say, "as long as we both shall live." Father was twenty-four and Mother was nineteen when they were married. The Lord blessed them with seven children—three girls and four boys.

When they began housekeeping, Father owned a good horse and buggy. Mother had received a pedal sewing machine as a wedding gift from home, a cow, and a fifty-pound can of lard. This was before Crisco, and they knew nothing about cholesterol; however, because they did a lot of manual labor, they burned up the fat by hard work.

Father had saved the amazing sum of $300. With it, he had to repair the house and buy furniture, vegetable seed, farming machinery, fertilizer, another cow, another horse, and a wagon to take the produce to market. They also needed money to live on until they started getting cash for vegetables they took to market. It would be June or July before they had any cash income.

Many people have heard the story that George Washington was so strong he could throw a silver dollar across the Potomac River at Washington. They seem to think it is impossible. Of course, it was much easier when George Washington lived, as a dollar went farther in those days.

Father said, "Our $300 melted away like dew in the June sun." How could they buy furniture, dishes, etc., and start a vegetable farming business with those meager finances? Who would even consider loaning them money with that small amount of capital? They bought six chairs, a sink, and a bedroom suite. The sink was a "dry sink" because those were the days before running water. It was made of zinc and provided a place to wash the dishes. There was a cupboard below and a sink above. This unit was all one piece, and at an antique sale today, it would probably bring about $1,200. The dry sink is currently in the home of their grandson, Kent Kohl. The zinc was pitted badly and has since been replaced with copper.

Father also "got a rare bargain" when he paid $1.65 for a wagon that was small but in good condition.

Father attributes their success to the Lord, and I quote from his book *STICK-TO-IT-IVENESS*, "When we started housekeeping, we started family worship. We read the Bible and had prayer every morning. We did not have much, but we did thank the Lord for what we did have. It helped us in years afterward."

It was March when they finally moved into their newly repaired house. That was just in time to start growing vegetables. Much of the farm was quite run down, but some parts were fertile. That is where they began to sow their seeds. Mother was afraid they would have to stoop all day sowing seed by hand, so she was glad when he got a little wooden wheel with a six inch drum that had adjustable holes in it. That simple machine reduced a full day of work to two hours.

Father had learned about vegetable farming while working in New York State. In those days, farmers only used 200 or 300 pounds of fertilizer per acre. They ridiculed Father for applying 2,000 pounds per acre, but when they saw the crops he grew, they stopped laughing and started using more fertilizer.

The hours were rigorous for a vegetable farmer. Father and Mother had to get up at daylight (about four o'clock) on Monday morning to get the vegetables ready for Tuesday's market. On Tuesday, Father would get up at two o'clock in the morning, feed the horses, eat a bite, and leave for Shamokin at three. After driving eleven miles, he would arrive at the curb market around 5:30 or 6:00. They were called curb markets because the farmers backed their vehicles up to the curb to display their produce on orange crates. Today, we would probably call it a sidewalk sale. They went to market three times a week and would get $2.50 to $10.00 per trip for their efforts.

Needless to say, Father did not need to take sleeping pills to go to sleep. However, there were no cars on the road, so when he started home, he could often get a little nap as the horses knew the way home. Horses had their advantages. However, none of us wants to go back to the horse and buggy days.

Let me tell you a true story about the advantages of going to see your girlfriend by horse and buggy instead of automobile. The friend who told me this said it happened about the year I was born, 1911. For several months, he was going to see a girl regularly who lived along the road that is now Route 147. He broke up with her and started going with another girl in the same community. He left the new girl's house about midnight. Since this was before there were any cars, and the horse knew the way home, he soon went to sleep. Now, if a driver of a car goes to sleep, they end up in the hospital. My friend woke at daylight and was embarrassed to find that the horse had taken him to his first girl friend's house. He said, "I got out of there in a hurry!"

Father joked that he invented the eight-hour day long before there were labor unions. Yes, eight hours before lunch, and eight hours after lunch.

Father was always looking for ways to improve anything at which he worked. He thought there must be a better way to do things. He took a correspondence course from Penn State on the use of fertilizer. Other farmers made fun of his "farming from a book." He realized that, to get the best prices, he had to harvest his produce before the others. Consequently, he decided to build a greenhouse in order to start the plants early. That way, he was several weeks ahead of everyone else. He got the customers first and kept them happy with the quality. He also discovered that if you gave them quality, they would pay a little more than the market price.

They started lettuce in the greenhouse. He put 200 pounds of fertilizer on one-tenth of an acre, though it cost him about six dollars, and he planted cucumbers between the rows. The neighbors thought he was crazy, but everyone was surprised that he got $65 worth of lettuce and $40 worth of cucumbers from that little patch. He needed a bigger greenhouse, so he built it himself, including calculating the amount of heat needed and doing the plumbing himself.

Father had borrowed the $800 to buy the farm from a man who only asked that he pay the interest. After three years, the man wanted his money. Every penny Father had made was reinvested in things that would take several years before they would produce significant income. It was also difficult for an outsider to see how installing an irrigation system and building a greenhouse would increase the opportunity to realize sizable profits later.

Father went to a rich man to borrow the money. The rich man came and looked over the farm and said he wouldn't put one cent into it. This rich man who refused to loan him the money invested his life's savings into something that was supposed to have above average income. He lost everything he had. His relatives had to keep him until he died so he would not go to the poorhouse.

Next, they went to a lady who had money to loan, and she promised them the money. Just as they were getting the papers ready, she heard that his father was sold out by the sheriff, and she backed out of the deal. When they had bought the farm shortly after their marriage, a bank had refused them money for the same reason. I would like to repeat that this problem was caused by alcohol. Parents, I hope you can see and realize that your reputation has a great effect on your children.

Father finally found a good Christian man that trusted him and loaned him the money. In 1904, when he was doing well financially, Father had a boil that turned into blood poison. The doctor told him that he had waited too long to come to him, and said he'd probably lose his leg, but he'd do the best he could. Father did not lose his leg, but he was sick for four weeks. He was sick in the spring just when they needed to plant the vegetables; they lost most of the summer's income.

Mother was carrying their first child, so she could not take care of the farm either. On August 5, the day after Father was twenty-nine, their first son, Andrew, was born. Up until this time, Father did not like babies. Of course, since this was his own son, it was different. He often took care of him in Sunday school and church as he seemed especially able to keep him quiet.

Because of Father's sickness, there was not enough money to buy the things they needed, so Father got a job in town during the winter months. He had to get up at 4:30 in the morning, eat breakfast, and walk two miles to the railroad station to get the six o'clock train, then walk one mile to start work at seven. He was on his feet all day, and he worked until six o'clock in the evening, walked a mile to the train station, rode another six miles, then walked two miles home, arriving there about 7:30. By the time he ate supper, it was time to go to bed. When spring came, he went back to the farm.

In those days, there was no radio, and they only had one time piece. Father tells of a night when their clock stopped. They tried to figure out the time by the almanac and the moon, but the moon was not shining, and they did not know how long they had slept. They thought it must be time to go to work, so father ate breakfast and left. As he was walking and got near the train station, he heard a train whistle. He was afraid he could not get there in time, and his heart sank. He did get to the station before the train left. However, it was the midnight train and not the six o'clock train. So he had a six hour wait. It is amusing now, but it wasn't funny to him then.

Father and Mother always believed that Sunday was the Lord's day. I quote from his book, "I remember on Saturday, I would come home at noon and work till midnight in the greenhouse, getting the ground ready and sowing the seeds. I would never work on Sunday. I felt the Lord was good to me and should be respected at least one day in seven. I know things did not always go the way I thought they should, but when things went wrong, and I would look back over them, I would see it was often my own fault. We kept up our family worship as it helped us through many difficulties."

When March first arrived, and it was time to start farming, he advised his employer several weeks ahead of time. The day he quit, they paid him cash. Father and Mother would not have any income for three months until they started selling vegetables. He carefully put the money in his pocket. He had only gone a few blocks when he could not find his money. He thought a pick-pocket had stolen it. It was Saturday noon, and he went home with a heavy heart. The money was never found, but because he had good credit, he was able to borrow a little money to take care of their expenses until the vegetables were ready to sell. Father always told us children, "If you owe a bill and cannot meet the payments on time, be sure to tell your creditor a few days ahead. Most creditors will respect you for it, and the next time you need money, they will loan it to you."

Business had been good; he had more demand for early vegetables than he could supply. He built the largest greenhouse in the area. The neighbors said it would collapse when they got their first snow storm. However, it lasted ten or fifteen years.

Any farmer will tell you that, almost every summer, there is a short period of time in which there is not enough rain. However, regular rainfall is much more essential for farming vegetables. Many of the crops have a brief critical stage when they need water the most. If they do not get water, the crop is drastically affected. Father was constantly looking for a way to insure a regular supply of vegetables. The most profitable time is when the competition does not have them.

Since a regular amount of water was necessary, Father looked into the possibility of irrigation. He was the first person in central Pennsylvania to install overhead irrigation. He soon found out what most people do; it takes a large and dependable supply of water for irrigation. He decided to drill a well. The neighbors said it was impossible to get enough water, but they found a plentiful supply at ninety-one feet.

While they were drilling, an old man came along and said, "That's right. You will need it, for it will not rain for six weeks." There is an old folk tale that says, "If it doesn't rain the day Mary goes over the mountain, it will not rain for six weeks." The date was July 15. It was already too dry for good vegetable crops. They laughed at the old man's tale, but he was right. It did not rain for six weeks! That was the driest year Father ever experienced.

They ran the irrigation pump twenty-four hours a day, except on Sundays, and the Lord blessed them with exceptionally good crops. They also got premium prices as no other farmer in the valley had nice vegetables. People came from all over the state to see the man-made rain. One old lady said, "I believe that is a sin. If the good Lord would have wanted it to rain, He would have made it rain. You have no business to interfere. The Lord may curse you for this."

Because of Father's success in using pumps to do what others said was impossible, a pump company offered him a good job traveling all over the country to figure pump specifications and to install pumps. Father turned that down, saying he would rather stay home with his family and grow vegetables than to make a lot of money and travel.

In the year 1908, my oldest sister, Mary, was born. Even though Father did not like children before their first child was born, he soon was a proud father of two.

Father and Mother were prospering and were able to pay off their debts. In the month of May, he took solid loads of lettuce to market. The one-horse wagon had to be replaced by a large two-horse spring wagon built to Father's specifications. Sometimes, Father had to hire two additional wagons to take the loads of beets, radishes, onions, and lettuce to market.

One particular incident stood out, and I will quote from his book, *STICK-TO-IT-IVENESS* (page 24), "We recall one man having a large hotel. He was a very fine man to deal with. He was a large man with a very fine personality. He always bought heavily and never paid me in the barroom or over the bar. One day it so happened that he did pay me in the barroom. The room was full of men drinking. He called me by name and asked 'Do you have your own farm?' I said, 'Yes, but it is not paid for yet.' He said, in a kind way, 'Keep going on the way you are and don't spend every cent you make. You will get your home paid for.' I never forgot that man or his advice. He did it in his barroom where there were a number of people spending their money just the way he said I should not."

Father says in his book, "We had worked very hard but saw success coming our way. It sure was gratifying and made us feel happy, and we sure thanked the Lord every day in our family worship and gave him the full day on Sunday."

To show what people of his day thought about Father's success, I would like to quote from Genealogical and Biographical Annals of Northumberland County, Pennsylvania, published in 1911.

John W. Furman, of Stonington, is senior member of the firm J. W. Furman & Brother, truck farmers, who occupy a leading place among the businessmen in their line in Northumberland County. Their place is known as the Hollis Dale Market Garden.

John W. Furman, born August 4, 1876, in Shamokin Township, was reared there and has followed agricultural pursuits all his life. In 1900, he located at Stonington, in Shamokin Township, where he bought the old Henry Klase farm, later owned by Peter Willour, this tract comprising twenty-one acres of very fertile truck land. He made vast improvements on the property since it came into his possession. In association with his brother, Freeman W. Furman, he does an extensive business in the raising and marketing of truck crops (vegetables), and the name of this firm stands for all that is progressive and up-to-date in that line. J. W. Furman and brother attend the Shamokin markets, where there is a steady demand for their garden stuff. Their work is carried on in the most intelligent manner. Their land is irrigated, they have erected a fine greenhouse, and everything about the place betokens the enterprise and advanced ideas of these young farmers who have won high standing among agriculturists in their section.

In the year 1911, the third child, Foster, was born. For ten years, Father had been going to market in the summertime. That meant three days a week he would get up at 2:00 a.m. in order to be at market at 6:00 a.m. Those hours were taking their toll. Not only were his hours of sleep very irregular but also the meals. Those two things were destroying his health. Father was thirty-five, and he and Mother decided they did not want to work those hours all of their lives. They decided to sell, move to another state, and see if they could be successful there.

I would like to summarize a few things before we follow their move to another state. Ten years earlier, my parents had moved to a log house in which it was not fit to live. The farm had not been worked for years. Ten years later, it was one of the most productive vegetable farms in the Susquehanna Valley.

This reminds me of a story. It was in the day before modern fabrics, and after wearing clothes a few times, they would need to be patched. Also, because there was not enough money to buy new ones, they would mend or patch them. Two ministers' wives were visiting. In those days, there was no radio or television, so they mended clothes while they talked. One wife said to the other, "I hear your church is growing, I wish our church would grow like yours." The other wife said, "Do you note I am patching my husband's trousers on the knees, but you are patching your husband's trousers on the seat?"

Father and Mother always realized they could not accomplish anything alone. However, working with God's help, they were accomplishing what seems like a miracle. Because theirs was a top quality vegetable farm, it was easily sold. When all the bills were paid, there was $3,000 and a faithful horse left, which confirmed their desire to move to another state.

Moving is sometimes a great venture. Also, it was a real challenge. Many exciting things happened to our hero and heroine. I will tell you about this unusual period in their lives in the next chapter.

Chapter 3
The Grass Isn't Greener
Years 1911–1918

How many times have you been discouraged and wanted to do something else? You look around you and see other people earning more money without working so hard. Perhaps you think you should try something else or change locations. The more you think about it, the more convinced you are that the "grass on the other side of the fence is greener."

Perhaps you are not familiar with this saying and do not really know what it means. I guess to really understand it, you must see a horse or cow in a beautiful green pasture. In fact, the pasture can be the very best. However, the cow will almost break her neck to get a few blades of grass that are on the other side of the fence. Before the days of electric fences, cows, just by sheer strength, broke the wooden rails or, if it was a wire fence, they could break the post by pushing hard enough. Of course, with electric fences, the cows stay away from the wire, or they get shocked. I've heard it is interesting to see a deer approach an electric fence for the first time. People who have seen it say the deer sticks out its nose to touch the fence. When it is shocked, it may jump as high as three to six feet like a coiled spring! You would laugh out loud; it goes straight up in the air.

Many people at middle age change jobs or locations in search of greener pastures. However, as you will learn as I tell of the life of my mother and father, the grass was not greener on the other side of the fence. My parents lost their life's savings and had to start over again. Sometimes, these changes are very traumatic and teach those involved some hard lessons.

The year was 1911; Father was thirty-five years old. He decided he did not want to continue to get up at two o'clock three mornings a week to go to market. He thought there must be an easier way to make a living. After visiting several states, he chose to move to Delaware. The address was Delmar, Delaware, but half of the town of Delmar is in Maryland. It is close to Salisbury, Maryland, the area called the eastern shore of Maryland. I wish he were here so I could ask him why he moved where he did. Father lived to be ninety-seven, and if I had it to do over again, I would have spent more time with both Father and Mother and asked them many questions about things with which they were acquainted. Dear reader, if your mother or father is living, spend time with them and ask them about how life was when they were your age. They will enjoy telling you, and you will get a blessing out of it. Once they are gone, it is too late to spend time with them.

One of the reasons Father may have moved to Delaware is because the winters are not nearly as cold there. Since it is between the Chesapeake Bay on the west and the Atlantic Ocean on the east, the water keeps the temperature mild. The average low temperature in the month of January is thirty-five degrees Fahrenheit. Their January temperature is about the same as our weather in March. Spring comes in March there, but not until April in Pennsylvania. The average temperature through winter and spring is about eleven degrees warmer than Pennsylvania. Since he wanted to grow vegetables for the fresh market, it was an opportunity to ship early vegetables into the Philadelphia and New York markets.

In 1911, it was a real problem to move. These were the days before trucks, and there were no moving vans. There were only two options. You could go by horse and covered wagon or by rail. Rail was a lot faster, taking about twelve to fourteen hours. The distance was about 240 miles. By horse and covered wagon, it would take six to eight days. Can you imagine what a trip of 240 miles with three small children would be like? The covered wagon offered some protection from the snow or rain, but very little from dust and temperatures extremes.

They decided to go by rail. Moving required a lot of planning and hard work. First, Father ordered a rail car into a rail siding at Sunbury. He needed the help of the neighbors to load several wagons and drive to the freight station. It took about three hours to get to the freight station and three hours to return. When they arrived in Delaware, they had a greater problem—to get things to their new home. However, since they did not have friends there to haul it, they paid the local livery man. Most towns had a hotel, and many of these hotels also had horses and wagons to rent. You could rent a horse and buggy and drive it yourself, much like the car rentals of today. However, to rent a team of horses and a wagon were different. They usually wanted you to hire their driver. I guess the big difference was you did not have to buy gas, but it was a lot more complicated than today. You couldn't just turn off the ignition and leave the team along the street. The horses had to be watered and fed. You would not dare to leave them unattended. In 1911, runaway teams killed people just the same as runaway cars do today. Sometimes it was difficult to get a team and driver on short notice.

Something else that complicated travel in those days was that there were no telephones, much less radio or television. The telegraph was the only source of fast communication. At that time, the telegraph office was located at the railroad station. It probably took more time and work to move the 240 miles in 1911 than it would take to move to the West coast today. Moving was a real challenge.

The state of Delaware was much different in 1911 than it is today. People in those days rarely traveled outside of the county in which they were born. Their knowledge of geography was very limited. At first, when Father told people he was from Pennsylvania, they would ask in amazement if it was in the United States. Delmar, Delaware, was also south of the Mason Dixon line. At first, it was a severe handicap; not only was Father a Yankee, but he was also a foreigner!

Since Father had been very successful in Pennsylvania, he thought he could make a success in Delaware. He was on the way to success, but, as I will tell you later, his bubble burst.

Father went to Delaware with about $3,000 in cash, a little furniture, and a faithful horse. You will have to understand a faithful horse was just as important in that day as a reliable truck is today. It is very difficult to say just what $3,000 in 1911 was worth in today's terms, but I believe it would represent more than $50,000.

When relocating, there are always extra expenses, and it usually costs more than a person figures. Too late, Father found that out. He soon needed more money. Since he was a Yankee and a stranger, it was hard to borrow money. They needed flour to make bread during the winter. In those days, families baked their own bread. To earn money, they grew lima beans in the summer and shelled them at night. The store paid them eight to ten cents per quart. That way, they were able to buy enough flour for the winter. It sure took a lot of lima beans to pay for the flour.

He soon found out that the first two farms he bought were poor and too far from town. The ground was almost pure white sand. We have a picture of us children playing in the sand. In fact, cars could not travel on it because it was so sandy. That type of soil is usually very poor, but he could grow nice watermelons. We have a picture of a watermelon standing on end beside my brother Andrew, who was six years old. The watermelon was almost as tall as Andrew.

In those days, only a few people with above average income could afford a car. To drive 240 miles to visit friends took more time and trouble than flying to Europe does today. It was quite an occasion to have two cars loaded with relatives and friends come to see us. We have a picture of these visitors eating watermelons. Since we did not have that many beds, my sister, Mary, remembers three people sleeping in the bed, while she slept at the foot. I remember all of the men sleeping in the barn. It was the early part of August, so there was no problem keeping warm. Even though I was only three years old, I can remember going out to the barn to call the men for breakfast.

On February 2, 1914, the fourth child, James George Furman, was born. February 2 is known as Groundhog Day in Pennsylvania. The old Dutch saying is that if the groundhog comes out of his winter home and sees his shadow, there will be six more weeks of cold weather. However, if it is a cloudy, blustery day, spring will come sooner. During the six years we were in Delaware, we made one trip back to Pennsylvania by train. Since I was only about two years old, I do not remember that trip. My older brother, Andrew, says that when they visited Grandma Eister (Mother was an Eister), he had his first taste of corn flakes. He thought they were the most delicious thing he had ever eaten. In 1913, prepared cereals were very rare. Also, Andrew and Mary remember going up the steep Reagan Street hill in Sunbury. Since the land in Delaware is as flat as a pancake, the hills were an amazing sight to the children. In fact, natives of Delaware who never traveled out of the state thought we were not being truthful when we told about hills like Blue Hill. Blue Hill is a cliff of about 400 feet opposite Sunbury overlooking the Susquehanna river.

In the spring of 1914, Father traded the two poor farms for a better farm closer to town. If he was to grow vegetables, it was very important to be close to a railroad station. Delmar, Delaware was on the main line railroad from Cape Charles, Virginia to Baltimore. In those days, there were stations in every town, even though they were only about ten miles apart.

The new farm Father bought had a good barn but no house. He nailed together a little shack to live in while he built the house. This he did by himself. When I visited Delaware recently, this house was still providing a nice home even though it was built seventy-five years ago by a farmer. Most houses in Delaware had no cellar but were set on several block pillars about a foot off the ground. Thus, snakes would often hide under the house. I remember a black snake about six feet long moving toward our house. Father got a garden rake to try to kill it. The snake climbed a tree and would lunge at father as he tried to hit it. The snake caused a lot of excitement as Father tried to kill it before it could get under the house.

Since a team of horses only traveled about four miles per hour, and the train was the only other means of transportation, you can understand why being close to a town was a great advantage. Another reason there were so many stations was because the steam engines needed wood to fire the boiler and water to run the steam engine. Some of the engines at that time only had enough wood and water to go about twenty miles. It was also the only way people could travel between towns. There was a train every several hours on the main line.

I mentioned there was a freight station every few miles. During the spring and summer months, there were commission merchants or buyers at each station. Each buyer bought fresh vegetables and fruits for several wholesale produce houses in Philadelphia, Baltimore, New York, Boston, etc. They would post what they were paying. If the produce arrived in good condition, they would pay the price agreed on, less their commission.

A train would start at Cape Charles on the eastern shore of Virginia in the morning (Cape Charles is about 115 miles south of Delmar) and pick up carloads of produce as it traveled north. The train would arrive in Delmar in the afternoon and then proceed to the cities, arriving about two o'clock in the morning.

Most of the commission merchants were honest men who bought fresh produce year after year. But there were a few crooks who would offer a little more money than the others. That way more people would sell to them. However, when the farmers got their pay a few days later, they were told the produce arrived in poor condition and had to be sold at a reduced price. When the commission merchant cheated enough farmers so that they would no longer sell to him, he would move to the next station and do the same thing there. Remember, there were few telephones, no radios, or televisions, and only one paper a week. News traveled very slowly, and a crooked man could hurt a lot of farmers before he was discovered. After Father was cheated several times, he decided to mark his produce. He also got on the train and arrived in Philadelphia while they were selling his produce. When he saw his produce sold, it brought the highest price. He identified himself and got witnesses to what happened. When he got back to Delmar, the commission merchant told him he had to sell his produce at a very low price. When Father confronted him with the facts, the merchant paid the full price. As you probably realize, every business or profession has its bad apples.

This also teaches a great lesson. Almost anytime an investment or business is paying a lot more than average, you better beware. We read of the thousands of people, particularly older folks, that someone had deceived and got their life's savings by promising them a high return on an investment. Beware of all schemes that try to make you believe you can get rich quickly. As my son, Joel, says, "If it seems too good to be true, it probably is."

On September 28, 1915, we got a telegram that Grandma Eister had passed away. Of course, Mother wanted to go back to Pennsylvania for the funeral. There were two problems. There was not enough money to buy the railroad tickets, and Father had blood poisoning. It was caused when a mule he was riding in from the field started to buck and threw my father off. Since the mule had a work harness on, Father's leg caught in the harness. Before he could free himself, he was almost trampled to death by the mule's rear feet. He got blood poisoning from those wounds. In 1915, they did not have the modern medicines which are available today. Many people lost their limbs and sometimes their lives from blood poisoning. The doctor told Mother she'd better stay home and care for the living rather then attend her mother's funeral. This was a very trying time for my mother.

As a boy of four or five, several incidents remain in my memory. There were no electric fences in those days. It was the job of my sister, Mary (who was about eight) and me to watch the cows and keep them out of the corn and vegetables. One day, there were about ten or fifteen calves (young cattle) that decided to run wherever they wanted to go. They did just that, and, even running as hard as we could, there was no way we could keep up with them. It seems funny now, and you probably would have laughed as you saw those young cows kick up their heels and run many times faster than we could. The young cows were having a good time, and I, as a five-year-old boy, was crying my heart out, running as hard as I could with a stick longer than I was tall. As I remember, we were not punished because the calves were beyond our ability to control. Sometimes, if we allowed the cows to get into the corn, we knew we would get a whipping. Taking care of the cows (or watching cows as it was called) gets very boring when you do it day after day, especially if you are five years old. One particular day, I was supposed to watch the cows for my Uncle Wilson (Freeman was his first name and Wilson his middle name) who lived next door. I was so tired of it, I went and told my uncle I would not watch his cows anymore. When my father heard about it, a couple of hits with a limber switch persuaded me I'd better change my mind.

Today, some so-called experts who really know very little about how to raise children would call that child abuse. However, a limber switch stings but does not do as much actual damage as the hand. I also remember that when I disobeyed Mother, sometimes she would make me get my own switch. We had plum trees that grew little shoots which made excellent switches.

I believe that God tells us how to discipline children in love. If you discipline your children in anger, you will get anger in return. Proverbs 13:24 says, "He who spares the rod hates his son, but he who loves him is careful to discipline him." Proverbs 23:14 says, "Do not withhold discipline from a child; if you punish him he will not die. Punish him with the rod and save his soul from death." If parents would follow the book of Proverbs today, it would eliminate most of the problems with drugs, sex, homosexuals, teenage suicides, etc. We tried to raise our four children by the Bible, and I can tell you it pays big dividends.

We went to the Melson Methodist Church, which was about three miles from our home. I remember one day we started out for a picnic. We went only a few blocks when it started to rain. We lived on Pepperbox Road, about one-half mile from State Line Road, which runs between Delaware and Maryland. When we got to the intersection, it started to pour. Father stopped the team and talked about turning around. We children just coaxed and coaxed him to go on to the picnic. We said, "Daddy, it's only dripping!" Today, you don't realize what a picnic meant to boys and girls then. It was the highlight of the year, almost as important as Christmas or Easter. We didn't even know what an amusement park was.

To me, a very interesting time was when the Gideon Zone 9 rally was held at Ocean City, Maryland, in 1971. I had the privilege to bring the Gideon message in Melson Methodist

Church. Before the message, I said, "This is indeed a great privilege. Sixty years ago, my father carried me into this church as a baby in his arms." When I spoke there, I was sixty-five, and a few of the people remembered my father. We had a nice visit after the church service.

I had the privilege of being asked to join The Gideons International in 1948. The Gideons place a million Bibles every nine days in 160 counties in over fifty languages. I have had the privilege of being asked to join many worthwhile organizations. Each of us only have twenty-four hours a day. I feel God would have us put Him first in our lives and then the family. After that, each person must decide how much time he will give to the church and other worthwhile organizations. The object of The Gideons is to win people to the Lord Jesus Christ through:

(a) the association of Christian business and professional men for service;

(b) personal testimony and personal work by individual Gideons;

(c) placing the Bible—God's Holy Word—or portions thereof, in hotels, hospitals, schools, institutions, and also through the distribution of the same for personal use.

After spending time with my family, the church, and the Gideons, I just do not have time for anything else. I have had the privilege of serving in many offices of the Gideons for forty-five years. The highest office I had was Chaplain for the Pennsylvania Gideons. If you, dear businessman, love the Lord, may I suggest you consider joining the Gideons. I believe the Lord will bless you through the Gideon ministry.

Father had a few good years. Vegetable prices were good, and he was reducing the debt he owed to the bank. He was growing watermelon, cantaloupe, strawberries, and sweet corn that was shipped into Philadelphia by rail. Father also grew tomatoes for the local cannery. In those days, there were tomato canneries about every twenty miles, as horse and wagon was the only means of transportation. In fact, Maryland and Delaware stood second in the nation in tomato production. Today, they stand seventh in the United States.

On October 1, 1916, Elnora Amelia, the fifth child, was born. Father had made enough money to pay off the mortgage. When he asked for a clear deed, the bank said some heirs would have to sign off. After several months and still no clear deed, he got an attorney. Upon investigation, he was told there were several heirs in England who refused to sign off. Finally, he got a friend from Pennsylvania to come to Delaware and check it out. He said, "Mr. Furman, you may never get a clear deed. My advice to you is to move out and start over again." The reason Father did not get his own attorney to search the deed before he bought it was because he bought the property from a state bank, and he thought they were honest. It taught him an important lesson—to always be sure any property you buy has a clear deed. It also cost him his life's savings.

Father decided the best thing to do was to move back to Pennsylvania. After selling the few things they had, he had $1,000, barely enough to pay transportation and a month's rent. Having lost almost everything was a very traumatic experience. It was as if his whole life fell apart, and he was a failure. Without any money, five small children to feed, and poor health, he was in a situation no one can understand unless they have experienced it personally.

At this point, many men turn to alcohol to drown their misery. Father, since he was a committed Christian and having seen what it did to his father, turned to God for help. In the next chapter, we will start the exciting story of going from $6,000 in debt to a business in which gross sales in 1989 were over $47,000,000.

With the help of God and hard work, it took twenty years before STICK-TO-IT-IVENESS SUCCEEDED.

Chapter 4
Starting Below the Bottom at Age 42
Years 1918–1928

Father and Mother arrived in Sunbury in the fall of 1917. What a problem—no money and five small children. In addition, Father was not in the best of health because of his financial problems. He was then forty-two and had to start all over again. Unless you have lost everything, you really do not know how traumatic it is.

This was during World War I and jobs were easy to find. Father's first job was on the railroad, but because of his weakened condition, he had to quit and take another job. He did not like living in town. He wanted to get back to the farm where the air was fresh and there was plenty of whole milk.

During the month of February, with snow on the ground, Father started looking for a farm. Without any money, he could not afford to buy a good farm. Also, these were war years, and there were not many farms for sale. It was a real problem to find one he could afford. Also, you must remember these were the days before cars. He rode the trolley from Sunbury to Northumberland and then walked over two miles to where the cannery is located today. Because he was walking, he could not visit several farms a day like you can when you have a car.

The farm had a good house and a large barn. The neighbors seemed to be prosperous. This farm had not been farmed for a number of years as the owner worked in town. Because of the snow, Father could not see how badly the farm was overgrown with weeds, briars and dewberry vines. Also, he could not tell that a lot of the land had winter springs on it. These winter springs kept many acres of the land so wet it could not be plowed early in the spring, unless the weather was unusually dry.

The price was to be $3,200 for 78.7 acres, a horse, and a cow. That is a lot of money when you do not have a penny and there are five children to feed. In today's terms, it would equal about $60,000. In those days, each township had its poor board to look after those who did not have enough to eat. Since the farm had not been farmed for years and was overgrown with briars, the neighbors were concerned that we would be a financial burden to the Township. They said that this farm was so poor that if a crow would fly over it, he'd better carry his lunch, and that a billy goat would starve on it overnight.

Mother had a maiden sister (Mary A. Eister) who had saved some money. She sympathized with my parents, so she bought the farm for them. The agreement was that they pay $10 down. The farm was deeded to her. Father was to pay $200 per year plus interest on the unpaid balance at 5 percent. If we defaulted on the $200 payment and the interest, we could be evicted. We thank the Lord for the compassion of Aunt Mary. She allowed us to live on the farm and farm it even though, for the next ten years, we did not pay any on the principle and were unable to even pay the interest some years. The agreement said if Father paid the sum of $1,600, then the farm was to be deeded to him and his wife, and Aunt Mary would take a mortgage for the balance.

We moved to this farm on March 18, 1918. Spring came early that year. Father remarked it was a fine day; the roads were dried off nicely. Remember, there were no paved roads. In the spring of the year, some sections were mud, ankle deep.

Since I was a lad of only seven, I do not remember much about World War I. All I remember was, on November 11, the church bells rang and the fire siren blew. We learned by phone that an armistice was signed. The phone was our only means of communication. I remember Father was farming on what we then called the four acres. Now that area is used as storage for tomato trucks, right behind where the scales are now located. My sister, Mary, and I ran about one-half mile to tell Father the wonderful news about peace. I still can see him stopping the team as we called to him at the top of our voices, "Peace has come!"

Soon after that, there were parades in Northumberland with bands, floats, and fire trucks. The soldiers from the local area marched as well as veterans of the Civil War. My, what a day of rejoicing and of welcoming our men home!

Since the fastest way home was by boat, it was many months before many of our men got home. My, how proud we were. Our men had fought a war to end all wars and had won. However, within twenty-three years, we would be in a war that was much larger and would last longer.

One nice November Sunday, some relatives came to visit us. We went for walk down over the lime kiln hill. It was a hot day, and we got thirsty. As a boy of seven, I drank some water from a creek that ran through the woods at the bottom of the lime kiln hill. Several days later, I got very sick for several weeks. Then it seemed that I was better and started back to school. About a week later, I became quite ill and was diagnosed with typhoid fever. They think I picked up the germ from that water in the creek. These were the days before antibiotics, and typhoid fever was a killer. The mortality rate was very high. Then Mother contracted the disease from me. Since typhoid fever was very contagious and often fatal, no one would care for the patients. We were moved to an isolated ward in Mary M. Packer Hospital on Fairmount Avenue in Sunbury. (In 1951, a new hospital named the Sunbury Community Hospital was built on North Eleventh Street in Sunbury.) My brother, James, got sick right after Christmas. After several weeks in the hospital, they decided his sickness was caused by too much candy at Christmas. In the same ward with James, who was only four years old, was a man by the name of Foster. James said, "That's a boy's name, it can't be your name!" I was seven years old and in the hospital. The ward had a lot of fun about Foster being a boy's name. James was in the hospital only about three weeks.

At that time, Father was working on the railroad. He started at six o'clock in the evening and worked until six o'clock in the morning. Since he walked about two miles to work and two miles home, it was about a fifteen-hour day. In the nine hours left, he took care of the livestock, ate, slept, and cut wood to keep warm. Remember, there were no chain saws. Trees were cut down with a crosscut which is a saw with a handle on each end for men to pull. Father said you got warm twice out of it—the first time by cutting it by hand and the second time from the stove. Those were long hours. If hard work killed people, surely Father was a prime candidate. However, he lived to be ninety-seven years old.

Part of this is published in his book *STICK-TO-IT-IVENESS*. A relative took the baby, Elnora, who was about two years old. That left Father with thirteen-year-old Andrew and ten-year-old Mary, who were a big help in getting meals and caring for the livestock, and four-year-old James.

Talk about dreary days—Father knew all about them. Both Mother and I were getting along fairly well in the hospital. One day, one of the nurses did not obey the doctor's order and gave the wrong medicine to me. I had a relapse, and they thought they would lose me.

Mother and I were in the same room. I was delirious, and I said to mother, "It would be so cold to be laid out in the cold,

cold ground." This really worried them. They thought it was a bad omen. However, a dedicated nurse took a special interest in me and, under her attentive care, I was nursed back to health.

There was no intensive care in those days and no intravenous feeding. Also, there was no hospital insurance. There were three members of the family in the hospital for a total of about 26 weeks. Can you imagine how far that would put you in debt? That was one of the reasons that, by the year 1928, even if we would have sold everything we owned, including our household furniture, we could not pay half our bills.

About the middle of February, Mother went home from the hospital. She was so thin and weak, she could not walk without help. I remember how lonely it was without Mother. About three nights a week, Father would walk the two miles to the trolley, ride it to Sunbury, and walk about eight blocks to the hospital. My, how I looked forward to his visits. By this time, I was allowed to eat a little ice cream. My, what a treat. The nights he could not come were very lonely. No one came to visit me except one of my cousins who lived in Sunbury. She came occasionally, and sometimes she would bring ice cream to me.

About the first of March, I remember Father coming for me in a horse and buggy. What a great day, after being bedfast for thirteen weeks! Father said I was so thin and weak I could not walk. He said he could easily carry me because I was nothing but skin and bone. Here I was, a lad of seven, who had to learn to walk all over again. I can still remember them putting the chairs in a row, so I could learn to walk.

Mother improved daily, and they wanted Elnora to come home. Her aunt had gotten so attached to her during those three months that she didn't want to give her up. Elnora was a lovely little girl and would capture any heart. Even though this aunt could afford to dress her better and give her a better education, etc., than Father and Mother could, they decided they wanted her home. The aunt brought her from Elysburg to Uncle John, who lived in Sunbury. It almost broke Father's heart when his little darling would just watch him but would not let him hold her. After watching him awhile, she suddenly ran to him and threw her arms around his neck. From then on, she just clung to him. She wouldn't even let anyone else put her coat on her. When she got home, Mother was so pale and thin that Elnora did not recognize her. This also was a heart-ache to Mother. For several days, our sister, Mary, who was ten, had to take care of her. However, in a few days, she warmed up to Mother.

That fall, before we got sick, Father had decided that, since he was close to Sunbury, he wanted to grow vegetables for the fresh market like he had when they first went housekeeping eighteen years before at Stonington. So he bought an old greenhouse. The glass, boiler, and pipe were worth moving. However, the wooden sash bars all had to be replaced. He got new ones made at the local mill.

Even though we were in the hospital, and Father worked twelve hours a day, somehow Father managed to build the greenhouse. When April came, he was ready to sow seed in the greenhouse. Even though our new home was only about fifteen miles from where Mother and Father began housekeeping, the neighbors had never heard of starting vegetables in a greenhouse. At first, they made fun of the idea. Father had experience and the knowledge of how to use manure and fertilizer and grew some very nice vegetables. The neighbors soon realized he knew what he was doing. Since we were only three miles from Northumberland, he could get there in about forty-five minutes with a team. This was much better than getting up at three o'clock in the morning, like he did at Stonington. Also, he sold directly to the stores instead of going to the curb market.

In order to have fields that he could plow early enough to grow early vegetables, he had to do a lot of draining. Mother said it seemed like he wanted to live in the ditch. I remember plowing the ditch as deep as we could with the walking plow. We dug the rest with a pick and shovel. That was real work especially when a lot of it was through hardpan with lots of stones as big or bigger than your head. Why did we do it by hand? The backhoe was not made until fifteen years later. In order to pay the interest on the farm, Father would work on neighboring farms or any place he could earn a little money.

In November, 1919, the sixth child, William, was born. As a lad of nine, I remember running to the ridge field (next to Ridge Road) to get Father to come to the house because Mother needed him. In those days, all children were born at home. Usually, a neighbor would come to be with the mother. Since the doctor came by horse and buggy, it took about an hour for the doctor to get there. Phone service was not very reliable, and, if the doctor was out on a call, it may take him several hours. Often the neighbor who was to take care of the mother for about a week had to deliver the baby.

DON'T QUIT

When things go wrong as they sometimes will,
When the road you're trudging seems all up hill.
When the funds are low, and the debts are high,
And you want to smile, but you have to sigh.
When care is pressing you down a bit,
Rest if you must, but don't quit.

Life is strange with its twists and turns,
As every one of us sometimes learns,
And many a failure turns about,
When we might have won had we stuck it out.
Don't give up though the pace is slow,
You may succeed with another blow.

Success is failure turned inside out,
The silver tint of the clouds of doubt,
And you never can tell how close you are.
It may be near when it seems so far.
So stick to the fight when you're hardest hit.
It's when things seem worse,
That you must not quit.

(Author unknown)

The next chapter tells of extreme trial and suffering. Yet God is faithful. Family worship is restored. God gives victory in spite of hardship.

Chapter 5
God Is Faithful

The Furman family experienced three major sicknesses in five years. In chapter four, I mentioned the first major sickness, typhoid fever, which produced major financial problems. If a family had no medical insurance, imagine what three major sicknesses would do to their financial situation! (Hospital insurance wasn't even available in the years 1919 to 1924.)

We were hit extremely hard by the flu epidemic that swept across America in the year 1921. All six children were sick at one time, and both Father and Mother got sick. My grandmother Furman came to take care of us. In those days, there was no central heating. I think all six of us were in beds in the living room because there was no heat upstairs. I remember Grandmother also got the flu and was in bed in the same room with us children. The medicine was green in color and tasted terrible. We laughed when we saw the face she would make when taking the medicine, so she would try to hide her face.

We had some very kind neighbors who came morning and evening to feed the chickens and pigs, and to feed and milk the cows. I remember the discouraging news when Bidelspach (a neighbor) told us all five of our pigs had died with hog cholera. That meant there would be no meat for us that winter. Also there would be no pigs to butcher to sell to pay the taxes.

During those dark days, the only meat we had to eat was what the neighbors sent in. What rejoicing when the rural mail carrier, who was everyone's friend, would say, "One of the neighbors butchered the day before, and they sent this meat for you." Many times, we would thank the Lord because of His goodness. Also, the neighbors would ask not to be identified. They really never knew how poor we were.

The flu epidemic was so bad that many people died. We thank the Lord that by spring we were all well again. Doctors came to the homes and had a lot more work than they could do. One case points to the problems the doctors had. Dr. Heilman was making calls at night. When he didn't arrive at one of the homes several hours after he was supposed to, a search party went to find him. They used what we called a bulls-eye lantern. We didn't even know what a flashlight was, as they were not invented until later. This bull's eye lantern looked very much like the head light on a train engine. They found the doctor asleep while his horse was eating grass along the side of the road. When the doctor awakened and saw what he thought was the headlight of a train coming toward him, he thought he was on the railroad tracks and jumped clear out of the buggy. You would have had a real laugh if you had seen it!

The third disastrous sickness happened to our family just before Christmas about 1922. Mother became very sick. I remember going for the doctor in a one-horse sleigh when the roads were drifted shut. Mother was sick all winter. The doctor came every day when her life hung in the balance. In 1922, sick people were seldom taken to the hospital. After she began to get better, the doctor came three times a week for most of the winter. I also remember taking the clothes about a mile for a neighbor to wash (there were no electric washers). About one block from the road I had to travel lived a family with two large, black dogs. These two dogs liked to run after horses. In the one-horse sleigh, as a mere lad of eleven, I could hardly control the horse who would run as fast as he could. The snow would ball up on his feet and fly back, some over my head, some hitting me. The hard balls of snow were about as big as a baseball. It was a real battle to control the horse and dodge the snow balls.

We had no money, so the doctor said he would take part of his payment in a ham. The ham looked alright, but when they cut into it, part of it was spoiled. So we gave him another ham. That meant we had no meat for the winter. The doctor attended mother several months but could not find her problem. Father said it did not seem fair that, when the ham was spoiled, he had to replace it, but the doctor got his pay, even if he did not know what was wrong with my mother. I remember the pastor, Reverend Ira Sassaman, visiting us and telling us afterwards how discouraged and depressed we were because of Mother's sickness. At one time, the doctor thought she had tuberculosis. It was a very dreaded disease in those days. We thank the Lord, when spring came, that He healed her.

Our extreme poverty caused a major depression for Father. With so many being sick so often, the family could not get together for family worship and for a time it was dropped. We children can still remember when Father was depressed, Mother saying, "Children, don't bother Father with anything. He isn't feeling well."

In fact, my older brother and sister remember those dark days very vividly. At times, it seemed God had forsaken us. Through those dark days, however, Father and Mother continued to take us to the little white Lutheran church a mile from our home. In those days when there was not even enough money to buy a two-cent postage stamp, they always gave us a penny for the Sunday School offering and one for the church offering. My sister, Mary, reminded me that one Sunday, Mother said to Father, "We only have a few pennies in the house, what shall we do? We need clothes and food." They decided to give it all in the church offering, even though they did not have any money coming in for almost a week. Even though our clothes were patched and the toes were out of our shoes, Father and Mother always took us to Sunday School and Church. I thank God that they took us instead of sending us. I have never known of a family that had family worship and took their children to Sunday school and church whose young people got involved in drugs and drinking. I am sure it may happen, but I believe those cases are very rare.

As I thought about the way my parents gave out of their poverty, I think of how opposite they were of the rich man in a church which needed a new roof. He said, "I want to be the first to give; I will give $50." (He could have probably given the whole $50,000 that was needed.) He was a fairly heavy man, and when he sat down with a thud, it jarred a piece of plaster loose which fell and hit him on the head. He jumped up and said, "I guess the roof needs to be repaired sooner than I thought; I'll give $500." Someone in the back of the church yelled, "Hit him again, Lord, hit him again."

As a committed Christian, how much should I give? The poem, "How Long Shall I Give?" expresses it better than I can.

> Go break to the needy sweet charity bread
> For giving is living, the angel said.
> And must I be giving again and again?
> My peevish and pitiless answer ran.
> "Oh, no," said the angel, piercing me through,
> "Just give till the Master stops giving to you."
> (Author unknown)

Many people would have given up and gone to the poor board (the type of relief they had in those days). Other people would have declared bankruptcy. However, Father believed in stick-to-it-iveness, as he said in his book. He often worked for someone else during the day and sawed wood by lantern light at night. We sawed the trees down by hand into lengths that could be loaded onto a wagon and hauled into the buildings. He had a two horsepower gas engine to drive a belt which ran a saw. After sawing wood one cold night, Father wakened after midnight and remembered he'd forgotten to let the water out of the engine. (This was before the invention of anti-freeze.) He knew it would freeze and burst the engine before morning. He said, "I bounced out of bed and got out to the engine in a hurry. It was not frozen solid yet, but I could not drain the water out. I was afraid the engine would not start, but I tried it, and it started right off. That soon warmed it up enough, and the water drained out."

I quote from Father's book,

> Not being with the family because of sickness and not having prayer to guide me every day, my faith began to waver. Although I did pray, it seemed I did not get as close to God as when we had prayer together every day.
>
> I was much discouraged. It seemed it was no use to do anything. It seemed everything I did went to nothing. It seemed God had forgotten us. A sick wife, large doctor bills, six children to clothe and feed on a poor farm sure was a struggle.

Trinity Union Sunday School and Trinity Lutheran Church was about a mile from our home. We all went the first Sunday we were in the neighborhood. They were very good people. They sure did a lot to encourage us. They were a great help to us in many ways. However, they were not able to help us much financially as they had financial struggles of their own. They did help us in ways more important than money could buy. I do not know how we would have made it without the help and support of the dear Christian friends at Trinity Lutheran Church in Point Township. There are so many I do not know, so I cannot name them all. However, I would like to name a few of whom my father said, "These men were like a father to me"—Asher Hoffman, Harvey Geise, Harrison Diehl, and Frank Geise. These men sold fertilizer to us on credit; they also signed our note at the bank when we were so far in debt it looked like we might never be able to pay. I want to pay a special tribute to all the dear folks in Point Township, for without their encouragement and support, this success story would never have happened. So, of course, this book would never have been written.

On Father's and Mother's twenty-fifth wedding anniversary, they had a heart-warming experience. The date was December 4, 1925. In order to keep body and soul together, Father worked on neighboring farms whenever work was available. Father was helping Asher Hoffman haul in and husk corn. That morning, he said to Mr. Hoffman, "This is our 25th wedding anniversary." Nothing more was said. Mr. Hoffman told his wife, and she called up Mother and invited Mother for dinner. Hoffmans lived just a mile from our home. Andrew, my oldest brother, took Mother in the horse and buggy to Hoffmans. In those days, when you worked on the farm, the farmer provided the noon meal which was called dinner. It was a real surprise to Father when he saw Mother there, and they sang happy anniversary to them as he entered the dining room.

For lunch at school, sometimes all we had was bread with a little butter on it. Sometimes, we would eat by ourselves so that other children would not know how little we had. Other children had peanut butter and crackers. The smell of peanut butter made me very hungry. A few years later, when things were going better, Father traded some produce for a twenty-pound wooden keg of peanut butter. That was a great treat to us. We were not allowed to have butter and jelly on the same piece of bread. The old saying was, "Before you can spread two things on your bread, you should own two farms."

When Mother got well, and we were together again as a family, Father said, "My wife insisted on family worship again; I was so discouraged, I felt reluctant. She insisted and succeeded. We got back to regular family worship. I thank the Lord thousands of times for family worship. I feel it brought me back to fellowship with God and was the means of our success." About this time, my sister Mary, who was about fifteen, attended a church meeting where they stressed family worship. She and Mother worked together to get Father to agree to family worship. We found that the family altar alters things, and so will you.

If anyone reading this book is depressed, or your family is falling apart, or you are about to give up on your marriage, may I suggest that together you as a family read at least one chapter from the Bible and pray together every day. Do you really want to preserve your home and have sons and daughters grow up free from such problems as drugs and sex? Family worship worked in our home, and I have seen it work in hundreds of other homes.

If all you are interested in is fame and fortune, you might as well lay this book aside. But if you are interested in starting your own business, running it by principles laid down in the Bible, you can succeed and enjoy life while climbing to the top. And you will also find this book to be interesting.

Father was despondent sometimes and felt the Lord and the whole world was against him. Regardless of how hard he tried, things went against him. He was so depressed at times, he didn't eat. However, God did not fail him in those times. I well remember that one of his favorite Scripture verses was Joshua 24:15, "But if serving the Lord seems undesirable to you, then choose for yourselves this day whom you will serve . . . But as for me and my household, we will serve the Lord."

I have mentioned Mother's strong faith several times. I believe Mother's strong faith was largely responsible for pulling our family through those difficult years. Perhaps your family is going through some very stressful times. I trust you will find my tribute in the next chapter to our mother a great blessing and encouragement.

Any success that has come to the Furman family can be attributed in a large part to three things:

1. The blessings of the Lord; even though we failed Him many times, we did try to honor Him. Scripture says in 1 Samuel 2:30b, "Those that honor me will I honor, but those who despise me will be disdained." We are a family of prayer, and Mother was a woman of great faith and prayer. It is still true that the family that prays together, stays together.

2. The whole family worked together and played together. We shared a common goal—to pay off the mortgage.

3. We all worked hard from sun up to sun down. As a child, I often wished we did not have to work so hard. However, I believe more lives are ruined by people who misuse their free time than by people who overwork. Because of our financial condition, which I will describe later, many of us did not have the normal time to play. Swimming was a rare treat. Instead of being involved in sports, we worked at home. We did not need to play games to use up our energy! I am not condemning sports, but there should be a balance. It would be better for many young people today if they had more work to do. I remember the Northumberland County Superintendent of Schools, Charles Hilbish, saying, "The student who has definite responsibility to do a certain job every day, regardless of circumstances, will always succeed and surpass one who can do as they please." I am reminded of the teacher saying to a pupil, "The devil always finds something for idle hands to do. Come here, I have a job for you."

Hard work is not enough. The Scripture says in Psalm 127:1, "Unless the Lord builds the house, its builders labor in vain. Unless the Lord watches over the city, the watchmen stand guard in vain." Unless the Lord blesses, hard work can destroy a person.

When Thou Passeth Through the Waters

Do you feel your heart discouraged as you pass along
    the way?
Does there seem to be more darkness than there is
    of sunny day?
Is it hard to learn the lesson as we pass beneath the
    rod,
That the sunshine and the shadow serve alike the
    will of God?
But to me there comes a promise, like the promise
    of the bow,
That however deep the waters, they shall never over-
    flow.

When the flesh is worn and weary and the spirit is
    depressed,
When temptation comes upon you like a storm on
    ocean's breast,
There's a haven ever ready for the tempest-driven
    bird,
There's a shelter for the tempted in the promise of
    the Word;
For the standard of the Spirit shall be raised against
    the foe,
And however deep the waters they shall never over-
    flow.

When sorrow comes upon you that no other soul
    can share,
And the burden seems too heavy for the human heart
    to bear,
There's one whose grace can comfort if you'll give
    Him an abode,
There's a Burden-bearer ready if you'll trust Him
    with your load;
For the precious promise reaches to the depth of
    human woe,

That however deep the waters they shall never over-
flow.
When the sands of life are ebbing, and I near dark
Jordan's shore,
When I see the billows rising, and I hear the water's
roar,
I'll reach out my hand to Jesus, in His bosom I will
hide;
It will only be a moment till I reach the other side.
It is then the fullest meaning of the promise I shall
know;
"When thou passeth through the waters, they shall
never overflow."

—*Henry Crowell*

Chapter 6
A Tribute to Mother

She was just an old-fashioned mother,
 She did not pretend to be "smart."
To care for her home and her dear ones
Was the wish that was first in her heart.

We were raised by the old-fashioned methods,
 So sparsely employed today.
 And when we so richly deserved it,
We were "spanked" in the old-fashioned way.

She taught us the old-fashioned virtue
 "A good name is far better," she'd say,
 "Than all of the wealth of the nation,
 And truth is the best any day."

She believed in the old-fashioned Bible,
 She trusted in old-fashioned prayer;
 She told us that Jesus would hear us
 If we'd speak any time anywhere.

Thank God for an old-fashioned mother,
 For the Bible and old-fashioned prayer;
For the old-fashioned faith that is looking
 For our Lord to appear in the air.
(Author unknown)

In many ways, this poem describes my mother, but I do not believe that the Bible and prayer are old-fashioned. I believe the Bible is just as true today as it was long ago.

Any praise I have given to my father should equally be shared with my mother because they worked together as a team. When Reverend Sassaman married Hazel and me, he told this story that may help some young married couples. A minister had told a young couple if their marriage was to be a happy one, they needed to pull together like a team. About a year later, the minister saw the husband on the street and asked him how things were going. The husband said, "You told us to work together like a team. That would be all right if there was only one tongue between us."

Mother and Father did not always agree, but they did work together. In fact, I believe Mother had a stronger faith than Father. On at least three occasions, he was despondent because of financial reverses and his and Mother's sicknesses. The family could not be together for family worship, but it was Mother who insisted that we begin reading the Bible and praying together. Father says that was a turning point in our family life. I believe the old saying that, "Behind every successful man is a dedicated wife." I believe it was Mother's faith that kept them taking us to church and Sunday School, even though the knees of our trousers were patched and our toes stuck out of our shoes.

I am sure many of you have mothers whom you love and admire. However, many of you have not had the privilege of having a mother with as strong a faith as my mother had. I would like to remind you that Mother had left a new house and a family that had an above average income. She left all of that to marry Father, a good moral man who loved the Lord. Father had been taken to church and Sunday School by a godly mother, but he had practically no money and a very uncertain future.

Mother was kind but firm. She had a quiet, persuasive way of asking one not to do certain things, and we children would obey. That persuasion was shown when she had said to Father shortly after they were married, "Please, Wes, do not smoke today." He never smoked again.

Both Mother and Father believed in discipline and frequently used the book of Proverbs as a guide, especially chapter 22, verse 15, "Folly is bound up in the heart of a child, but the rod of discipline will drive it far from him." And chapter 29, verses 15–17, "The rod of correction imparts wisdom, but a child left to himself disgraces his mother. When the wicked thrive, so does sin, but the righteous will see their downfall. Discipline your son, and he will give you peace; he will bring delight to your soul."

Our parents taught us by example as well as precept. They told the truth and expected us to do the same. Some parents teach their children to lie, like the father who took his son on the train. Anyone under six years of age could ride free. He told his son to say he was five. The conductor thought he looked big for five and said, "How soon will you be six?" The boy said, "As soon as I get off the train." Parents, if you do that kind of thing, do not expect your children to tell you the truth.

That reminds me of a young son who was whipped for a rather serious violation of his father's direct instructions. After the whipping, the father said, "Son, this whipping hurts me more than it does you, but I do it because I love you." The boy looked up through his tears and said, "Father, I wish I were big enough to return your love."

First as a father, then a grandfather, and now a great grandfather, I realize that truly my parents' discipline was for my good. I think some of the whippings I got did a lot of good. We had several plum trees that grew long thin sticks, and they were very limber. They were called "suckers." Although they did not do as much harm to our body as a spanking, they surely did sting. When Mother wanted to teach us a lesson which we would remember, she would make us cut our own switch.

The Sunday after a girl was baptized, she said to the pastor, "I thought when I was baptized, it would take away evil thoughts." The pastor said, "I should have held you under the water longer."

Parents, one word of advice. Never discipline your child in anger, or you will get anger in return. Discipline in love, and you will eventually get love in return.

Mother was a very hard worker. She was also able to teach us to enjoy working and realize its rewards at an early age. I can remember Mother praying for each of her seven children by name. When we were away, she would wait up for us or, if she did go to bed, she spoke to us when we came home. Perhaps the following poem describes what I mean.

MOTHER
She always leaned to watch for us,
Anxious if we were late,
In winter by the windowsill,
In summer by the gate.

And though we mocked her tenderly,
Who had such foolish care,
The long way home would seem more safe,
Because she waited there.

Her thoughts were all so full of us;
She never could forget,
And so I think that where she is,
She must be waiting yet.

Waiting till we come home to her,
Anxious if we are late.
Watching from Heaven's windowsill,
Leaning on Heaven's gate!
—Margaret Widdemar

I believe that Proverbs 31:10–12 describes my mother much better than I can: "A wife of noble character who can find? She is worth far more than rubies. Her husband has full confidence in her and lacks nothing of value. She brings him good, not harm, all the days of her life." Also verses 28 through 30: "Her children arise and call her blessed; her husband also, and he praises her: 'Many women do noble things, but you surpass them all.' Charm is deceptive, and beauty is fleeting; but a woman who fears the Lord is to be praised."

The next chapter tells of the exciting life down on the farm.

Chapter 7
Down on the Farm
Years 1918–1928

At the age of eighty-three, I look back over the years from 1918 to 1930. My, what a lot of changes have occurred! They tell me that in my lifetime there has been more scientific advancement and knowledge than occurred in the previous two thousand years. I will try to tell you about some of the "good old days" that older people talk about.

In the Pennsylvania Dutch country, the preacher was often invited to Sunday dinner by one of his congregation. In those days, chicken was the most expensive meat. When the preacher came for Sunday dinner, chicken was usually served. That was a big event in our home as we were too poor to have chicken except on special occasions.

On one occasion, the farmer took the preacher out to the barn while the wife finished getting the dinner. A rooster was on the barnyard fence crowing his heart out. The preacher said, "Why is he crowing so loudly?" The farmer said, "You would crow too if you had as many sons in the ministry as he has!"

Were they really the GOOD old days? How would you like to do without electric lights? Think of traveling by horse and buggy at about four miles per hour. Today you can average over sixty miles per hour on interstates, and it takes less time to travel to the West Coast by air than it used to take to go the thirty miles to Williamsport by horse and buggy. Think of the space shuttles traveling about 24,000 miles per hour!

Can you remember when there was no refrigeration? The farmers kept the cream or milk in a milk can dropped by rope into the hand dug well. Many farm home sites were picked where there was a cold spring having running water with a temperature of fifty to sixty degrees. Everything perishable was kept in the spring house. When you needed those things, instead of reaching into the refrigerator, you had to go 50 or 100 feet to the spring house. If you had no spring house, the next best thing was the cellar or the well. If you lived in town, you had an ice box. The ice was delivered about every other day by the ice man.

Can you remember the days before computers or even the electric adding machine? Then you punched the figures in and pulled a crank to add up the things at the cash register. Since there were no copy machines or computers, it required scores of secretaries to copy over figures and accounts. I remember when I was chief executive officer of our company, it was usually the twentieth to twenty-fifth of the next month before we had a sales analysis. Now I marvel that the day after the month closes, we know our total monetary sales for the month. The printout shows several hundred items. Each one is compared to the last two years, as well as percentage of movement, not only for the month but also the year-to-date totals. They are so much more accurate today. When a secretary copies it over, sometime figures would get transposed, so all the figures had to be checked over very carefully to see that they had not been transposed, or had an extra zero added, or were missing a zero. Today, once it is in the computer correctly, it never changes.

Have you heard the sayings about the cracker barrel? They came from the fact that crackers, flour, sugar, corn meal, and many others things came in a barrel. The store owner weighed out the amount you wanted; many times, you had to bring your own container.

Instead of buying canned or frozen vegetables, you bought Mason jars, cleaned your own vegetables, and canned them on the cook stove in a wash boiler. There were no prepackaged groceries of any kind. Instead of going to the store every day to get something for a special recipe, you were lucky to go once a week. Instead of buying bread, most housewives baked their own bread. Remember those delicious home-made pies?

In those days, all the plowing was done with a team of horses or mules. If you had a good team, you could plow an acre per ten-hour day. Now, we have tractors that plow sixty or more acres per day. Then the grain was cut with a cradle. When I was a boy, they were just starting to use binders. Side hills that were too steep were cradled by hand, and the outside round was cradled to avoid waste by the binder running down the grain. The binder put it in sheaves. The sheaves were placed in shocks of about twelve to twenty sheaves for about a week to dry. When dry, usually the sheaves were hauled into the barn to be stored until the thrashing machine would come to the community.

The thrashing machine was pulled by a steam engine. It looked a lot like the old steam engines they used on the railroad at that time. It took a lot of preparation. The engine required soft coal. The steam engine required more water than the average farm well could supply. Thrashing also required five or six extra people. So you asked your neighbor for help, and then when they needed help, you did the same for them. It was up to the farmer to provide two meals a day. Not only was it the best of food, but there were also two or more kinds of pies for dessert. My, how we boys enjoyed those big meals!

Field corn was cut by hand in October and tied in sheaves. The sheaves were put in shocks of about ten to twelve sheaves. In late October or November, the corn was husked by hand and thrown on piles. It was hauled to the corn crib and shoveled off by hand. Fifty bushels of shelled corn per acre was considered a good yield. In the year of 1990, our farm manager, Sam Rovenolt, was awarded a nice plaque for the best yield on a five-acre plot in the state of Pennsylvania. It was a whopping 228.5 bushels of shelled corn per acre!

Hunting season for rabbits, squirrels, and pheasants started on November 1. We tried to get as much corn husked as possible before November 1, so we could go hunting. Many times, we could get four rabbits, several squirrels, and a pheasant in a day. To be considered a good farmer, you needed to be done husking corn by Thanksgiving.

The reason it was said that the farmer went to bed with the chickens and got up with the chickens was a matter of necessity. Remember, there were no electric lights! I think of the rooster who said, "I liked the good old days when dawn came sneaking in from the east. Now when the electric lights come on, they hit you in the eye with a bang." Many times, the farmer did not have an alarm clock. Of course, since the rooster crowed about dawn, that took the place of an alarm clock.

Many preachers did not receive a very large salary. Much of their living was given to them in farm produce. They often got too much of one vegetable when the crop was good. Many country churches had what was known as Harvest Home. It was usually about the first Sunday in October. The whole pulpit area would be decorated with fresh fruits and vegetables and canned food in Mason glass jars. All the fresh vegetables were given to the preacher and the canned things taken to the church orphanage. There was the case of the preacher who was very thin. However, the horse he drove was rolling fat. Someone asked him why he was so thin and his horse so fat. He said, "It's this way, I feed the horse, but you feed me!"

Johnny, who was four years old, came to his mother at about eleven o'clock with a stomach ache. His mother said, "Have you eaten anything since breakfast?" He said, "No." She said, "Maybe it's empty." About three o'clock that afternoon the preacher came and, while the mother was answering the phone, the preacher complained of a headache while talking to Johnny. Johnny remarked, "My mother said, 'Maybe it's empty.' "

Our church in the country only had preaching on alternate Sundays. The reason was the pastor preached at St. John's Lutheran Church in Northumberland in the morning. In the afternoon, he would preach one Sunday at our church, and the following Sunday he would preach at our sister congregation, Grace Church. Reverend Sassaman was our pastor. However, when it snowed, the car stayed in the garage and someone from the congregation went for the preacher. Hazel's father, Mr. George Epler, got Reverend Sassaman with a team of horses hooked to a bobsled. After getting the preacher, he stopped on the way to church to get his family. While the team was stopped, the snow slid off the tin barn roof with a roar which caused the team to jump forward. The seat was an eight-inch board laid across the bobsled box. When the team jumped, Reverend Sassaman fell backward with his feet up in the air. After he got up, someone asked him, "Are you hurt?" He answered, "No, only my dignity."

In the summer, many farmers got up at 4:30 or 5:00 in the morning. They immediately went to the barn and fed the horses and cows. After that, they milked the cows. Some cows were very difficult to milk if you did not feed them first. Many people used a three-legged stool to sit on while milking, and they would hold the bucket between their legs. We had a four legged stool with a place on it to set the bucket. If the cow gave a twelve-quart bucket full, she was considered to be a pretty good cow. Today, the average cow produces three times as much milk as they did then. Mr. Dean Stuart of Corning, New York, recently told me he had a cow that produced seventy-five quarts of milk a day! However, he milked four times a day instead of two.

Talk about cows giving milk! I think of the preacher in college who was asked to milk the cow of his landlady while she went away. He said, "Don't let anyone kid you that a cow gives milk. You have to take it from them!"

When the milking was finished, it was carried to the milk house. Before the days of the cream separator, the milk was left undisturbed for about twelve hours. Then the housewife took a flat type of utensil and skimmed off the cream that had risen to the top. Cream will not rise to the top on pasteurized milk. About 1922, we got a De Lava cream separator which we turned with a crank. We kept the cream in the well as that was the coolest place we had. When we got enough cream, we would put it in a barrel churn to make butter. It looked like a barrel with an axle fastened in the middle on each side. When the lid was off, you fastened it with a hook so it could not turn and spill the cream on the floor. Once I took the lid off without fastening it. You guessed it! It turned and spilled all the cream on the floor. Tragedy! There went a whole week's income. If you lost your weekly pay check, you would feel like we did. It is true, it is no use to cry over spilled milk. However, we went without some necessary things because there was no money to buy them. After the butter was made, we took it to the local store to get the week's supply of groceries. The story is told of a lady that took her butter to the store. She confided to the store keeper that a mouse drowned in the cream. She said, "You can sell it to someone else. What the mind don't know, the heart don't grieve." She asked the store keeper to trade it for someone else's butter. He went to the back and changed the wrapper on it and gave her back her own butter without her knowing it. The next week when she came in, she said, "Whose butter was that? It tasted just as good as mine!" The store keeper quoted her saying, "What the mind don't know, the heart don't grieve!"

By about 6:30, you were ready for a farmer's breakfast of eggs with bacon, ham, or sausage. Since you had already worked an hour or two, you were hungry and did not worry about cholesterol as your work burned it up.

Overnight guests were expected to eat with the family. Mother had too much work to do; she could not get more than one breakfast. That way, they also were present for the most important part of the day—reading from God's Holy Word, then prayers by one or more of the family. Father was very particular that everyone attended "Family Worship."

After breakfast, we went to the barn to finish the chores. Usually the horses were curried or groomed before breakfast. To do a good job on three horses took about half an hour. If we got done too soon, Father would look at the horse and say, "It looks to me as if you threw the curry comb over the horse and caught it on the other side." Sometimes we had to do it over. In those days, many people took as much pride in keeping their horse looking nice as people do today with a new automobile.

In spring or summer when the weather was right, we tried to be on our way to the field by seven o'clock in the morning. Since we did not have a watch, we usually worked until we heard the noon whistle at the factories in town. It was three miles away, but horses did not make noise like tractors do, so we could easily hear the whistle. You always finished the round you were on. When it was a long field, it might be 12:30 when you left the field. Many farmers had a large bell which the wife would ring when dinner was ready. It became known as the dinner bell. On the farm, dinner was at noon and the evening meal was known as supper. Believe me, after walking behind a plow or harrow for five hours, you were ready for a big meal. My! How we longed for that noon whistle! Of course, the horses always walked faster when going toward the barn than going to the field. Some of the advantages of a team over a tractor was, in warm weather, the horses needed a five minute break every hour. I remember the pleasant time we had with our neighbors when we took the break for the team the same time as the neighbor across the fence. Remember, there was no radio, no television, and very few phones. As we visited while

63

the horses rested, we learned many things from our neighbors.

Usually you only worked the team a total of ten hours per day. However, since we were growing vegetables for the fresh market, we often got up at four o'clock in the morning and worked until after eight at night.

Did you ever wonder why the big old houses have three or four chimneys in them? Some houses had a stove in almost every room. It was necessary to sleep with the windows open because the lamps and stove used up oxygen. Also the coal stoves would sometimes give off sulphur fumes that could be deadly if the damper in the stove pipe was closed too tightly. Many times, the stove pipe went up through the floor into the bedroom and then entered the chimney. That provided some heat for the bedroom. Many people have died from fumes from stoves. Also, many fires have been started when someone put something too close to the stove pipe in the bedroom.

In those days, the deceased were usually kept in the home the night before the funeral. They had what was called a wake, where several people would sit up by the casket all night. Some of the reasons were to keep evil spirits away and, in some of the poorer homes, to keep the rats away. Some wakes were preceded by a family meal with plenty of liquor, where sometimes the watchers drank a little too much. At one particular wake, three men were watching the body and drinking when one of them fell asleep. The other two thought they would play a trick on him, so they took the stiff out of the casket and put the sleeping man into it. At daylight, the man woke up, looked around, pinched himself, and said, "If I am living, I should not be in the casket, but if I am dead, I shouldn't have to go to the bathroom."

We were one of the first in the community to have running water in our house. Before the days of the automatic pump, Father built a water reservoir on a slight hill above the house. It was just high enough to give us water in the bathroom, which was upstairs. You might not think that was a big deal. But do you realize before you had running water, there were no bathrooms or inside toilets, and you had to go outside to the outhouse? Another name for the outhouse was privy or outside toilet. Our outhouse was about 300 feet from the house. During the day, you were expected to go to the outhouse unless you were sick, regardless of how cold it was. At night, most people used a chamber pot, which was kept under the bed. Of course, that had to be carried out to the outhouse during the day. No one was ever accused of sitting in the outhouse reading a book when temperatures were below freezing or close to zero. I well remember running through drifting snow to go to the outhouse.

Most outhouses had two holes that were cut in a board with a hand saw. Those seats were not very comfortable either. A wooden building about five-by-five feet was set over a hole in the ground. There were no D.E.R. (Department of Environmental Resources) regulations. However, in the farming country, there may only have been one family to over 100 acres, so contamination was not usually a problem. As a boy, we did not know what toilet paper was. We often used old Sears & Roebuck catalogs. When the catalog company started using colored or coated paper, one farmer complained that catalogs were not even any good for toilet paper anymore.

There are many stories about the old fashioned privy. One that actually happened was about an older man in the community whom the young boys liked to tease. Every year on Halloween, about three boys would get behind the privy and push it over. Of course, this was always done at night. After that happened about three years in a row, the man figured out a solution. He moved the privy forward about two feet in front of the hole in the ground. Then he put a light covering of straw over the hole. Guess what happened when the boys got behind the privy to push it over? That was last year they bothered that man.

Another story that is told is about some boys who upset the privy with their father in it. Soon afterward, he accused them of doing it. They tried to blame it on their neighbors. Finally, they owned up to it, and he decided to give them a whipping. They said, "When George Washington cut down the cherry tree and he owned up to it, his father didn't punish him because he told the truth." The father said, "But George Washington's dad was not in the cherry tree."

Before we had running water, we had to carry all the water in and then carry it out again. We pumped it all by hand. Just to pump enough water for ten cows and four horses took over half an hour! Also, the watering trough never ran over. After we had running water, sometimes we would open the spigot and go do other work and let the watering trough run over. Since water was almost always short, that could cause major problems. Father used to say, "I never saw the watering trough run over when you pumped water by hand."

Without a shower or bathtub, how did you take a bath? Also, there were no bathrooms in most houses. Since you had to heat the water on the kitchen stove and carry it to your bedroom, you didn't take a bath as often as you do now. The saying that you took a bath Saturday night whether you needed it or not was not too far from the truth. Recently, my sister reminded me of one cold Saturday night when I was home from school in Philadelphia. We only had heat in the living room and the kitchen. While the family was in the kitchen eating supper, I had carried warm water into the living room and was taking a bath. Of course, they all knew I was getting ready to go see Hazel Epler. (We were married about two years later and have had a wonderful life together for fifty-seven years.) About the time he knew I would be undressed, my younger brother James slipped out the back door, came to the front door and rang the door bell. I quickly grabbed some clothes and went into a cold side room and called for someone else to open the door. Of course, we all had a good laugh about that.

When I think of my boyhood and some of the pranks we played, I am reminded of the grandfather who grafted five different colors of apples on a tree planted where there had been a wood pile for years. He was so proud of that tree, he asked the county agent to include it in the farmers' tour that fall. In the meantime, his grandsons had bought some oranges, grapefruit, pears, peaches, and bananas and tied them to the tree. As the grandfather and his guests were walking to the tree, the grandfather said, "I want you to see the amazing fruit that a tree planted in an old wood lot will produce." He wanted to play humble and did not look up as they approached the tree. His guests laughed and said, "John, do you mean to tell us a tree planted in an old wood pile will grow oranges, grapefruit, peaches, pears, and bananas all on the same tree?" When he looked up, his eyes almost popped out. Finally, the grandfather said, "My grandsons have been up to some pranks."

We used a 2.5 horsepower gas engine to pump the water. I remember one cool morning, I cranked the engine. The crank fit over a key in the drive shaft. I had on a ragged coat. When I leaned over to turn the lubricant on for the cylinder, my ragged coat caught on that key and wound my coat around it, pulled my neck down against the fly wheel, then started whirling me around! Praise the Lord the engine was set up on railroad ties. That gave enough room for my body to fly around without crushing me. Otherwise, I would not be here to write this book. Since the engine was cold, the extra load stopped it. My brother was hit by my feet as I flew around. I had some bumps and bruises but was able to go to school. Believe me, I was a lot more careful around engines after that!

In the winter time, we did not get up until six. We carried the lantern to the barn for light. I remember well the many times we were cautioned to always be careful with the lantern and hang it a special place to avoid any chance of fire. Many barns were burned down because a lantern was upset and the kerosene spilled out and caught on fire. In fact, the great

Chicago fire that burned more than half of Chicago, I am told, was started when a cow kicked over a lantern. Also, we were warned not to carry old style matches which were called barn burners. If we lost one, a mouse or rat might chew on it and start a fire.

On a cold wintery morning, the animals in the barn kept it warmer than our house was. Sometimes the fire went out in the kitchen stove. Many times, we did not own gloves and were glad to start milking, as the cows' teats were warm, and they warmed our hands. I never really liked to milk. I still remember the hand cramps I would get. Of course, if you did it regularly, your hand muscles would get used to it. Today, cows are milked by machine, and the milk is pumped to a cooling tank.

My oldest brother, Andrew, finished grade school in 1920. You had to pass a special exam to enter high school. He passed the special exam and wanted to go on to high school. However, some of his classmates tried to discourage him from going to high school. They said, "You dress so poorly, the town people and the teacher will make fun of you." At that time, only about 60 percent of children went to high school and graduated. Father and Mother wanted all of us to have a good education. They said, "We will be sure all of you get through high school. However, we are so poor, if you want to go to college, you will have to work your way through." All seven of us graduated from high school. Andrew, Mary, and James graduated from college. The rest of us went to Bible College for a year or two and some took some special courses at local colleges.

While I was going to high school, during the spring, we rushed to get ground plowed. We would often get up before daylight, feed the horses, get a quick breakfast, and try to get to the field at daylight. We worked several hours until it was time to get ready for school. Then we put the horse in the barn and got ready for high school. I would ride a bicycle three miles to the high school. As soon as school was out, I rode the bicycle three miles back home. When I got home, I would get the horses out and work until dark. That left a little time to study. Even though some of us wanted to play basketball and be involved in other school activities, that was not possible. There was just too much work to do on the farm, especially in the spring. Also, sometimes the young people's organization from the church would take trips to local parks. However, if there was work to do on the farm, we stayed home.

I remember Carl Riggs, a very close friend, wanted to see the Penn State campus as he was thinking of going to school there. He asked me to go along with him. We were planting early tomatoes for market. Father said he just could not spare me for a day. So Carl Riggs said, "I will help plant tomatoes for a day without pay, and we will both go to see Penn State campus the next day." Not many friends will work a day without pay to help their friends.

In those days, there were no paved roads in the country. When roads were icy or too muddy to ride the bicycle, we walked the three miles to the high school. We did not need gym classes to get exercise.

I failed to mention that up through eighth grade, we went to Stone School, a one-room schoolhouse in the country. One teacher taught all eight grades. There were five schools in Point Township. That way, most pupils did not have to travel more than two miles to go to school. Except in very bad weather, most students walked. If we went by the road, it was a mile to the stone school from our home. When temperatures were below zero, with a wind chill factor of twenty degrees below zero, that was a long way to walk for a six or seven-year-old. When it was cold and windy, we would take a little different route so we could walk through the woods about one-third of the way. It seemed a lot warmer in the woods as there was very little wind among the trees.

The one-room school in the country was very different than high school in Northumberland. I failed algebra the first three months in high school. Then Professor Danowsky, the school principal, started to teach the class. From then on, I was on the honor roll in mathematics. When I graduated from high school, I was awarded a $100 scholarship to an engineering school, Rensselaer Polytechnic Institute, and a gold medal for having the highest grade in mathematics and science in the high school. In high school in Northumberland, we had a very fine teacher, Boice Bristor, who taught mathematics and public speaking. A good teacher really makes a big difference!

The course I took in public speaking taught by Boice Bristor was a great help to me in business. I also had the opportunity to participate in several class plays. Those things helped me a lot in the business world. However, when I graduated at the age of sixteen, I was the youngest and smallest of my class. Also, I was voted the most shy and least likely to succeed in business of anyone in the class. The Lord delights in taking nobodies with very limited ability like myself and using them to His honor and glory. I trust that any success the Lord has seen fit to give me and my family will be used to His honor and glory. In view of the above, I was surprised to receive the Alumni Award of the Year at the annual alumni banquet of Northumberland High School in 1993. It reads:

Alumni Award
Presented to
Foster Furman
For Outstanding Service to Alumni
Church and Community
1993

In accepting the award, I thanked the committee and the many in the room who worked for us and helped to make our success possible. I also was surprised to learn that I would have received the award in 1992; however, I was in Michigan attending the wedding of our granddaughter, Esther Severn. As a result, the award was given to Attorney Donald Steele.

The next chapter will tell the exciting story of how the business started with 360 glass jars of tomatoes cooked on a cook stove in a wash boiler in the kitchen of our home. What a thrill to see the business grow over the years. Today, Furman Foods is the largest family-owned vegetable cannery in the state and the largest tomato processor east of central Ohio.

Chapter 8
Big Oak Trees From Little Acorns Grow
Years 1921–1929

By 1921, Father had established a good fresh vegetable business with the local grocery stores. There were very few chain stores and no supermarkets, but there was a neighborhood store every four or five blocks. Each of these stores would buy two to ten baskets of tomatoes for the local housewives who did their own canning. Father had built a greenhouse. He would sow tomato seed in March and have tomato plants in pots with blossoms and little tomatoes on before planting them in the field in late May, after the danger of frost was over. This way, he would have tomatoes for the fresh market three weeks before anyone else. I remember one year, on June 6, we almost lost our entire acreage of tomatoes when the temperature dropped to thirty degrees.

Anyone with a garden knows that sometimes during the summer, many have more tomatoes than they know what to do with. The total amount that the local stores could buy at one time was 100 to 125 baskets (each basket held sixteen quarts). The managers of the neighborhood stores said, "We can't use any more now, but if you bring them back next winter, we will sell them for you." That is just what Father decided to do.

Little did he imagine that those 360 glass jars of tomatoes would grow into sales of almost fifty million dollars per year!

When Father moved to Delaware, it looked like he had made a big mistake. However, the success the tomato canneries had while he lived in Delaware encouraged him to try canning tomatoes in Pennsylvania. But how could he do it without any money to build a factory and buy machinery? The old saying, "Where there is a will, there is a way," proved to be true.

In those days, the only way to heat water for washing was in a wash boiler. This was a container about twenty-three inches long and twelve inches wide. We had a wash boiler and a cook stove in our kitchen. The wash boiler would hold fifteen Mason glass jars. In 1921, Father and Mother canned 360 Mason glass jars of tomatoes. Now we process 36,000 cans at one time compared to fifteen in 1921. Pennsylvania tomatoes had much better flavor than the canned tomatoes on the grocery shelves. Father and Mother were also very careful to use only the nice, whole, red tomatoes. Furman quality tomatoes soon created a demand. Father always emphasized quality. He said, "If you lose an order because of price, but people like your quality, they will come back. But if you lose an order because of quality, the price will not bring them back."

There is no substitute for quality. When a pastor was sick, he called a friend to speak for him. The friend explained why he was there. In the children's sermon, he wanted the children to understand what a substitute was. He pointed to a beautiful stained glass window and said, "Suppose you were playing ball alongside of the church and a ball broke that window. Since the window had to be ordered special, they closed the hole up with a piece of cardboard. That would be called a substitute." After the service, a lady greeted him and said, "You are not a substitute; you are a real pain."

I quote from Father's book, "We needed a faster way to cook them, so I brought my resources into action again. To scald the tomatoes for peeling, I had a wire basket that I made. We could scald half a bushel at a time. That was very hard work, to lean over a boiler of hot water holding a half bushel of tomatoes. We had to hire a few women to peel tomatoes. My wife's Sunday School class peeled tomatoes. They put the money in the treasury of the class. That helped with the finances of the church."

In 1924, Andrew, the oldest son, graduated from high school. Mother wanted to go to the graduation, but my youngest sister, Alice, was born the day before. Andrew said that was his graduation present.

As the demand kept growing for canned tomatoes, the merchants wanted them in tin. In 1924, we bought a little hand sealer from Sears & Roebuck Company. By working really hard, you could seal two cans a minute. For a larger container to cook the tomatoes in, Father cut the end out of an old oil drum and riveted ears on them to hold the drums above the fire. For a fire place, he took old metal boxes in which they made ice and cut a hole in them with a cold chisel. He made baskets of wire and metal to hold the cans. We fastened a block and tackle to an overhead beam to lift the baskets out of the boiling water. Tin was so much easier to use. With glass jars, you would not dare put them in boiling water or they would break. Starting out with luke warm water took almost twice as long to sterilize tomatoes, compared to dropping tin cans in boiling water. We used wood to heat the water. It was a lot of hard work to cut the wood by hand.

Why did we turn the sealer by hand? We had no electricity on the farm. Remember, Lindberg did not fly across the Atlantic until six years after we started canning. In 1921, when we started canning tomatoes, you could buy a spanking brand new Ford for $395. You could only drive a few hundred miles without a flat tire. That made it necessary to have a tire pump as standard equipment, as well as pliers, a monkey wrench, a screw driver, and a jack.

Before we had electricity, we used a gas engine to pump water and saw wood. We also got a larger sealer and ran it with a gas engine. Total production for a year was about 250 cases. To expand, we desperately needed electricity. Did you ever stop to think how hard it would be to get along without electricity? However, the cost to build a power line was about the same per mile regardless of the number of customers. Because of the low number of customers in the country, our minimum monthly rate was sixteen times higher than an average home which was one dollar per month. To reduce the cost, we dug the holes for the light poles. Doing this by hand was hard work. We dug twenty-five holes five feet deep in the stones and the clay which we called hardpan. We used a crowbar about eight to ten feet long to loosen the dirt. When the hole was over two feet deep, the ground was lifted to the top with what we called a spoon. The handle was almost straight with a round spoon on the end. Sometimes, we used a half stick of dynamite to loosen the ground. I remember getting severe headaches when I handled the dynamite. We also hauled the light poles. By doing this, we were able to get the minimum rate down to about $12 per month. Today, the $12 looks like peanuts; but then, we were so poor, that amount of money looked like a mountain. The first year, we had so little electrical equipment, we only used three dollars worth of electricity per month. However, we soon got enough electrical equipment to use up the minimum.

It was a great day in 1927 when Father held up my little sister, Alice (about three years old) so she could pull the chain to turn on the lights. Now, with electricity to run the machinery, the pace of growth picked up. We bought a Max Ams sealer and put a one-third horse-power electric motor on it and were able to seal four cans a minute. We doubled production. Wow! We thought we were going places! Actually, we were making progress. From about 1926 to 1928, we increased pro-

76

duction four times to 1,000 cases per year. It is amazing that the machines which put the lids on the cans at speeds of 520 per minute use the same method today as was used on the hand machine to seal two cans a minute in 1924.

Until 1926, we had been doing the canning either out under the trees or in the kitchen. The canned tomatoes were stored in the cellar. Our first building was a cheap frame building, sixteen-by-forty feet. We cooked the tomatoes outside, but peeled the tomatoes and stored the canned tomatoes in this building. There was not any money to buy other equipment. They say, "Necessity is the mother of invention." The Lord had given my Father a very inventive mind. If he needed something, since he had no money to buy it, he made it. He bought lots of used pulleys, scrap iron, pipe, old gear boxes, stainless steel pipes, and many things from junk yards that other people discarded. He used these things to make machinery he could not afford to buy. For the first ten years, most of the equipment was second-hand or home-made.

In the days before V belts or direct-drive motors, all of the machinery was driven from a line shaft. The line shaft usually ran the length of the building. It was a steel shaft on which you placed pulleys wherever you wanted to run a machine. The line shaft was driven by a steam engine or a motor. You ran a flat belt from a pulley on the shaft to a pulley on the machine. That meant the machinery had to be set parallel to the line shaft. Any engineer or person who ever worked with flat belts will tell you they have to be much tighter than a V belt, and machinery must be lined up perfectly or the belt will run off. To help with traction, we used a special substance to rub on the belt to make it stick to the pulley. If you wanted to run a machine in the opposite direction from line shaft, you would put a twist in the belt. A twisted belt usually had better traction than a straight belt. Today, most machines have an individual motor on them. You can set them at any angle and any place you can get electric wire to them.

If Father needed some pulleys he could not afford to buy, he would take a block of wood, cut it as round as he could with an ax, then bore a hole through it to put a shaft in it. Then he would turn it down with a chisel as he ran it, like they do on lathes. The rims on the Ford cars were much like the truck rims today. He took three rims, fastened them together with flat iron, then fastened wire screening on them to use for a rotary washer. This was before the days of the electric welder. All iron was fastened with bolts. That meant all the holes had to be drilled with a drill. This was a very slow way compared to electric welding. Before we got electricity, the holes were all drilled with a hand-turned brace and bit. You really needed a sharp bit when you put pressure on the brace by hand. Also, we used a cold chisel and hammer to cut holes in metal tanks. To cut strap iron or angle iron, it was sawed off with a hand hack saw. It took a lot of time and hard work to build machinery.

I do not believe that hard manual labor does as much damage to one's health as mental stress. As C.E.O. of a growing company for thirty-three years, I know about hard work and stress. In those thirty-three years, sales have increased from $200,000 to over $11,113,000. That increase was in real dollars, as inflation was less than 1 percent per year.

In order to supplement our income, Father took a job driving a school bus. We also needed a bigger truck. Father bought a truck with seats that were easily removed. The aunt that loaned us the money to buy the farm was very patient with us. We were not able to pay even the interest, not to mention the fact that we should have been paying something on the principal. For a number of years, it took everything we had just to keep body and soul together. All we had for many a supper was corn meal mush and milk. Sometimes, we didn't even have any butter, sugar, or syrup to put on it. Breakfast often consisted of fried mush. We usually had all the milk we could drink. To get good corn meal to make the mush, we would roast ears of corn in the oven, shell it by hand, and grind it in the small grinder we had.

After we got electricity, before we could put in an automatic pump, we needed more water. Father made several round cement rings about eight feet in diameter. We dug a well by hand below the house in an old creek bed. We needed the cement rings to keep the gravel from flowing into the well as we dug it. As we dug the gravel out from under it, the ring would drop down and keep the gravel out. To get the gravel and soil up to the surface, we rigged up an old winch and pulled the soil up by hand. My, that was hard work!

In order to dig the second well to about twenty feet deep, we needed a better way to get the soil to the surface. Father's inventive mind took some track that is used for hay forks in the barn and put it above the well. We used an old oil drum, cut the end out, and put an axle in the center. When the drum was full of gravel and water, we used a horse to pull it up as if we were storing hay in the barn. For safety to protect us in the well, we kept an eight-foot plank to stand behind just in case anything fell. I am sure today the Occupational Safety and Health Administration (or O.S.H.A.) would not allow it.

My oldest brother, Andrew, really wanted a college education. Since he had to earn all the money himself, how was he to do it? While he was in high school, he bought seventy-five pullets (young laying hens). That reminds me of the young house wife who went to the grocery store and asked the store keeper for a chicken. Not knowing what kind she wanted, he asked, "Do you want a pullet?" She said, "Can't I carry it?" At first, Andrew thought there was a lot of money to be made. Father helped him to build a chicken coop twenty-by-fifty feet. Andrew did well for a few years. However, for several years, he lost money. He decided he would rather teach than raise chickens. So three years after he graduated from high school, he sent in his registration to Bloomsburg State Teacher's College. In those days, if you had twelve college credits, which you could get in one year, you could get a temporary certificate. So, after one year of college, he taught school at Leck Kill, Pennsylvania, for two years. That was in the lower end of Northumberland County. Many of the people spoke Pennsylvania Dutch in their homes and some of the first graders had trouble understanding English. The children would curse in Dutch on the playground. Since Andrew did not understand Dutch, he did not realize what was happening until he got a complaint from the school board. To continue teaching, he had to go back to college for a year to get a permanent teaching certificate. The two years he taught school, he got $85 per month. He decided he would teach school for a career, so he went back to college for a year. Thus, he was able to get a job in the local school called Joseph Priestley School.

Mary, the oldest daughter, had an accident on February 12, 1925, on her way to school. We were walking down the steep part of the hill above the present Priestley Elementary School when she slipped on the ice. She hurt her knee so badly she was unable to go up and down the steps at school. In those days, there were no ramps for wheel chairs. If you had a physical handicap, you could not get an education unless you could afford a private teacher. It took a lot of courage for Mary to go back to high school five years later. N. A. Danowsky was the principal of the Northumberland school system. He gave Mary a lot of encouragement. Mary was now past twenty-one and father had to pay her tuition. She went back to high school in January of 1930 as a junior. It was very difficult to start in the middle of the year, five years after the accident and to graduate a year-and-a-half later. That took more work and study than most people are willing to do. However, she wanted an education bad enough to work hard to get it. She showed the stick-to-it-iveness that characterized my father. Father set this forth in his book by that name. Instead of graduating two years before me, in 1926, she didn't graduate until 1931. When she graduated from high school, she went on to Bloomsburg College. When I graduated from high school, Mary was working for a clothing store. She was able to buy me a blue surge suit for graduation at a discount. I will be forever grateful. We were so poor that Father and Mother could not buy me a suit. We all worked together as a family.

When I graduated from high school, Father said, "If you want to go to college like your older brother, you will have to work your way through." However, he said, "If the family works together, I believe there is a future in the canning business. I am afraid if you spend four years in college, since I am not very well, we will loose the business before you graduate. You will have to make that decision." Soon after this, a doctor who was much younger than Father, said to him, "You will never live to be an old man." Father was fifty-four at the time, but he outlived the doctor by many years. Father was ninety-seven when the Lord took him home.

It was a big decision—should I continue to work on the farm, go to college, or seek other employment? For several years, I worked at home in the spring, summer, and early fall. The first winter, I worked at the Ford dealership in Northumberland, Mertz Motor Company. In the office during March, they trained me to calculate the previous day's business. I had to check to make sure that the gallons of gas sold, both cash and charge, agreed with the meter on the pump, etc.

When April came, I wanted to get back to the farm. We needed to plant tomatoes in the spring so we had tomatoes to can during the summer. When I gave two weeks notice that I was quitting, they said, "It is alright to help your parents, but you are due for advancement here if you stay. You have your own future to look after; if you go back to the farm, you will never amount to anything." I want to thank the Lord for directing me to help Father and Mother. I am sure natural wisdom would have caused me to make the wrong decision. Within fifteen years, Mertz Motor closed up; but by that time, the cannery was making real progress. Father sold canned tomatoes to Hoover Mercantile Company, who had a branch in Sunbury. He was able to get me a job with them for one winter. That winter at the wholesale house was good training as I learned something about the business from the buyer's point of view.

I realize it was only the Lord's guidance that prompted us children to stay home and work to pay off the mortgage. When you realize that our debts were twice our assets, from a business standpoint, it was hopeless. As a family, we realize now only the Lord knew how much He would prosper us.

The year was 1928. Even though the economy as a whole was very good following the first World War, we, as a family, were in tragic financial condition. When figuring up our financial condition after graduating from high school, the records showed that if we sold everything, including household furniture and dishes, we could not pay even half of our debts!

Furman tomatoes soon gained a reputation as the best tomatoes in local stores. They had a distinct fresh flavor. They were nice, red, ripe, whole tomatoes. One buyer said that they were so nice it looked like they were hand-made. We received many letters stating Furman tomatoes were as good as their own home-canned and, in fact, when they could get such nice canned tomatoes, they would not go to the fuss of canning their own.

Owners of the neighborhood stores said that if we could can other vegetables with the same high quality, vegetables that taste as good as fresh, that they could sell them. In response to customers' suggestions, we added stringless beans (green and wax), peas, corn, beets, and mixed vegetables.

To supply the increased demand, we had to find a faster way to cook or sterilize the tomatoes. We bought a used twelve horse power, locomotive-type steam boiler. We continued to fire this with wood. The first telephone cable, or lead line as it was called, was run over Montour Ridge, a mountain about a mile from our plant. They needed to cut a path forty feet wide through the woods to run the cable. We could have this wood by cutting it up. That boiler sure took a lot of wood. With the new boiler and a retort forty-eight-by-sixty inches, we were able to increase packing by five times or 5,000 cases.

A food broker from Wilkes-Barre bought several cans of Furman tomatoes after a storekeeper told him Furman tomatoes were better than any he had ever sold. He called and made an appointment to see Father. He said, "If you will pack them next summer, I will get you a firm order at a firm price before April 1." We figured our cost and decided we could make a little money at the price he suggested. So we took what was known in those days as future orders. It was by far the largest order we had taken up to that time. They were to be shipped out from September until May.

By the year 1934, our production was up to 14,000 cases. From the years 1928 to 1934, we had increased production by 14 times. This happened during the Great Depression. To look at the figures now, they look very small. Words cannot describe the long hours, heartaches, and disappointments that those figures represent. I wish I could draw you a word picture, how we worked from daybreak to sundown. When night came, you were too tired to do anything but go to bed. Sometimes, I was so tired I cried myself to sleep.

However, neither can words express the tremendous joy and excitement that comes from the victories we had. After about twelve years of not even being able to pay the interest, our interest payments were up to date. At long last, it looked like we might be able to start to pay off the mortgage. Since we had not fulfilled the agreement and had really only paid $10 on the property, my Aunt could have ejected us at any time. The hope that someday we as a family would be able to pay off the mortgage looked like it might become a reality, and it gave us new courage. The hope of victory and fulfilling a family dream was very exciting! In fact, it was just as exciting to us as Penn State winning the national championship in football over

Miami in 1987. Of course, the fact that seven of the third generation and three of the fourth generation hold degrees from Penn State emphasizes how important both of those victories were to us.

Earlier, I had mentioned the three serious sicknesses that hit the family in three years, and Father's depression about losing his life's savings because he could not get a clear deed to a farm after he'd already paid for it. We now thanked the Lord for the victories He was giving us.

Hard work is not enough. The Scripture says in Psalm 127, "Unless the Lord builds the house, its builders labor in vain. Unless the Lord watches over the city, the watchmen stand guard in vain." Unless the Lord blesses, hard work may destroy you.

In our wildest dreams, we never imagined that Furman Foods would one day be the largest family owned vegetable cannery in Pennsylvania. Today, we have a better than two-to-one current ratio. Banks offer us all kinds of incentives to do business with them. As I mentioned before, it took a lot of blood, sweat, and tears before we realized how much the Lord blessed us.

The next chapter will tell the exciting story of how a whole family worked together to see their dream come true—paying off the family mortgage. What a relief to know you owned your own property after struggling almost twenty years. During the dark years mentioned above, it seemed as if that day would never come. Today, I find it difficult to find words to describe our joy. Truly, large oak trees from little acorns grow.

The Great Depression of the early thirties made it very difficult. We couldn't go any lower. Owing two dollars for every dollar we had in assets means we were at the bottom looking up when everyone came sliding down. Read about the heartaches, hard work, blood, sweat, and tears that led to victory.

Chapter 9
The Great Depression
Years 1928–1941

October 29, 1929, Black Tuesday—in less than thirty days, stocks lost 40 percent of their value. One company's stock dropped from $113.50 per share to $4.00 per share in one day. The president of the company jumped to his death from a ledge of a New York hotel. The papers were full of suicides of people who lost their fortunes. Since wealth was their god, they had nothing for which to live.

It seems that some of the hardest people to win to the Lord are the very successful men who call themselves self-made men. My dear reader, are you at the top of your profession? You don't think you need God? My friend, are you too proud to admit that you are a sinner? Will God have to take away your gods—money, prestige, position, business—to get your attention? God may have to take away your health, your wife, your son or daughter to get your attention. God says in Luke 9:23–26,

> If anyone would come after me, he must deny himself and take up his cross daily and follow me. For whoever wants to save his life will lose it, but whoever loses his life for me will save it. What good is it for a man to gain the whole world and yet lose or forfeit his very self. If anyone is ashamed of me and my words, the Son of Man will be ashamed of him when He

comes in His glory and in the glory of the Father and of the holy angels.

My dear reader, if you have never accepted Christ as your Saviour, the Bible says in Mark 16:16, "Whoever believes and is baptized will be saved, but whoever does not believe will be condemned." I would love to see you in heaven. If you are not sure of heaven, please lay this book aside right now and read the Gospel of John and also read 1 John 5:9–13, which was written that you might know that you have eternal life.

You may be interested in a few news items of the years following the stock market crash taken from the *New York Times*:

January 4, 1931: 500 farmers storm Arkansas town, demanding food for their children.

June 17, 1932: Pictures of bread and soup lines.

June 18, 1932: 10,000 veterans march on Washington demanding bonus.

March 4, 1933: President Hoover's last day in office, the banking system of the United States collapsed.

Not quite three and a half years had passed since the stock market crash had plunged the United States, and most of the world, into the worst economic debacle in Western memory. Industrial output was now less than half the 1929 figures. The number of unemployed, although difficult to count accurately, had mounted to something between thirteen and fifteen million, or a record high of 25 percent of the labor force. Hourly wages had dropped 60 percent since 1929, white collar salaries dropped 40 percent. Farmers were getting five cents a pound for cotton and less than fifty cents a bushel for wheat.

March 6, 1933: Roosevelt orders a four-day bank holiday and later made it a full week. This was to stop "runs" on banks. People were hoarding their money.

March 13, 1933: Many banks reopen today but with hoarding barred.

September 14, 1933: Announcement of the National Recovery Administration Board, or NRA.

May 21, 1935: Roosevelt set $19 to $94 for monthly relief wages.

September 1, 1939: German army attacks Poland, cities bombed, ports blocked. Danzig is accepted into Reich.

The Depression was ended not by the government's efforts but by the beginning of the Second World War.

The real effects of the Depression did not hit our area hard until 1931. Many banks that in normal times were in good financial condition had to close their doors because the depositors started what was known as a "run on the bank."

In 1931, the Farmers & Mechanic Bank in Northumberland closed. Father had a little money in it. He had issued checks to pay bills. When the bank closed, people expected him to pay them cash. Where was he to get the money? I do not remember how he paid them off, but I do know that the bank paid most of their depositors off in small installments over several years. The North Branch Title & Trust Bank in Sunbury also closed.

Financial conditions continued to get worse. Many businesses did not survive. Profits in the food business were very low; however, people always need to eat. They may not be willing to pay much for what they eat, but they must eat, so we actually prospered.

There is a book about the depression that described our family, *We Had Everything But Money*. We had plenty to eat most of the time as we lived on the farm that had all kinds of fruits and vegetables, as well as milk. We also had a happy family. There was plenty of room to play. We had good neighbors whom we could see every Sunday. We had many things money cannot buy.

Money Will Buy
A bed but not sleep.
Books but not brains.

Food but not appetite.
Finery but not beauty.
A house but not a home.
Medicine but not health.
Amusements but not happiness.
A crucifix but not a Saviour.
A church but not a heaven.
But what you cannot buy
you can receive as a gift.
(Author unknown)

"For the wages of sin is death; but the gift of God is eternal life in Christ Jesus our Lord" (Romans 6:23).

Father was always trying to do something new and different than others. In the early thirties, he tried marketing the following soups: chicken noodle, chicken, chicken corn, vegetable beef, and tomato. We packed the soups in #2 cans, the same size cans in which we pack tomatoes. It was expensive to get machinery for the can size other soup packers use. Of course, Campbell and Heinz monopolized the soup business. We never could get any worthwhile volume, so after about five years, we gave up on soups. Father also made a whole wheat cereal which was much better than Grapenuts. It was a delicious cereal. Even today, I wish I could get some cereal as good as Father made. However, that market was controlled by a few companies then as it is today. After a few years, we discontinued the cereal. We put a lot of work and effort into those items. It is hard to express in words the trials and distress we went through when these items into which we put so much work did not succeed.

We were doing everything by hand, which was very expensive. I quote from Fathers book, page 45, "Peas were picked by hand. Then, we hired a lot of women to shell them. That sure cost money. We heard of a small machine run by an electric motor to shell peas after they were picked. I found the cost, and they were very expensive. I thought, if someone else could build a machine, I could too. I felt what had been done can be done again. I found the principle the machine worked on, so I went to work. I had it ready when the next year's crop was ready. We planted a lot of peas and had boys pick them. It did very well. We used it several years. It sure cut expenses." I remember when Father would be building machines, he was so interested in what he was doing that he would work on them after supper as long as he could see.

The stringless beans were snipped by hand, which was very slow. The corn was husked and cut off by hand. To be fair with those people who worked hard, instead of paying by the hour, we paid by piece work. Many people will work fast when things come to them on a belt, but if they have to pick it up, they are very slow unless they are paid based on production. Before we went to piece work, it was a real problem and took a lot of supervision to get production out of some of the workers. As we told them to work harder, I am reminded of the foreman who was told, "What is your hurry? Rome wasn't built in a day." He replied, "But I wasn't foreman then."

Many years between 1918 and 1932, we were not able to pay the interest on our mortgage. However, the canning business was growing and profitable. About 1932, we were able to pay all of the back interest. My Aunt Mary was about eighty years of age and not in good health. To avoid complications when she would pass away, she deeded the farm to Father and Mother. We had worked the farm for fourteen years. We had the interest paid up-to-date, but the $10 down in 1918 was all we had paid on the farm. Aunt Mary took a mortgage for $2,400 and a note for $800. We just praise the Lord that Aunt Mary had not ejected us as the agreement called for.

About the year 1930, Father lost his voice. The doctor told him that it was caused by goiter. He went to the Geisinger

Hospital. A specialist there told him the goiter was not causing it. Later, his voice returned but they didn't find out why. When they said they would not operate for the goiter, Father decided to be operated on for a double hernia. He had suffered with a hernia for years. While Father was in the hospital, Mother and we children tried to run the farm. It was late May, and we were planting tomatoes for the canning factory. Cut worms had cut off as many as 85 percent of the plants. Also, one of the horses had died. My, what a trying and discouraging time. At first, we did not tell Father, but he sensed something was wrong and got the whole story from us. He told us to get wheat bran, mix some molasses and parris green (an insecticide) with it and spread it on the fields in the evening. That killed the cut worms, and we replanted the tomatoes and got a good crop.

My oldest brother, Andrew, taught school in the winter but worked with us at home in the summer. My oldest sister, Mary, often worked as floor lady in the cannery. In 1934, Andrew married Mercy James. Also, my younger brother, James, graduated from high school and went on to college to study for the ministry.

Wonderful Things That Happened at Furman's

While the economy of the world was struggling, the Lord was blessing us, and we were growing. About 1933, we had a good crop and needed more money for cans. We went to the local bank. Mr. Charles Steele, the president, was out of town. He was also a United States Senator. Since we already had borrowed as much money as the banking laws allowed, the cashier did not have the authority to loan us more money. Father found out what day Mr. Steele would return and went to his home and asked him for the loan.

Mr. Steele said, "According to your financial statement, we could not loan you a penny. Also, you only have a $1,000 life insurance policy. You are an honest man, and, if you live, I know you will pay us. You have always paid your bills, and if you were not able to meet a note on time, you would come a day or two before it was due and advise when you could pay it." He also said, "You are in the food business, and people always eat! So, based on those things, I can tell you, you will get the loan even if your financial statement does not warrant it." I never forgot the remark about life insurance. When we took over the business, we always carried enough life insurance to cover most of each person's interest. That was a great help in getting bank loans.

Aunt Mary, who had loaned us the money, was a maiden lady, and she died in 1933. I quote from Father's book,

> We knew they would want to settle the estate. We were paying the interest but nothing on the principle. The heirs were a little sore. They did not visit us and did not know what we were doing. When Aunt Mary died, I knew what would come, so I began to figure. We knew my wife would get a little out of the estate. There were nine to divide it among, so it would not be much, but it would help. We found that if we would sell all the livestock which we could spare and our canned goods, we could pay off the mortgage. With my wife's share, it would make a neat sum, so we could easily borrow money. We asked a party to loan us the money. They really knew more about our business than our relatives and looked the thing over. I told them about how much we would need. They gave it readily.

The relatives had been contemplating what they would do. They did not want to throw us out with our big family. They sent one of their number to see what arrangements could be made. We just informed them we could pay it off. That was a pleasant surprise for them. They sympathized with us and did not want to cause us any trouble. It made them feel good that we could settle it so easily.

The records show that on November 30, 1934, the Northumberland National Bank gave us the $1,500 loan and took a mortgage for that amount so we could settle the estate. Also, on November 18, 1936, we were able to pay the mortgage off. Praise the Lord! What a day of rejoicing that our family goal of paying off the mortgage was finally realized. VICTORY! VICTORY! We finally had a clear deed to the property.

Nineteen thirty-six was the year in which the second most important event of my life happened. Hazel Epler and I were married. What was the most important event of my life? Earlier, I mentioned the Lutheran Church in our community. When I was about twelve years old, Reverend Sassaman had a week of evangelistic services. One night, when he preached on 1 Samuel 3, telling how Samuel was called to the Lord, the Lord asked me to surrender my life to Him. The reason I mention this as more important than my marriage is I doubt very much if Hazel would have married me if I did not know the Lord. The details of our courtship, marriage, and fifty-fifth wedding anniversary are in chapter 19, "The Women in My Life."

I have made many mistakes and often have not walked as close to the Lord as I should have, but praise God He was faithful and always brought me back to Him.

The third most important event of my life was going to The Bible Institute of Pennsylvania in Philadelphia during the winter of 1932. It was at Bible college that I learned how to study the Bible and communicate it to others. In fact, it did so much for me that my two younger brothers and two younger sisters all went to The Bible Institute of Pennsylvania, which later became Philadelphia College of the Bible.

One request I made of all my children was that the first year out of high school, they take one year at a Bible college. After that, they could pick their school and their vocation. I think going to Philadelphia College of the Bible did more for our children than any other thing I know. Many of our grandchildren also attended Philadelphia College of the Bible. The records show that twenty three of my relatives have attended there. I also had mentioned that I decided to help Father and Mother instead of going to college. At the suggestion of my older brother, Andrew, I went to some Saturday courses at Susquehanna University and also took a course in accounting by correspondence. All of my children have four years of college and one has seven years.

My, how times have changed. I have a flyer advertising grocery items. It is dated October, 1933. It lists thirteen grocery stores in Sunbury and four in Northumberland. Prices for a Furman's #2 can of corn was two for $.25; mixed vegetables, two for $.19; tomatoes, three for $.25; and string beans, three for $.25. Today, there are only six grocery stores in Sunbury and Northumberland. A 303 can of tomatoes sells for $.57 and corn for $.63. A #2 can was one pound, three ounces.; a 303 can is one pound.

The Lord blessed us. We hired food brokers in many of the cities of Pennsylvania. The quality was so good that demand continued to grow. The 12 HP boiler mentioned earlier had to be replaced in 1935 with a 45 HP steam boiler which was hand-fired with soft coal. We also bought a number of forty-by-sixty inch pressure retorts.

Before this, we were only boiling the corn at 212 degrees Fahrenheit. We did this many years without any trouble. However, one year over half our corn blew up. We lost over $1,000 which was a large sum to us in those days. The spoiled corn would develop tremendous pressure in the can before it would blow the end out or the side seam open. I remember seeing a can shoot up into the air eight or more feet when it exploded. Someone said, "I wonder if they canned popcorn." We called the can company's quality control department, and they advised us since corn was a non-acid vegetable and the pH was so high, that often boiling would not sterilize it properly. We thank the Lord no one got sick or got botulism poisoning. Today, the law requires that any vegetable with a pH above 4.6 must be pressure cooked at 240 degrees or higher. Most botulism cases are in home-canned foods where they use boiling water instead of pressure cookers.

Every year, sales and production grew by about 10 percent. About half of the growth was in new items. The other half was increased production of items we were already canning. Every increase meant we needed more steam. For forced draft, we put a large blower on the boiler. I can remember the fire doors getting so hot they warped and had to be replaced every few years. Also, when I stirred up the fire and threw shovels of coal on it, sometimes it would puff with fire coming out and singe my eyebrows.

We also needed more buildings. The sixteen-by-forty foot building we built in 1926 was too small. In 1931, we added a twenty-four-by-twenty-eight foot shed-type, open building. The posts were spaced so we could put three-by-six foot hotbed sashes on the building to close the factory up on the cold mornings in late September. The hotbed sashes were used to protect the tomato plants from frost in the early spring, thus we got double usage from them. This saved us a lot of money.

The home-made cookers were too small by then, so we bought several forty-by-sixty inch open retorts. However, for the cooling tank, Father took an old 500 gallon gas tank and cut the end out of it with a hammer and cold chisel. That was really hard work. We could not afford anything else. We used crates with three tiers of cans weighing about 420 pounds. To get them in and out of the retort, we bought a wooden crane. This had a handle with an arm about thirty inches long. As we lifted the crate, a ratchet kept it from dropping. However, when we lowered the crate, we had to control it. I weighed about 145 pounds and that was really hard work. One day, my hands slipped off the handle! I jerked my head back so the handle which was revolving at a high rate of speed would not hit me on the chin. The handle knocked my hat off. People who saw it said I was as white as a sheet. If that handle would have hit me on the chin, I doubt if I would be here to write about it.

After a few years, Father put an electric motor on the crane. He put a small pulley on the motor and a large pulley on the crane. A six-inch flat belt drove the crane. When not in use, the belt hung loose. To use it, he made a belt tightener which, when we pushed, would tighten the belt to make it drive the pulley on the crane. He got his idea from something he saw in a grain mill. We did not have the motor running when we wanted to lower a crate. We held the belt tightener so the belt would slip on the one pulley. That way we could lower the crate just as slow as we wanted to. That sure made a hard job easy.

We needed to save money wherever we could. For storage, we put the canned vegetables in the cellars of the homesteads of Norman Geise and Foster Furman. We also used the wooden garage built next to the factory.

This was before fork lifts were invented. We used a roller track to convey it to the area where it was stacked by hand. After stacking fifty-five-pound cases for ten hours to a height above your head, you didn't need to worry about cholesterol.

I mentioned the whole family worked together. My youngest sister, Elnora, after graduating from high school, went to Bible college one spring term. Since she worked as floor lady at the cannery during tomato season, she could not go the fall term. She was the floor lady for about seven years. Chapter 11 tells of her marriage to Norman Geise.

Our sales were pretty good in the soft coal areas of western Pennsylvania. We would deliver canned vegetables to the company stores and other grocery stores in a stake body truck. We brought coal back for fuel to fire the steam boiler. At first, we shoveled the coal off by hand. However, as better equipment became available, we had special stake bodies made with a hoist under them. It was so much easier to dump a load of coal than to shovel it off. Having a load both directions gave us a good freight rate into the area.

The next chapter will tell of the struggle to produce canned vegetables for our brave boys fighting in Germany and Japan. Also, at age sixty-five, Father decided that government regulations were too much for his nerves, and he decided to retire.

Chapter 10
The Second World War
Years 1940–1943

World War I was supposed to be the war to end all wars. Yet twenty years later, Hitler started an aggression that led to World War II.

On New Year's Day of 1940, even though Germany had clamped an iron fist around Europe, and Japan was raping China, most Americans were peaceably preoccupied with their own affairs. Hitler had sent his Panzers (tanks) into Poland in September of 1939 and, by so doing, had embroiled himself with those two bastions of democracy, Britain and France. Many Americans thought it was a phony war. A poll conducted in December, 1939, showed that 67.4 percent of the American people were opposed to taking sides. On September 16, 1940, the first peace-time draft in American history became law. In a speech prior to the 1940 election on October 20, Franklin Delano Roosevelt said, "I have said it before, but I shall say it again and again. Your boys are not going to be sent into any foreign wars." In November's election, Roosevelt got twenty-seven million votes compared to twenty-two million votes for Wendel Wilkie. Thus, Roosevelt broke the 144-year-old tradition against being elected to a third term.

In mid 1941, the danger to Pearl Harbor became very real. The long-standing rivalry between Japan and the United

States for Pacific supremacy was further aggravated by announced plans for broad expansion of Nippon's Greater East Asia Co-Prosperity Sphere. In July, President Roosevelt brought matters to a head by freezing all Japanese assets in the United States. Months of negotiation followed. In closed meetings on November 22, the militarists in Japan's Imperial Palace said, "We will wait until November 29, and after that, things are automatically going to happen." While they were still negotiating on November 26, six radio-silenced aircraft carriers stole out of the remote Kuriles north of Japan and headed for Pearl Harbor along the untraveled northern route. On the morning of December 7, 1941, they struck Pearl Harbor at 7:55 while it was still asleep. In 110 minutes, 2,400 men were killed and hundreds wounded. Eight big battleships were destroyed, three light cruisers were sunk or damaged, and 188 planes were destroyed. The Japanese lost twenty-nine planes, only one third of what they expected to lose. War was declared and four bloody years lay ahead.

During the war, most males between the ages of eighteen and thirty-six discovered a fateful notice in their mail.

> Greetings. Having submitted yourself to a local board composed of your neighbors for the purpose determining your availability for training and service in the land or naval forces of the United States, you are hereby notified that you have been selected for training and service therein. This local board will furnish transportation to an induction station. You will there be examined, and if accepted, you will then be inducted into the land or naval forces. If you are employed, you should advise your employer of this notice. Your employer can then be prepared to replace you if you are accepted or to continue your employment if you are rejected. Willful failure to report promptly to this local board at the hour and on the day named is a violation of the Selective Training and Service Act of 1940, as amended, and subjects the violator to fine and imprisonment.

Many men enlisted, feeling it was their patriotic duty. Also, by enlisting instead of waiting to be drafted, they had an opportunity to pick their type of service. Most of the drafted men ended up being foot soldiers.

That was fifty years ago. Some of my relatives describe it as, "war is hell." However, the war finally ended, whereas hell, as described in the Bible, lasts forever. Books and friends can tell you more about the heartaches, tears, broken dreams, homes broken up, and pain that only war can cause. Many wives, children, parents, and grandparents cried themselves to sleep at night because loved ones were called into the service. Who can describe the agony of waiting to learn if a loved one survived when the ship they were on was torpedoed; the long nights of waiting to hear from a son or daughter in the service? College careers were interrupted. Marriages were postponed or perhaps moved up several months, so they could be married before leaving for Europe or the Pacific. How families dreaded the telephone call or a rap at the door by an official of the armed service to say, "Your son or daughter is missing in action and presumed dead."

The draft that was passed on September 16, 1940, fourteen months before we got in the war, was already working when war was declared. To that extent, we were partially ready.

Nothing that happened at home can be compared to the suffering, heartaches, etc., of the soldiers and families of those who were asked to give the supreme sacrifice for their country. However, we on the home front faced our own hardships and challenges. We were a small growing company. All of our key employees were young men, and, therefore, subject to the draft. I was thirty at the time, but I had a double hernia which gave me a physical deferment. Also, as plant manager of a food processing plant, I had an occupational deferment. Before the next canning season, Paul Geise, assistant plant manager, and three key men, George Byers, Al Sassaman, and John Sulouff, would be in the service. In addition, a lot of our part-time employees went into the service. We were able to get two deferments for the factory—Thomas Lee Stahl and John Slear.

Our government had learned from the first World War of the need for a good food supply. That was the reason for giving draft deferments to farmers and food processors. I believe it was Napoleon Bonaparte who said, "An army moves on its stomach." It was in the early 1800s that thousands of French soldiers were perishing miserably from scurvy and slow starvation because their diet of smoked fish, salt meat, and hardtack did not sustain them.

Napoleon made a frantic appeal to all patriots. If anyone would devise a method of ensuring fresh, wholesome food for French armies and navies—at all times and under all circumstances—a grateful government would present him a prize of 12,000 francs, and then the war could be won on well-filled French stomachs.

This appeal inspired Nicholas Appert to experiment for fourteen years. At last, he found that if he put food in airtight bottles and immersed the bottles in boiling water for varying periods of time, it would keep the "processed" food in edible condition. He received the 12,000 francs in 1809. This was the beginning of the food processing industry.

For almost 100 years, the cans were made by hand. Small pieces of food were forced through a small hole in the can and then it was soldered shut by hand. It was about the year 1901, the year President McKinley was assassinated, that the open top or sanitary can was invented. This allowed whole fruits and vegetables to be filled through the top. The lid was put on the can with a double seamer much like it is today, almost 100 years later. The first sanitary cans had a side seam that was crimped and soldered. About 1964, or thirty years ago, when it was learned that the lead in the solder could be harmful, they started electric welding of the side seam. Most spoilage happened at the side seam or where the lid crossed the side seam. This change has eliminated 95 percent of the spoilage. The fact is that previous to 1950, a swell allowance of one-fourth of one percent was taken off the price. Today, all food cans are entirely free from lead. About 1987, they started making an extruded or two-piece can. Except for those few changes, the sanitary can and putting the lid on by double seaming is about the same as it was 100 years ago.

Here are some quotes recorded from government officials:

"I should like to emphasize that every person working in the food industry is just as important to the war effort as any person working in an ammunition or airplane factory, or just as important as the soldier on the battlefield." Colonel Paul Logan, U.S. Army.

"The canning industry is not a cut-back industry," Brigadier General Carl Harding, Office of Q. M. C. said to the Chicago Processors' Conference. "I again wish to emphasize the necessity for every pound of preserved food in 1944 that can be produced. The need for canned fruits and vegetables for a man (soldier) overseas is more than double the need for a man at home."

In the years 1939 and 1940, we modernized our plant. In the years from 1933 to 1940, we built three more open-shed type buildings with a total of about 2,500 square feet for processing. We increased production from 25,000 cases in 1939 to over 50,000 cases in 1941. That was doubling production in two years. The Lord was good in getting us ready for the war years that started in 1941. Getting enough employees was a real task. J. W. Furman once said, "Some give their lives; some give their blood; I will give my sweat and hard work. I would rather have a tired back than an empty stomach."

I was amazed to see in the records that in 1941, fifty acres of tomatoes only produced 250 tons or an average of five tons per acre. We hand picked them four or five times. I also noted that the farmer with the best yield only got seven-and-one-half tons per acre. Our best yield in 1991 per acre was forty-three tons on hand picked and thirty-nine tons per acre on machine picked. In 1992, Furman Farms broke all records for large acreage by producing an average of thirty-five tons per acre on a total of 107 acres.

Our plant was built to pack 40,000 cases, but in 1943, we packed 69,000 cases. I lived within a block of the cannery. I well remember my daily schedule was to go to the factory about 5:30 in the morning, stoke up the soft coal, and turn on the blower on the steam boiler. We hand fired at that time. I would return home, get breakfast, and get back to the factory by 6:30 to stoke the fire up again so we would have steam to operate the factory by seven o'clock. I would take about thirty to forty minutes for lunch and thirty to forty minutes for supper. Then I would work until the factory shut down about one or two o'clock in the morning.

Our oldest son, Franklin, was about five years old at that time. He could not understand why I spent so much time at the factory and had very little time to play with him. In fact, he almost came to hate the factory so much that, when he graduated from college, he considered working for someone else. We told our children that at least I was with them on Sunday. Also, they got to see me a few minutes as we ate dinner and had family worship at the supper table, while many children did not see their fathers for years and many of their daddies never came home.

We also had employees that worked up to twenty-two hours a day. One man, Bill Dreese, slept in the barn. After several days of twenty-two hours each, he fell asleep on his feet while forking pea vines into the pea viner. Since the closest restaurant was three miles, and gas was rationed, my Mother fed any employee who worked past the supper hour. Often, she did not know if there would be two or twelve until an hour before the meal.

On an application to the draft board in 1944 for continued deferments, it shows that from April 1 to November 1, the following people worked seventy hours or over per week—John Slear, Lee Stahl, Arbor Neidig, and Howard Reitz. To average that many hours over seven months means that, during the peak season, they worked up to twenty hours per day. During pea season, the field crews sometimes would start at one o'clock on Monday morning.

Our closing machine was running at 100 cans per minute. The women and many employees worked a twelve to thirteen hour shift. However, I, as well as many key employees, worked through both shifts. Lee Stahl, a retort operator and maintenance mechanic, started at 4:30 in the morning and often worked until 2:00 the following morning. We always closed down Saturday evening in time for the wash-up crew to finish before midnight. We believe Sunday is the Lord's day, a day when people should go to church and rest. Since many of us worked up to twenty hours per day during the week, guess what we did on Sunday afternoon!

We believe the Lord blessed us for believing that it is more important to go to church and Sunday School than to can peas on Sunday. Also, it was more important to rest on Sunday afternoon than to can peas. I well remember that two canneries in Bloomsburg ran on Sunday because the hot weather was maturing peas so fast they thought they would lose them if they closed down on Sunday. Since their employees were working almost day and night, by the time Wednesday came, many of their employees were so tired they could not work. The farmers brought the peas to the cannery, but there was not anyone to can them, so they lost hundreds of tons of peas and thousands of dollars. The fact of the matter is, they both went bankrupt within ten years. Our employees rested on Sunday and worked hard enough the next week to take care of our whole crop. So we made out a lot better than they did because the Lord blessed us for taking Sunday off.

One particular trying incident stands out in my mind. One night, an inexperienced workman was steam cleaning a chain elevator. He got the steam hose caught in the elevator, and it literally tore it into eight or ten pieces before I could stop it. It was two o'clock in the morning, and we needed to start working on the peas at six o'clock. To me, it looked like an impossible repair job. I believe I actually cried. I called my brother, Bill, who had an agriculture deferment but did welding for the factory. When he looked it over, he said, "You go home and get some sleep; it will be ready to go by six o'clock."

In addition to the men mentioned before, the draft board gave agricultural deferments for Norman Geise, William Furman, and K. James Kohl. We operated two farms and also harvested peas and beans for other farmers. Agricultural deferments were based on sixteen units of production.

What did J. W. Furman Cannery contribute to the war effort? On a government form I found in the files was the following information dated March 24, 1944:

      Beans, snap ....4,850 doz. for Navy
      Peas...................................10,592 doz. for Army
      Tomatoes ....27,978 doz. for Navy
      Beets ....3,326 doz.

This was 50 percent of our production.

John Sulouff was in England when he saw a can of our beets. He was surprised and overjoyed. It was almost like a letter from home. He picked it up and yelled, "I work at Furman's Cannery."

The acreage we contracted for in 1944 as compared to 1991 was:

	1944	1991
Green Peas	145	600
Sweet Corn	100	0
Tomatoes	110	2,100
Green & Wax Beans	60	1,200
Beets	60	0

To help recruit employees, the government sent us the following figures, showing how much of our pack the war department needed: every other tomato, every third ear of corn, every other bean, three out of five cases of beets, two out of every five cases of peas.

We found another way to encourage workers so they would feel they were helping in the war effort and thus be proud of what they were doing. Each day, we would put on a piece of cardboard the number of cases produced the previous day and how many soldiers that production would feed for one meal a day. Producing 798 cases of tomatoes per day would feed 119,700 soldiers one meal. If we produced 1,090 cases of peas per day, it would feed 163,650 soldiers one meal. If we produced 588 cases of beans per day, it would feed 88,200 soldiers one meal.

In early 1944, the draft board canceled all previous deferments and reclassified some of our key employees as A-1 even though we had contracted for the same acreage of vegetables as we canned in 1944. Due to the danger of not having enough key employees, we wrote to each of our growers. I quote parts of the letter dated April 4, 1944. "Selective service considers it more important to the welfare of our country to take two of our key employees and put them in the army, rather than leave them in our factory to process the vegetables grown on the farms. . . . Due to loss of key men, we are forced to reduce our acreage from 20 to 40 percent depending on the vegetables. Please change your contract to read as follows. . . ." We are thankful that, through the help of the Army Quarter Master procurement service, we were able to get those key employees deferred and make a normal pack of canned vegetables.

We shipped a lot of our canned vegetables overseas. They needed to be packed in Solid Cardboard V-2 cartons. A V-2 sleeve was put over the case, and they were strapped with steel straps. Sometimes, they were stored outside in the weather.

Or in the unloading operation, I am told they were thrown on the beach where they might get wet. The solid cardboard would not fall apart if the cases got wet.

At the end of December 1941, Secretary of Agriculture, Claude Wickard, startled Americans by suggesting that because commercial farms were busy feeding the Army, United States civilians who wanted fresh vegetables on their tables should plant victory gardens. With that, millions of Americans who didn't even know what a hoe was, dug up their yards and planted vegetables. They were called Sunday farmers. In 1943, the victory gardens produced at least one-third of all the fresh vegetables consumed in the country.

For a people almost totally unused to any kind of wartime sacrifice, WPB Directive No. 1 to OPA Jan. 1942—instituting rationing—came as a shock. Suddenly, United States citizens were stuck with a mess of little books and stamps that limited the food and gas they could buy!

Gasoline rationing was especially unpopular. When the average driver received an A card limiting him to a mere three gallons per week, he started to cheat. By the end of the year, most drivers realized it was not patriotic to cheat and began to abide by the law. Of course, there were long lines at the gas stations.

Since there were more buyers than we could supply, our sales people worked in the factory and, thus, did not need gas to travel. I have been reading that, at the beginning of 1944, farmers were not allowed any gas to haul their vegetables to the cannery. It took a lot of letters and telephone calls to straighten that out.

The customer had to give stamps as well as cash to the grocery store clerk. The store gave the stamps to the wholesaler. The wholesaler deposited them in the bank, like money. When he bought the canned vegetables from us, he made out a check for stamps, just the same as he did for money. Then we had to write checks to the government to cover all we sold.

Some point values were as follows:

Hamburger ....7 points
Butter..16 points
One can of carrots ....6 points
Peaches...18 points

What a headache! Grocers had to cope with some four-teen billion points per month. I remember the trouble of try-ing to balance the stamp account at the end of the month against what we had sold. If you have trouble balancing your bank account, that is a picnic compared to ration stamps!

We had to get ration stamps for the sugar we needed to pack peas and corn. Just to buy simple supplies like buckets and bushel baskets, we needed orders from the government. In my letters to the Office of Price Administration in the summer of 1945, I read that we had a larger pack of peas than normal, and we had to apply for additional sugar for the larger pack. Of course, the canning of peas could not wait until government red tape was cleared. So we canned the peas and used the sugar we were allotted for corn. We were able to get additional sugar for the corn that we packed in August and September. My, what a hassle!

Since orders far out paced supply, price controls were in-troduced in 1942. We had to send to the Office of Price Ad-ministration the average price at which we sold each vegetable, as well as each grade, for the year 1941. For the next four years, our ceiling price would be controlled by the figure we sent in. Each year, we were allowed to add certain increases for sugar, cans, labor, and raw vegetables. We had a few items on which our prices were below cost of production. In some cases, we were able to get a reasonable increase. In other cases, we just had to quit packing certain items because we lost money. Talk about paper work and headaches! You don't know anything about it until you have been through a war.

During the years 1942 through 1945, prices rose very little under price control. The comparison of prices below helps one to realize how much inflation we have had since 1945. Prices below are from a list of December 14, 1945, which I sent to Office of Price Control. Everything was packed in #2 cans which was 1.22 times bigger than a 303 can. As families became smaller, the can sizes were decreased. I converted the price from a #2 can to a #303 can in order to give correct comparisons:

Price per case of 24 cans	1945	1991
#303 Furman Tomatoes	$2.34	$10.00
#303 Furman Whole Kernel Corn	2.54	11.50
#303 Furman Sweet Peas	2.50	10.00
#303 Furman Green Beans	2.22	8.50
#303 Furman Kidney Beans	1.72	7.95

Prices paid for vegetables per ton		
Fancy Peas	$97.00	$257.49
Fancy Stringless Beans	96.00	191.92
Tomatoes	27.59	95.25

We wrote to the National War Labor Board in June of 1945 asking permission to raise our minimum wage to $.55 per hour. In 1991, the minimum wage was $4.25.

Victory in Europe; Germany signs peace treaty in General Eisenhower Headquarters at 2:41 a.m., May 7, 1945. Victory in the Pacific; Japan signs peace treaty aboard battleship Missouri in Tokyo Bay on September 2, 1945.

You who saw the victory parades after the Gulf War in 1991 and had family members come home have an idea what it was like. However, you have to remember, this last war only lasted a few months, whereas some of the boys in World War II were away for several years. There were parades and great celebrations. The biggest difference between the two wars was that we lost over 400,000 men in World War II and less than 100 in Desert Storm. (In comparison, we lost 58,000 in Vietnam.) Thus, as in other wars, there were many families who waited in vain for their sons and daughters, fathers and mothers, who were buried on foreign soil and also buried at sea.

Price controls, rationing, and the draft were ended toward the latter part of 1945.

In addition to an all-out war effort, some other things happened at Furman's. My younger brother, James, was ordained as a Baptist preacher and married Edna Beck from Altoona. They met while they were both attending Juniata College at Huntingdon, Pennsylvania.

K. James Kohl started to work driving horses on our farms. He loved farming and wanted to share his dreams with someone. Guess what? He fell in love with my youngest sister, Alice, and they were married in 1943.

J. W. Furman, founder of the business, reached the age of sixty-five during the war years. An uncle, Dave Wilhour, owned a house in Vero Beach, Florida. He invited Father and Mother to visit him. Father and Mother spent a few weeks in Florida in 1942. He and Mother liked the warm sunshine and oranges. They rented a house for several months in 1943. It seems the older you get, the more cold weather bothers you. Also in 1943, homes were not insulated like they are today. Most rural homes did not have central heating or electric heat.

Uncle Dave Wilhour had a mortgage on a home right next to him in what they called the Pennsylvania Colony. The owner was several years behind in his payments. He wanted more money than Father was willing to pay. After a number of letters, finally the man agreed to sell it for the unpaid amount on the mortgage. People could not get gas to travel to Florida, so homes were hard to sell. Father got a good buy and completed the purchase in the fall of 1943. He really sprang a great surprise on us when he told us about it and asked if we would be interested in buying the business.

Father grew up in a business climate with very few government controls and regulations. It was very difficult for him to accept price controls, wage controls, and rationing. He said, "It's just too much for my nerves."

I remember one particular incident. We were running mixed vegetables which was a mixture of carrots, potatoes, tomatoes, celery, sweet corn, etc. The state inspector came about the middle of the afternoon. The ladies would clean enough celery, carrots, etc., for a given number of batches before putting it in the cans. Waste such as corn husk, etc., was sitting there in containers. In those days, we cleaned everything by hand. The inspector looked in his book and said that waste is to be stored in silos. We explained that we removed the waste at noon and would clean everything up at the end of the day. He insisted it was to be put in silos. He proceeded to write up a negative report that could have possibly resulted in either a hearing or closing us down, as he would not renew our license. This was serious. Just before he left, he called Father aside and said that "so and so" was running for the Pennsylvania House of Representatives. If Father would contribute to his campaign, he would make a good report, and Father would get his license. This was against Father's principles, and he would not pay bribe money to anyone. Father believed, as we do, that if you want good laws, it is very important to visit and know your government officials regardless of their political affiliation. Since Father knew the representative, he called him and said, "Do you know inspector 'so and so' is trying to raise money for you by threatening to send reports that may prevent our license from being renewed?" The politician was very upset and assured Father that this inspector was doing this on his own and would be fired.

I believe it was in November when Father asked us to buy the business. Father and Mother left for Florida after Christmas in 1943. We children had some big decisions to make. How would we pay for the business? What was a fair price for the business? Father wanted to divide his estate equally among his four sons and three daughters. Where would we get the money to pay the three children who were not part of the business?

Since Father could not get gas to drive to Florida, they went by train. In the first letter written from Florida on January 2, 1944, he described their trip. A trip to Florida in 1944 was as big as a trip to Israel is today. In fact, it took almost as much time.

Even though he was retired, he continued to get up about 5:30 every morning. His neighbors teased him that he got up early so he would have more time to loaf. In his letters, he would tell about sowing peas, string beans, lettuce, and radishes on January 1. So you see, even though he was sixty-seven, he still loved to grow vegetables. He continued to grow his own vegetables until he was eighty-eight. When they could no longer go to Florida because of Mother's health, he sold the property.

Father and Mother wrote one or two letters every week. In every letter, he asked about the grandchildren, or babies, as he called them. They also shipped a lot of oranges. Since the oranges and grapefruit were tree ripened, they were much sweeter than what we could buy in the store. One time, he shipped over twenty-five bushels of oranges and grapefruit. He told us to be sure the babies got all the fruit they could eat and then sell the balance. For the fruit we sold, he received $1.50 for the fruit, $.29 for the basket, and $1.40 for the express cost, for a total of $3.19. He also told of planting fourteen orange trees and two grapefruit trees. He thanked the Lord that he remained healthy long enough to pick fruit from them. Many of the letters told of them going fishing. He fished more in one week in Florida than he had in his whole life. In 1944, Florida was a fisherman's paradise. They caught 50 to 100 fish per day. Some would get forty-five pounds per day. The last I fished in this area in 1988, three of us only caught five to ten fish.

I would like to review some of the highlights of the Furman family, beginning with our move to Pennsylvania. J. W. Furman had lost everything. A sister of my mother bought a farm for $3,200 for us to live on. Father only paid $10 down. For many years, he did not even pay any interest. By the year 1928, because of three major sicknesses, our financial condition was hopeless. We owed over $6,000 and, if we had sold everything, including household furniture, we could not have paid half of our bills. By the year 1933, we had the interest paid up to date. My mother's sister died, and we were able to borrow $1,500 by getting a mortgage from the bank. We were able to pay the balance to her estate so they could settle it. A year later, the family dream came true; we were able to pay off the mortgage. In 1944, when J. W. Furman retired, he sold the business to two sons and two sons-in-law for $42,789.20.

In the next chapter, read about the challenges and hardship of the next generation buying out the business.

Chapter 11
The Changing of the Guard
Year 1944

<u>The Winds of Fate</u>
*One ship drives east and another drives west
With the selfsame winds that blow.
'Tis the set of the sail
And not the gales
Which tells us the way to go.*

*Like the winds of the sea are the ways of fate,
As we voyage along through life:
'Tis the set of the soul
That decides its goal,
And not the calm or the strife.*
—Ella Wheeler Wilcox

What a challenge! To change from a one-man ownership to a four-owner partnership was a big adventure. The father of one of the partners said a partnership is a "blankety-blank" poor ship to sail in, especially since it was a family partnership. We had many obstacles to overcome.

Where would the partnership get the money to buy out the business? Even though Father's estate was very small, he wanted to divide about half of it among the seven children.

Since four were in the new business, that left two brothers and one sister to pay. Also, it is often hard for a new business to get credit, especially when the new owners are all young people. The cannery business is a seasonable business, requiring large sums of money for cans and labor during the growing season. Customers wanted canned vegetables the entire year. The loans would be paid off during the spring and early summer.

Another challenge was the fact that we were all young. We all wanted our own homes. We either had small children or were just starting our families. If you have ever started your own business, bought a home, and started a family all at the same time, you know it can be very stressful financially. Where was the money to come from to pay the mortgage? In those days, there was no hospital insurance. How would we pay the doctor bills? We had a real struggle financially. However, we had gardens and grew most of our own vegetables. We got the canned vegetables we needed in the winter from the cannery. Our food cost us very little. If we couldn't grow it, we would do without. Also, we lived a very conservative lifestyle. In the early years, if we would have spent money too freely, Furman Foods would not exist today.

Babies cost money, and they got sick then, just as they do now. However, family values were different in 1944 than they are today. Most people wanted three or more children. Children and grandchildren were considered a gift from God as we read in Psalm 127:3–5: "Sons [or daughters] are a heritage from the Lord, children a reward from him. Like arrows in the hands of a warrior, are sons born in one's youth. Blessed is the man whose quiver is full of them." There always seemed to be too much month left at the end of the money. Regardless of our tight financial condition, most of us believed in tithing. Any success we may have had, I believe, is related to the fact that, if we put the Lord first in finances, as well as other things, He would bless.

In spite of all the problems we faced, we had a lot going for us. First and foremost, we were all committed Christians. We started a practice which we are still following after almost fifty years. All our board meetings are opened with Scripture reading and prayer. Our meetings with our employees are opened with prayer.

The second hallmark that made our business distinct and different than most businesses is something that I believe had a lot to do with our success. Not only did most of us tithe our salaries as individuals, but the partnership minutes show that whatever profits the partnership made, we gave 20 percent to the Lord.

Also, we believed that Sunday is the Lord's day. We, as individuals, believe it is more important to go to church and Sunday School than it is to attend sporting events, etc. We followed our father's principles that it is more important to go to church and Sunday School than it is to can vegetables on Sunday.

The third thing was we all knew what hard work was. All of us had worked many years for my father. The youngest, Jim Kohl, had worked for J. W. Furman for seven years before the partnership was formed. I, the oldest, was now thirty-three, and I helped to take care of the cows when I was only four. As we would say then, we all knew the business from the ground up.

The legal forming of the partnership, J. W. Furman Cannery, is dated February 2, 1944. K. James Kohl was twenty-three when elected secretary of J. W. Furman Cannery. He is better known as Jim. He started to work in the fall of 1936 driving horses. Jim belonged to the same church and went to the same young people's activities that my sister Alice did. It was just natural that they would want to share their dreams, hopes, and lives together. They were married in the fall of 1943. Since Father and Mother bought some property in Florida and spent the winters there, Jim and Alice moved into the homestead until Father and Mother came back in April. Jim and Alice

cared for the livestock that winter. In 1948, they bought a lot
from the partnership to build a home. It was about a half mile
from the factory on a hill overlooking the factory and Tuckahoe
Valley.

The fact that Jim grew up on a farm where he took care of
cows and horses was a great help. He was also familiar with
planting and harvesting crops which was invaluable training for
him. It was hard work following a walking plow all day. This
was the day before tractors. Everything was done by horses—
plowing the ground, dragging, and harrowing three or four
times. This was necessary to prepare a level seed bed since
vegetable crops require more soil preparation than grain crops.
He planted stringless beans and sweet corn with a two-row,
horse-drawn planter. Peas, oats, wheat, and rye were sown
with a grain drill about eight feet wide. We needed to plant
five bushels of pea seeds per acre. In order to do that, we had
to buy special sprockets for some drills. When we started growing tomatoes, we planted them by hand. However, by 1944, we
were using a horse-drawn one-row planter. Peas were harvested by cutting them with a hay mower that had special
guards and a windrow. Stringless beans and tomatoes were
picked by hand. Jim drove the team to harvest wheat, oats,
and rye with a grain binder that put the grain in sheaves. Jim's
seven years of experience working for Father was good training for the job he was given in the partnership as farm manager.

William Furman, who was twenty-five, was elected treasurer. In 1940, he married his childhood sweetheart, Dora
Propst. Dora also grew up in the same community. She attended the same church as the rest of us. Her home was about
three miles away. One night, Bill ran out of gas at her home.
He tried to get home by putting some gas in the tank that was
in a can at her place. However, there was some water and
dirt in it, and he only got part way home. He had to walk
about three miles home on Sunday morning. Dora's neighbors had a lot of fun teasing them about it.

In the spring of 1940, Mr. Yoxheimer, the neighboring farmer, decided to sell his farm. He gave Father the first chance to buy it. We were glad to buy it as their property was only several hundred yards from our house, just across the creek. The house and barn were less than a half mile from the cannery. That was an ideal place for Bill and Dora to begin housekeeping. On April 1, 1940, they bought the house and barn from Father and moved in during August of 1940.

Bill had worked for Father as a boy of four or five. He helped to take care of the cows and horses. In those days, the children started helping on the farm almost as soon as they were able to follow their father to the barn. William milked cows, took care of the horses, pigs, and chickens as a boy. Working with their father is an experience every boy should have. Of course, not every boy can grow up on the farm; however, working with dad, they learn many things that are not taught in school. Rarely does a boy or girl get into trouble if they can work with their father or mother. William inherited his father's engineering ability. Also, working with Father, he learned how to build things. This training with Father was invaluable. As a small company with limited financial resources, we needed to build as many of our machines as possible. He was to become the plant engineer, for even though he had no formal training, he learned how to figure speed ratios, size of shafts, pulleys, and horse power required to drive machines. He built most of the machines in the winter.

He also went to welding school. The electric welder revolutionized machine building. Instead of spending hours drilling holes with a hand brace and bit, and using bolts, we could weld parts together in a few minutes. Before we bought Father out, William was also in charge of the 300 to 400 teenagers we had picking beans in the summer. Many a teenager earned money picking beans and saved sizeable amounts toward their college education. This was good training for Bill as he was made plant manager in 1947, which included personnel. After we had a full-time personnel manager, Bill continued as plant engineer until his untimely death in August of 1976 of a brain tumor.

Norman Geise married Elnora Furman in 1940. He was elected vice president. He was twenty-seven and grew up on an adjoining farm. He also had two brothers who started to work at Furman's as teenagers. All of them worked at Furman's until they retired. Norman lived about a half mile from the cannery. He went to the same church, same Grange, and same young people's meetings as my sister, Elnora. Perhaps that had something to do with him becoming part of the family. They bought a plot from Father on the Yoxheimer farm. The Lord timed Father's buying of that farm just in time for both Norman and Bill to live on it.

Norman and Elnora built a very modest bungalow-style house. It was located about 250 yards from the factory building in 1940. However, warehouse #11, built about 1980, was within eight yards of their property. The loading dock built on warehouse #6 was within about 100 yards of their house. When we started loading trucks around the clock, the noise often wakened them, and they wished they had built a greater distance from the factory.

As a farm boy, Norman worked with his father and learned to do many things. He started to pick beans and tomatoes for Father almost as soon as he could carry a basket. The experience in the field with growing crops was invaluable training for him. In the new partnership, he was to be the canning crop specialist. He oversaw signing the contracts with the farmers for all the vegetables we needed for canning. His job was to decide what varieties of vegetables to grow, order the seed, and see that each farmer got the varieties that would grow best in his soil. He would also tell them when to plant it, how much fertilizer to use, which herbicides, insecticides and fungicides to use, and when to apply them. He also had a high and low thermometer to register temperatures. The growth of vegetables is very dependent on degree days, and if rainfall is normal, you can tell within a few days the time when a crop will be ready to harvest. A degree day for peas is the number of degrees the average temperature for the day is above 40 degrees Fahrenheit. The contracts also stated that a farmer should harvest the crops the day Norman specified.

The upkeep of the trucks was under Norman's supervision. He also delivered merchandise to the stores in Williamsport, Danville, Bloomsburg, and Harrisburg. About this time, we discontinued the truck routes and sold only to wholesalers and chain warehouses.

I was thirty-three when I was elected president. My duties included being general manager and sales manager. As a boy, I watched cows, milked cows, drove teams, and worked at every conceivable job, including picking tomatoes. In the factory, I oversaw the ladies peeling and processing of tomatoes while I was scalding tomatoes and firing the steam boiler by hand. Sometimes, I cased and stacked them in the warehouse after they were canned. I also labeled cans by hand, loaded trucks, and delivered to the stores and wholesale houses in a straight truck.

About 1938, I started going with Father on most of his sales calls. We did not pack anything in the winter, thus leaving me free to help on sales calls.

Also, I was plant manager, which at that time included hiring, firing, and all that goes with personnel problems. I said when I retired there were only about three things around the cannery that I never did. I never learned to weld, drive a tractor trailer, or run the computer. At the age of seventy-six, I bought the word processor on which I am writing this book.

From the ages I have mentioned, you can realize we were a relatively young team. However, all of us had worked at the cannery since we were teenagers. Most of us had worked at our particular jobs for three to eight years. We had a lot of experience for our ages. In fact, collectively, we represented fifty-three years of accumulated experience. When I looked over the old-time books, I found there was only one employee older than I was, and that was Lee Stahl, thirty-five. We are thankful that my father J. W. Furman lived many years and was glad to give us some good advice.

The financial statement of J. W. Furman in 1943 shows the following:

Assets	Liabilities
Accounts receivable $11,350.27	Accounts payable $10,168.41
Canned vegetables 44,854.35	Notes payable.............24,458.70
Machinery and livestock....13,211.69	
Buildings and real estate......8,000.00	
Total assets $77,416.31	Total liabilities..........$34,627.11*
Net worth $42,789.20	

(* includes the profit sharing notes of the four partners of $14,292.50)

Based on today's values, that amounts to about $162,598. He divided $66,500 (based on 1992 values) equally among his seven children, leaving him only $96,090 (based on 1992 values) on which to retire. Remember, there was no Social Security or other benefits for retired people. That meant that the interest was only about $8,000 (based on 1992 values) a year on which to live. The agreement provided them with a house and utilities and all the milk and vegetables they could use. They had to live on a very tight budget.

The figures below show the results of the whole family working together.

1991 Net Worth of Furman Foods $10,620,922
1991 Net Worth of Furman Farms $8,422,476
Total Net Worth $19,043,398

Even today, when people ask me if I own Furman Foods, I say the banks, fifty-one of my relatives, and I own it. Please note, I list the bank first. As a Christian, I should say the Lord owns it but allowed us to manage it for thirty-two years.

To get today's values, I took the prices that five vegetables were selling for in 1944 compared to today. Today's prices are 3.8 times higher than in 1944. In checking wages, I found they are 10.6 times higher than they were in 1944. In those days, there were no social security, unemployment benefits, sick leave, vacations, free uniforms, health or hospital insurance, profit sharing or pensions, or 401(k) matching funds. Today, those fringe benefits add over 25 percent to our wages. The total rate per hour including fringe benefits went up 13.5 times from 1944 to 1991, whereas the prices of vegetables went up only 3.8 times. Probably the biggest reason for canned vegetables selling so cheaply is because of the mechanization that took place. In 1944, food took 24 percent of a person's disposable income. In 1991, it takes less than 12 percent. Food is a real bargain. Father used to say the problem isn't the high cost of living as much as it is the cost of high living.

In 1928, when I started to work for Father, I had faith in him. Also, I had a belief that if we ran our business according to God's principles, He would bless us. Since Father owed two dollars for every dollar with which he had to pay, about all he could give me was my room and board. I also had use of the family car. However, with five drivers and only one car, it created problems. I was able to save any money I earned in the winter working elsewhere.

The 1937 time book showed that most of our men were getting 22.5 cents per hour. That included Jim Kohl and Norman Geise who were to become part of the partnership in 1944.

In 1940, Norman and Bill both got married. Their wages were $18 a week; mine was $20. We worked as many hours as necessary to get the work done; during the summer, it was usually 60 to 70 hours per week.

The year I was married, Father agreed to give a note to me for 10 percent of the profits. In 1940, when William and Elnora were married, each of us was given notes for 15 percent of the profits. We had an agreement made that all of the children signed stating that, "These notes are to be deducted from net worth of estate before division of the estate." To anyone reading this book who have their children working with them in a business, may I suggest to all involved that you have a signed agreement that rewards the children that stay with you on the farm or in the business. It proved so successful for our family that when our sons, the third generation, joined the business, we gave them a percentage of the profits in the form of stock.

This type of a signed agreement can save a lot of misunderstandings. It also saves a lot of hard feelings when settling the estate. When we settled Father's and Mother's estate, there was no wrangling or hard feelings. One of my brothers-in-law who was involved in settling his father's estate said, "I wish we could have settled my parents' estate so peacefully."

The capital of the J. W. Furman Cannery formed the twenty-seventh day of January, 1944, was $24,250. Today's equivalent would be about $90,150. The profit-sharing notes mentioned above ($14,292) were almost 60 percent of the capital for the partnership. Each of the four partners was given $2,500 by Father. That amounted to $10,000. Ownership was as follows:

Foster Furman	$7,250	.299%
Norman Geise	$6,500	.268%
William Furman	$6,500	.268%
K. James Kohl	$4,000	.165%

The three children that did not come into the business were Andrew, Mary, and James. We gave notes to each one of them for $2,500. We gave Father a note payable on demand of $10,000 and a mortgage of $15,000, both with interest at 5 percent.

Something that I believe helped to promote harmony and thus contributed to the success of our business was the following: "No one partner may at any time or times own more than thirty (30%) percent of the total cash investment unless an amount of more than thirty (30%) percent is agreed to by a majority in number of the partners." Since each partner shares in the profit in the same percentage as his investment, the closer the investment is for everyone, the better incentive it is for everyone to go all out to make it succeed. Ten years later, the ceiling was changed to 28 percent and the bottom to 22 percent. From 1944 to 1963, all of the partners, including the president, received the same wages.

In December 1945, the wages set for 1946 were $75 for two weeks. We worked ten to twelve hours per day, including Saturday in the spring and summer. We were allowed to take Saturday afternoon off in the fall and winter. The bonus for partners was to be $1,350 for the year which was about $.10 per hour above our highest paid man. The year 1946 was the first year that the partners were allowed three weeks of vacation with one week of sick leave.

Another policy that has been very helpful is in effect even today. Each officer shall devote his full time to the exclusion of any other employment. Many businesses suffer and a lot of dissension is created when one of the officers gets involved in outside activities. Even though they may devote as much time to the business as others, it can create suspicion that they are dividing their time and efforts. Several times, we have had to ask officers to obey this rule to avoid serious dissension.

The total pack in cases of each item in 1943:

Peas	16,166
Stringless Beans	14,347
Corn	3,770
Tomatoes	29,223
Tomato Juice	390
Mixed Vegetables	1,962
Carrots	180
Red Beets	2,885
Grand Total	68,923

123

Tomatoes were our biggest volume item. Our biggest day's run in 1943 was 1,001 cases of tomatoes. Our biggest day's run of tomatoes in 1990 was over 15,500 cases. Tomatoes are by far the largest volume item we pack. They make up 72 percent of our fresh vegetables and 42 percent of our total pack. In chapter one, I told about our first two buildings. As the demand for quality canned vegetables grew, we needed more room. About the year 1936, we added another shed-type building to the end of the present building. Again, by the year 1940, we added twelve feet to the width on both sides. About 1942, we added another twenty-by-twenty foot building to the end. We had a total of about 3,000 square feet for manufacturing space. Can you imagine what all of these shed-type buildings looked like? I will have to admit, they looked more like chicken coops than a canned-food processing plant. Of course, today they would be condemned by both the Food and Drug Administration and the Department of Labor and Industry. Actually, in those days, most tomato canneries looked like chicken coops. You really have to see the early pictures to appreciate it. We wanted and needed a new canning factory.

We wanted to pack dry beans in the winter, but we needed a closed building. Our canning buildings and warehouse were only built to handle about 45,000 cases. It was a real hassle to can over 68,000 cases in those crowded buildings. We stored cases of canned vegetables in cellars of all our houses, as well as in the basements of barns. The big trouble with that was the cans rusted. Also, it took a tremendous amount of labor to move them back for labeling. All of this was done by hand. However, labor then was only $.55 per hour.

In 1943, we built our first cement block warehouse which measured 50-by-100 feet. I am sure some of my readers think that was no big deal. However, when you know Father had bought a hand-operated block machine and a cement mixer operated by a gas engine, you can realize what an undertaking it was. This machinery was put in the boiler house of the greenhouse, and we made blocks in the winter time. By working very hard, two people could make about twelve eight-by-sixteen-inch cinder blocks per hour. The quality of the blocks left much to be desired. It took many days of hard labor to make the thousands of blocks needed for the warehouse. Also, remember that each block had to be lifted by hand several times until they were cured and ready to use.

We cut the wood for beams and rafters out of our wood lot. Did you ever try helping on a two-man cross cut saw? Try it if you want to really know what hard work is. While cutting timber, we were surprised to see two flying squirrels glide out of a tree when it was falling. They were very pretty and graceful as they spread their wings, which are similar to bats' wings. The logs were hauled about a mile to a local saw mill by team and wagon.

The footings were dug by hand and then concrete was mixed with a mixer run by an electric motor. Father bought a used surveying transit which he used to check the grade for tile draining. He showed us how to lay footings and shoot levels.

We hired Stuck Brothers to lay the blocks, but we did most of the other building ourselves. It was a very rough building, but it was used to house our labeling equipment until 1983 (a time period of about forty years) when we outgrew the building. There were wooden posts every sixteen feet. When we started using forklifts in 1963, we had real problems working around those wooden posts.

As mentioned, Father grew lettuce, beets, tomatoes, etc., for the fresh market all of his life. Soon after we bought the business, we quit growing those vegetables for the fresh market. We found the canning business more profitable. We just did not have enough time to do both. We still continued to use horses in farming until 1950. All of us raised our children on milk from a few cows we kept. Keeping cows required someone to do the barn work on weekends. About the mid-sixties, we found it cheaper to buy our milk. When we had plenty of our milk available, we often made an eight-quart freezer of ice cream. I remember when Franklin came home while attending Philadelphia College of the Bible, we would have peanut butter on bread and ice cream for several meals. One time, I went to our local doctor for a physical exam for a large insurance policy. Both my sugar and cholesterol levels were extremely high. Dr. Freidline said, "What in the world have you been eating?" When I told him, he said, "I am sure it tastes good, but if you want to pass your exam, you will have to return to a normal diet for a month and then come back." I followed his advice and passed the exam. In fact, even though both my sugar and cholesterol levels are on the high side most of the time, he said, "If you only use one pat of butter and one dip of ice cream, you can enjoy them all of your life." I appreciated that advice. I am past eighty-three years of age now, and my annual physical check-up showed both sugar and cholesterol levels to be normal.

In 1943, sales were about $200,000. The next chapter will tell of the ecstacy of victory, the struggles to keep up with mechanization, and canning enough to reach $1,000,000 in sales in 1958.

Chapter 12
Growth and Challenges for the Partnership
Years 1945–1958

The only place where success comes before work is in the dictionary. We had a lot of hard work ahead of us. We knew that and looked forward to the challenge.

One of the first challenges faced by the partnership was to change from a wartime footing when the government took 50 percent of our production. We went from serious shortages to surpluses in a few months. On September 5, 1945, rationing was ended. That was only three days after the peace treaty was signed with Japan. This was done in an unbelievably short time, and we were very thankful for it. Price controls were ended; what a relief to get rid of the government's red tape!

One of our greatest problems was that we had thousands of special V-2 solid cartons that the can company had purchased for us. At that time, we received all of our cans in cartons. After many telephone calls and letters, the government agreed to pay the can company, as well as us, for all of the extra expenses for the cartons.

What would we do with the vegetables the army released to us? We had spent many hours and phone calls to keep our customers informed. All this paid off when we went from shortages to surpluses as most of our customers were pleased with the services we had given to them during the difficult war years. The pipe lines were dry, which absorbed most of the first year's surplus.

Because of our extremely crowded condition, we were not able to over-pack. As a vegetable packer, we made out better than many. I know of a neighboring packer who grew much faster than we did. However, about 85 percent of his business was with the government. Fortunately for the owners, they made a quick sale just before the war ended. Within six months of the new company take-over, the army orders were cancelled, and they had a major layoff. The fact of the matter is, the owners got three times what the plant was worth after the war ended. It was so bad that many companies did not survive. That teaches an important lesson: "Do not put all of your eggs in one basket." That principle has helped us in our business. We had opportunities to get larger orders if we would reduce our price a little to large chain-store companies. We could have grown much faster and run our new plant to capacity, but then they would be able to control so much of our business that they could name the price, regardless of profit. We did not want any customer to control more than 10 percent of our business. Every customer is important, but you can still survive if you lose only 10 percent of your sales. One hundred small customers are worth a lot more than four big ones.

Not only were we crowded to the point that we could not operate efficiently, but we needed to run our plant twelve months out of the year if we were to attract good employees. In January of 1946, we started planning to build a modern cement block factory to replace the open sheds. That presented a real challenge. In the fall of 1946, we needed to put cement footers in before freezing weather. We did not have the money to hire a contractor, so we drew up the plans ourselves for a building 70 feet wide and 100 feet long; 7,000 square feet to replace 2,500 square feet. We were canning red beets in the old factory while we dug the footers and ran the cement foundation. For inexperienced builders like ourselves, it would have been a lot simpler to lay out the building on a new site. Because of the warehouse and boiler location, we needed to build on the site of the old building. Father was seventy-one years of age but in good health. He helped us to shoot the grades, picking various points outside the building area and leveling them with points in the building area. It was a real victory for us when we found, after doing 240 feet of wall, that we were only out of level a little over an inch. We had a former contractor construct the building. He put the footers in for a wall to separate the boiler room from the balance of the building. He was off by four inches in seventy feet. That made us feel pretty good that we had been off only one inch in 240 feet.

The logs for the two-by-eight rafters were cut by hand out of our woodlot, the same as the lumber for the warehouse built a few years earlier. We used steel posts in the middle and steel girders to support the rafters. We would rather have had a building without posts. However, by using a few steel posts, we reduced our building cost by about 25 percent. With proper planning, the four posts in the center of the building were not a real problem.

June 19, 1947, was a BIG DAY when the first cans of peas were run through the new plant. HOW BIG WAS IT? How do you describe the emotions you have when you achieve an accomplishment you have dreamed about for several years? It was exciting, planning a new plant and seeing it become a reality. I believe that some of you who started keeping house in a small house trailer, or perhaps an apartment, know something about the emotions we experienced. You always dreamed of the day when you could build your own house. About five years later, your first child is due. The Lord has been good to you in providing health and good jobs. You have been able to save a little money. You spend hours going over floor plans and deciding how to build—what a great day when you and your family move into your own home that you planned and helped to build! If you have done that, then you know something of the emotions we had and the celebration of our great accomplishment!

Our biggest day's production of peas that year was 1,879 cases packed on July 2. The comparison figures were 14,538 cases of 16-ounce peas packed in the year 1990. That first year in the new plant, we added kidney beans and butter beans to our line. The total pack in 1947 of all vegetables was 82,919 cases.

To process the increased production, we needed three additional retorts, or a total of six. Our new plant had space for ten retorts, so we thought we had plenty of room for expansion. The old wooden crane did not have a big enough circle, so we bought a steam crane; that was much faster and safer.

For several years, we continued to use old gasoline tanks for cooling. However, by 1956, the two cooling tanks took so much water that we bought a cooling canal about 110 feet long. The crates were hung on hooks that were pulled along through the water at a very slow speed. The cooling canal reduced our use of cooling water to about half of what we were using. Water is a precious commodity, and we needed to save as much as we could. This also gave us more room for retorts.

The new enclosed plant made it possible to pack beets and carrots in January and February and dry beans and fruit juices until the middle of June when peas were ready. VICTORY! By 1951, we attained our goal of running our plant twelve months out of the year.

Sales exceeded one million dollars in 1958. Based on today's values, that would equal about four million dollars. In 1991, we had several months that sales were over four million dollars per month. This was a great milestone in the history of our company. When my generation took over in 1944, sales were about $200,000. In fifteen years, we had increased sales five times. That shows a growth rate of over 14 percent a year. The main thing making that possible was the ability to operate twelve months out of the year.

We made a very important decision in 1949. It was the addition of #10-size can, or food service pack, in peas, stringless beans, kidney beans, butter beans, beets, mixed vegetables, and carrots (listed in order of volume). This, I believe, contributed more to our growth than any other single decision. Today, foodservice sales often contribute to over half our profit.

However, to pack #10-size cans, it involved getting additional special retorts equipped to cool #10-size tins under pressure. If we did not use pressure cooling, the cans would buckle from the internal pressure. Not only did it spoil the appearance of the cans, but they would leak, making them unfit for sale. Of course, adding the retorts required additional steam. We bought our first coal stoker in 1945 and installed it in our 45 HP boiler. By installing a stoker, we increased the capacity of our boiler almost 50 percent. Having an automatic stoker also eliminated a very hard job of hand feeding the coal into the boiler.

We had also added peaches to our line. We packed tree ripened hand-peeled Alberta peaches in two-and-one-half size (28-ounce) cans. Since they were tree ripened, they had the flavor of home-canned peaches. For a number of years, they made a big hit, and the demand far exceeded the supply. But by the year 1963, because of high labor cost, we had lost money for three years. Another problem about canning peaches was that the biggest crop usually came at the same time as tomatoes. Therefore, there was not enough labor available.

At lunch time, the women packing the peaches usually put all of the peaches that were peeled in the can, so they would not turn brown. One day, there were a few buckets of peaches that were not put in cans before lunch. My brother, Bill, told a new employee to turn the buckets upside down

131

over the peeled peaches so they would not turn brown. People laughed until they cried when they saw the new employee stand there a few minutes then start to turn the full buckets of peaches upside down on the table. What a mess; peaches scattered everywhere! He was supposed to take empty buckets and turn them upside down over the peaches.

We considered putting in automatic pitters and machine peelers to reduce our labor cost. This also required twice as much water as we had available. Also, we could not find a reliable supply of peaches in sufficient volume to cover the overhead. My daughter, Jane, was at Philadelphia College of the Bible at the time, and the students named her "Peaches," because they liked them so well. In view of losing money and other problems, we discontinued peaches. Today, even after twenty-five years, people still talk about those peaches and wish they could get some.

Another new item was Bak-N-Beans which contained large limas and a slice of bacon in tomato sauce. Since there were more large limas in the can than bacon, we would not be allowed to use the word "bacon" first. However, since Bak-N-Beans was a new word, we were able to get a copyright for it. It really is a clever name that describes a very good product. Bak-N-Beans sell well in Pennsylvania Dutch country, and I am sure, if we could afford the advertising which the national brands use, it could be a volume item.

In 1944, the year the second generation took control, there were thirty-seven vegetable canners in the state of Pennsylvania. The next twenty years would see twenty-six of those vegetable canners go out of business, leaving a total of eleven, or an average of more than one going out of business each year. Actually, 70 percent of the vegetable canners either went out of business or were bought out by other canners over a twenty-year period. It was a major challenge to mechanize as fast as new machines became available. One of the main reasons so many canners went out of business is that they did not mechanize fast enough to keep up with the times. As I write this book, I marvel at what the Lord did for us. Only His direction and wisdom made it possible for us to sell one million dollars worth of products in such difficult times and make a profit.

The second generation laid a firm foundation of going from a very poor financial rating to the best in the industry. By 1985, we were the only family-owned vegetable canner left in the state of Pennsylvania.

We joined the National Canners' Association and the Pennsylvania Canners' Association. (Today, these are known respectively as the National and Pennsyvlania Food Processors' Associations.) By attending these meetings, we were able to keep abreast of the latest developments in technology and mechanization. Another big advantage of belonging to the National Canners' Association was their coverage of product liability. They do it for a fraction of the cost of insurance companies. The National Canners' Association investigates every claim. Since most of the cases involving trouble with canned food are fraudulent, by fighting them, it has held cases to a minimum. The most serious charge we ever had was about twenty-five years ago. A woman in the coal regions got food poisoning and died after eating a meal that included a can of our tomatoes. The National Canners' Association was able to prove that the meat she ate was the cause of her death. We received a lengthy brief of the case.

Some of the changes that made it possible for us to pack a million dollars worth of vegetables in one year were the great advances in mechanization. Every year after our fresh pack was over, we would sit down and plan how we could cut costs. Getting vegetables ready for canning was very labor intensive. We would go to the National Canners' Convention where the latest equipment was on display. Many times, we could not afford to buy, but we would get ideas. If we could not make it ourselves, we would buy good used equipment. If the labor saving would pay for a piece of equipment within two years, we figured we could not afford to be without it. If it would pay for itself in three years, it was a good investment. If it took more than four years to pay for itself, the need had to be so great that we could not operate without it. Even though we put in the most efficient labor-saving machines, we rarely had employee lay-offs. Usually, we just increased production that much more.

Some of the labor-saving machines were labelers and casers. Before 1950, we cased the vegetables by hand out of the retort crates. We stored them in the warehouse until we knew what label to put on them. A man took them out of the case and labeled them by hand. Around 1950, though, all of this changed. We bought an unscrambler that would set all the cans on end, then run them through a twister to roll them into a caser. When we knew what label would go on them, they were poured out of the case unto another unscrambler that would put the cans on their side and roll them into a labeler. After they were labeled, the cans rolled into a caser and then into a case sealer. That increased the speed of labeling to about four times faster than by hand and also reduced the cost of labeling to less than half of what it was before.

To keep up with demand, we needed to grow more beans and tomatoes. At that time, they were both picked by hand. There was not enough local help available, so we hired a crew leader from Wilkes-Barre in 1950. For the first several years, we housed the migrant laborers at a building in Northumberland on Priestley Avenue. Later, we built cabins for them behind the factory. For stringless beans, we used 300 to 400 boys and girls from nearby towns. Many boys and girls started to pick beans at about ten years of age and would continue to pick until they were old enough to work in the factory at age sixteen. It was hard work. However, I could name many boys and girls who earned money to go to college by picking beans. Some went on to become teachers or county school superintendents.

Since the young people went to school or college, we could not depend on them for picking tomatoes because the biggest crop usually came after they went back to school. Very few local people would pick tomatoes, so we got crews from Florida and Georgia. Some years, we would get good crews; other years, we got poor crews.

We did not allow alcohol in the camp, but, of course, some got it in. They would go to town, come home drunk, and start fighting over the women in the camp. Many well-meaning people made appeals to give them blankets, etc. The fact of the matter is, the more money and free things they got, the worse off they were. After a good week's pay on Saturday, it was sometimes Wednesday before they were sober enough to work. In the meantime, the beans or tomatoes they were supposed to pick spoiled.

The constant trouble we had with migrant help pushed us to buy mechanical bean pickers in 1959. One machine did the work of 200 hand pickers. The machines did not get drunk or sick. Many of the migrant workers were good, dependable, moral people. However, when 15 percent got drunk, they spoiled it for everyone.

Norman Geise was in charge of migrant labor; he was called at all hours of the night to settle arguments. Sometimes his life was in danger. I seldom got involved, but on one occasion, I saw the man he was talking to had concealed a knife in his hand. Norman was greatly relieved when we quit using migrant labor and went to mechanical harvesting.

In 1954, we bought our first forklift. The cases were stacked on 32″ by 40″ pallets. At that time, the industry had not yet established the 48″ by 40″ pallet as standard, and there was no pallet exchange program. In fact, when loading trucks, the cases were taken off the pallets and stacked on the floor. It was not until 1975 when it became standard procedure to deliver canned vegetables on four way 48″ by 40″ pallets. We would exchange pallets with the customer. Exchanging pallets not only saved a lot of labor, but a forklift could unload a truck in about a half hour compared to three hours by hand. Of course, the same was true when loading trucks. Customers liked it because of the labor savings, as well as it not tying up their dock so long. When they exchanged pallets, they could unload five times as many trucks in a day.

When we started using forklifts, we really eliminated one of the hardest jobs in the warehouse. Up until that time, we moved cases on roller tracks and had an elevator with a rubber belt to stack the cases when it got too high to reach from the floor. A case of twenty-four 2.5 size cans weighed fifty-five pounds. These men really earned their wages stacking them as high as they could reach for ten hours a day. Today, forklifts are used for moving almost everything.

Previous to building the new plant in 1947, I carried the tomatoes in wire baskets from the scalder to the women who peeled them. The peelings, cores, etc. dropped down on a special wood table Father had built. Women stood on each side with a drag chain in the middle. We turned a crank by hand to deliver the waste into the hopper of a special pump to move them up into an old 500-gallon tank. This tank was mounted on a wagon. When it was full, a team of mules would be hooked to it to take it to the field for fertilizer. About ten women stood on each side of the table. Standing on the cold cement was not very comfortable. The women asked for a board to stand on. One afternoon, I put a one-inch thick board down for them to stand on. The best peeler we had at that time was a very nice lady we called Sweet William. Next to her stood a very greedy woman who complained about everything. After I placed the board on the floor, Sweet William leaned over to the other woman and in her Dutch brogue said to her, "Did you hear ve got a raise at lunch time?" The greedy lady eagerly asked, "How much?" Sweet William said, "Vone inch."

When we built the new plant in 1947, we put in a system similar to a merry-go-round for the tomato peelers. We could not afford to buy a manufactured one. It was much easier to build one with square corners.

Recently, we had a retirement party for one of our best mechanics who helped to build much of the machinery in our new plant. Kenneth Dunkleberger worked for us for forty-one years. One of the men said that my brother, Bill, who was plant engineer, and Ken would visit other factories or machine shows. When they saw something that would improve our plant operation, they would measure it and take some notes. During the winter, they would build the machines themselves. Some of the machines they built would more than double production per person. It was mentioned at Ken's retirement party that many of these machines worked better than some of the new machines we purchased. The tomato peeling table they built with a Laporte chain worked very well. At one corner, the scalder delivered the tomatoes into twelve-quart dishpans. A man stood there and put them on a Laporte chain that delivered the tomatoes around the table. When a lady needed tomatoes, she would pull off a dishpan.

For coring and peeling the tomatoes, we used a special knife called a spoon because of its shape. The special coring knife increased production. The ladies dropped the peelings into their dishpan and put the peeled tomatoes in a bucket next to the dishpan. When a lady had peeled all of her tomatoes, she would put the dishpan with peelings on the chain which conveyed it to a place where someone would empty the skins into a hopper. When she got her bucket full, she placed it on the chain that delivered it to a table close to the filler. She then got an empty bucket from a shelf above the chain. The buckets were numbered, and someone marked down the number of each bucket they peeled. It was necessary to have the buckets numbered as we paid by the bucket; also, we could check which peelers left skin on or crushed the tomatoes too much. Some would put their bucket on the belt when they were not full. At first, we used granite pans and buckets. However, each time they fell, some granite would crack off. We wanted to change to aluminum that would not crack and would last ten times as long. That was during war time, so we had to get a special order from the government to buy them.

Father learned soon after starting the business that some women would work just as hard when getting paid by the hour. However, some would only peel half as many tomatoes on hourly rate as they would on piece work. To be fair with the women who worked hard, we paid them by the bucket. We also had to compete with other canners and, if we were to sell our product, we had to have the right cost.

Before 1953, we used a rotary-type blancher for peas, string beans, and dried beans. Most vegetables needed to be blanched three minutes at about 180 degrees. The rotary blancher was actually a large drum with a screw in it that pushed the vegetables through to the other end. Our rotary blancher was only about eight feet long. We needed a bigger blancher. Pipe blanchers, where the product is pumped through a pipe, were just coming into general use. We were fortunate to get a used pipe blancher at a reasonable price.

In February of 1954, just as I was ready to get into my car while visiting our broker in Pittsburgh, Jack Fuch called me to come back. He wanted to talk about packing a forty-six-ounce drink called Reymer's Blend. That was our entry into the juice business which became a high-volume item. H. J. Heinz bought the Blend name around 1959. We continued to pack for them for about eight years until they decided to pack it themselves.

Our biggest volume was fruit punch, a special mixture of fruit juices. We also packed orange, grapefruit, grape, and pineapple-grapefruit juice drinks. All of these were good volume until the dry mixes for drink, which were much cheaper, took over the market around 1975. I think the fact that we could sell them at four cans for a dollar had a lot to do with the volume. When inflation raised the price, volume on some of the items was so low, we discontinued packing them. Another reason that made the drinks so attractive to us was that the big runs of juices were in the spring when we needed something to fill production time to keep our year-round employees busy. Since that required large volumes of sugar, we put in a liquid sugar system. My! It was so much easier to have an electric motor to unload the sugar compared to unloading 100-pound bags of sugar one by one. The use of liquid sugar also proved very good for packing four bean salad and tomato catsup which we added later.

When we decided to pack forty-six-ounce fruit juices, we knew that we needed another warehouse. The warehouse of wooden construction had posts every sixteen feet and didn't work well with forklifts. In September of 1954, we decided to build our first fireproof warehouse. It was seventy-two feet and four inches wide. By working with the steel company, we discovered that, by using two rows of posts every twenty-four feet, we could save 25 percent more than a clear-span building. We spaced the distance between the posts so we could get six rows of pallets per bay. That way, the posts really did not cause very much trouble. Our total warehouse space in our old frame buildings was 10,000 square feet with a roof height at the eaves of about twelve feet. We needed a nineteen foot clearance to make full use of our forklift stacking. Since I was responsible for the finances, I was inclined only to build a warehouse of 8,400 square feet. I made the mistake of saying it would take us years before we would need a warehouse of 11,800 square feet which would triple our warehouse capacity. My business partners reminded me thirty-five years later about that foolish statement and laughed about it. As it turned out, we actually built the larger warehouse and had to build another one in five years. We usually built another warehouse every five or six years. In 1955, the actual cost per square foot was $2.37. Warehouse number thirteen was completed in 1990 with 50,250 square feet and cost $13.53 per square foot.

This warehouse was more expensive because it has loading doors with seals and locks so trailers cannot run away from the dock when forklifts enter. At the old loading docks, we had several frightening experiences of trailers rolling away from the docks with forklifts part way on. Fortunately, no one was killed. As I look over the old depreciation schedules, it is amusing that the warehouse built in 1944 providing 5,000 square feet was listed as the BIG warehouse. The warehouse built in 1990 was ten times as big.

Until 1954, our cans were delivered in cases by trucks. My youngest sisters, Elnora and Alice, remind me that one of their first jobs as teenagers, when Father owned the business, was to take cans out of cases and place them on a track to roll to the can washer and then to the hand packing table. We all worked together to make our business successful. I will tell you more about my sisters in chapter 19, "The Women in My Life."

Our closing machine was running about sixty cans a minute. At that speed, one person could not put the cans on the track fast enough. The answer to that problem was to get the cans in bulk in the trailer. Another advantage was that we could get more cans on a load, thus reducing our freight cost. They were unloaded onto the can track that delivered them into an elevator with a can fork that held fifteen 303-size cans. With a can fork, one person could feed up to 120 cans per minute.

The original twenty-by-fifty foot frame building, which was built about 1924, was replaced with a cement block building about 1944. We stored the empty cans on the second floor. That way, they could roll by gravity to the hand packing table. Most of the cans were fed right out of the trailer into the can line. However, since it took different types of can linings for different products, it was often necessary to store some cans. We also needed an extra supply in case the trailer did not arrive on time. In response to that need, we added a third story in 1952.

In addition to factory and warehouse space, one of the greatest needs was a plentiful source of water. We drilled five wells within two years and then four more wells within eight years or an average of a well per year. We only put pumps in four of these wells. While we were hunting for a site to drill, a water witch (as they were called) stopped and told us we were drilling at the wrong place. He said he would tell us where to drill. So he walked over the field until the rod in his hand turned down. He said "Here is a strong stream of water under this spot." So he put a stick in the ground to mark the place. Then he said, "I will go out here about 100 feet and cross the place at right angles to see if I get the same results when I cross this spot." While his back was turned, my brother-in-law, James Kohl, moved the stick off to the side about fifteen feet. Guess what! He walked to the stick instead of the place he had designated before. We have laughed about that many times. Of course, we disregarded his advice. I don't think we ever told him the trick we played on him. As I have observed water witches work, I believe there is something to their claims, but I do not think they are dependable when a large volume of water is needed.

We hired a geologist from Bucknell University. He stated that maps show the ariskiny sand is close to the surface. That usually contains natural gas and water. He told us if we drilled at the right spot, we could probably get enough natural gas to supply the need for our factory. The places he picked for water were below where Franklin built later; they were a half mile from plant. The geologist thought the well would produce over 500 gallons a minute. When we started test pumping the first well we had drilled, it looked like we had 400 gallons a minute. However, after about four hours of pumping, it only produced about seventy-three gallons a minute. Then the geologist from Bucknell picked another site about 500 feet from the first well. When we test pumped it, the level in the first well dropped. The underground streams were tied together. The two only produced 108 gallons per minute. Also, the second well was sulphur water. The volume was not sufficient to cover the cost of piping it a half mile. When we asked for his bill, he said, "My predictions were so far off, I will make only a minimal charge."

The well driller said, "Let me pick the spot; if I don't get several hundred gallons per minute, it won't cost you anything. However, if I get water, the rate will be a little higher." The spot he picked was about 500 yards below the factory on land we had purchased to put our waste lagoon. He got less than 100 gallons per minute. We never put a pump in it. For the next well, we got Dr. Parizek from Penn State University to pick the spot. It was above Norman's house and tested ninety gallons a minute with 200 feet drawdown. That was the best well up to that time.

In fall of 1955, we were approached to pack a coconut chocolate milk drink. It was a special secret formula and tasted very good. It looked like it had great potential. However, the man promoting it was strapped for money. It required that we buy an homogenizer and other expensive equipment. We would also have to invest a lot of money. We prayed a lot about it as individuals and also as a company because the investment was large enough that, if it failed, it would seriously affect our financial ability to expand our vegetable canning. In January of 1956, we finally voted to proceed. However, we had been praying that the Lord would close the door if it was not the right thing to do. We had an agreement drawn up. The day we were to sign the agreement, the man came and said, "You are good honest folks and have worked hard. I will have to be honest with you. You are too nice a people to get involved in this because you may lose a lot of money. I think we'd better cancel the whole thing." We thank the Lord for protecting us from a deal that could have ended in disaster. Only the Lord knew the future. I have always thanked the Lord that He moved this man to back out. This was outstanding guidance from the Lord. There are a number of times the Lord directed us just what to do.

Before 1947, we filled all of the cans by hand. That year, we bought a used five-pocket pea filler that took the place of four women. Ten years later, we bought a used ten-pocket filler so we could produce enough peas, corn, and dried beans to meet the demand. Since stringless beans did not flow freely, we had to buy a different type of filler.

Computers were unheard of. All records of cases sold were recorded by hand, and we wanted records on each customer. All invoices were figured on a hand-operated adding machine. Ursula Lehman recently reminded me she punched the keys and then pulled a lever. Next, each invoice was typed by hand on a manual typewriter. We got our first electric typewriter in 1956. We had good secretaries, but sometimes when copying, they would transpose figures. Now if you put it into the computer correct the first time, you do not need to be concerned with it being wrong when it reprints. It was often the twentieth or twenty-fifth of the month before we knew how many cases we had sold, how much each customer bought, or what was left in our inventory to sell. The same was true of cash receipts and expenses. To do it the old way, I presume it would take ten times as many secretaries as we have today.

Those were busy days for all of us. We were all raising families. We must always remember that our families are more important than our jobs or businesses. It seems that people who are managers or are starting their own business have more of a problem deciding how much time to spend with families. If you spend too much time in your business, you may find, after climbing the corporate ladder, that it is leaning against the wrong wall. You may lose your family, even your wife. You end up being lonely when you retire. I hope none of you will be as devoted to your business or any hobby as a certain man was to his golf game. On one particularly beautiful morning, just as the tenth hole, which was along the road, was reached, a hearse went by. This man took off his cap and stood at attention until it disappeared over the next hill. His partner said, "I didn't know you had that much respect for the dead." And the man replied, "It's too bad. If she would have lived another week, we would have celebrated our twenty-fifth wedding anniversary."

For many years, Father & I had attended the Pennsylvania Canners' Convention. In 1956, I was elected to the Board. I will never forget the first Board Meeting. In those days, the four or five leading can companies would take turns hosting the Board of Directors the night before the convention. One year at the dinner, I sat at the end of the table. The waiter started with me and asked what cocktail I wanted. I declined to order any. After going around the table of about twenty people, I was the only one who hadn't ordered. He said, "Everyone else is having a cocktail, can I bring you one, also." I said, "No." I was the new kid on the block and some of the other canners started teasing me. The executive secretary was a heavy drinker. He said, "We need someone on this board that knows what he is doing. You leave Furman alone." They never said anymore about it. They usually held the Board Meeting on Sunday afternoon before the convention. When I got my next notice that the Board Meeting would be on Sunday, I wrote back and said I have more important things to do on Sunday. When you hold your Board Meeting during the week, I will attend. They changed the Board Meeting to a weekday and continued on a weekday for over thirty years.

By the year 1956, Father had reached the age of eighty and Mother was seventy-five. They were both in good health. He would drive around home, but we were all glad when he decided it was too far for him to drive to Florida. It was decided that each of us would take turns taking Father and Mother to Florida and bringing them back. We would be given an extra week's vacation every other year. Each of us was glad to get to Florida and usually stayed an extra week or two.

Having reached one million dollars in sales, or about 420,000 cases, we wondered how long it would take to reach our next goal—to pack one million cases, more than double our pack in 1958. How many years do you think it took? We still worked more hours than most of our employees. Those were exciting years, which the next chapter will tell about.

Chapter 13
Dreaming of a One Million Case Pack
Years 1958–1969

How many is a million cases? If placed end-to-end, they would reach from Northumberland to thirty miles past Richmond, Virginia, or 260 miles. How much food is in a million cases? It would feed every man, woman, and child in the city of Harrisburg a four-ounce serving each day for three months. On the way to reaching our goal, many exciting things happened. In 1958, we added 5,000 square feet more to our production area, making a total of 12,000 square feet.

We incorporated under the name of Furman Canning Company in March of 1961. Franklin Furman, the first of the third generation, joined the company. We purchased 340 acres of river bottom from Mr. Bittinger in 1964. In 1965, we incorporated the farms under the name Furman Farms, Inc. which purchased all the farm land and both the canning and farming equipment.

In 1966, we purchased a continuous cooker for $250,000, which included installation. In 1968, more of the third generation joined the company: David Geise, Joel Furman, and James F. Kohl. In 1969, William Furman, Jr. was the fifth of the third generation to join Furman Canning Company.

We also had to add two warehouses with a total square footage of 31,000 feet.

147

<u>Why We Needed to Form a Corporation</u>

By the year 1960, three of the partners had children with dri-ver's licenses. In a partnership, if any of our children had an ac-cident and the parent did not have enough insurance and equity to cover the liability, they could reach over into all of our estates. Of course, the same was true if the company had financial problems; as a partnership, the creditors could take our homes and everything we had. It was a big challenge and a lot of work. Even though there was much less paperwork and taxes were lower in a partnership, the financial risks were just too high to continue as a partnership. So, as of March 7, 1961, we formed the Furman Canning Company. Furman Canning Company bought all of the inventory of canned veg-etables, other current assets, trucks, automobiles, and office equipment. Furman Canning Company assumed and paid certain liabilities, accounts payable, notes payable to banks and individuals, and accrued payroll taxes. The total amount was $179,583.65, the assets having a fair market value of $347,718.43. Shares of stock were issued to cover that amount.

The officers of the Corporation remained the same as in the partnership:

President	Foster Furman
Vice President	Norman Geise
Secretary	K. James Kohl
Treasurer	William Furman

In June of 1961, my oldest son, Franklin, graduated from Penn State University with a degree in horticulture; he ma-jored in food technology.

Franklin actually started for the company about fourteen years earlier, picking beans, hoeing, pulling weeds, etc. on the farm. When he was 16, he did manual labor in the fac-tory. While in college, he worked in our quality control de-partment.

When he graduated from college, the big question Franklin faced was if he should come and work for us or get some experience at another factory. He also asked me if he should look at a job with someone else. Bird's Eye asked him to visit their plant in New York State. I said, "Even though we need you, it is better for you to find out what they have to offer than to realize, at a later date, you wished you had." The personnel director at Bird's Eye told Franklin after the interview, "I have been instructed to hire someone from Penn State, and you are the one I want." They told him at the end of a year's training, he would probably be given a position of plant manager in another state. As he advanced in their company, he may be moved every several years. Franklin planned on getting married that fall. The prospect of moving every few years did not appeal to him. Also, the opportunity at Furman's might not be open a few years later. We were overjoyed when he decided to work for us.

Franklin was the first to join our company with a college degree. How were we to gauge what to pay him? Other companies had offered him a lot more money. He started at 10 cents per hour below our highest paid man, our warehouse foreman. The second year, he got the same as the foreman. After that, the raises would be gauged by how he fit into the organization.

It was agreed that, at the end of three years, we would review whether or not the children of owners should share in the profits by getting shares of stock. It was difficult for some of the officers to realize that, if we were to grow, we needed children to come into the business and the younger generation needed a college education and should be paid accordingly. It was of the Lord that Franklin's disposition was to trust us. All I could do was promise him we would pay him a fair wage after seeing what his generation could do. Being the first one, he had many challenges the later ones did not have to deal with.

We desperately needed someone to develop and manage a quality control department. Our pack in 1961 was a little over 500,000 cases. As general manager as well as sales manager, my checking of samples was a hit-or-miss affair. I would cut samples when I had time, or ask someone else to do it. Our quality standards were not well defined. A Pennsylvania Dutchman would say, "We flew by the seat of our pants."

Franklin's employment at the cannery was interrupted by his duty with the Air National Guard in Germany during the building of the Berlin Wall. He married a fine girl named Esther Teske who was a registered nurse at Geisinger Medical Center in Danville. In October, he left for a year in Germany. While Franklin was in Germany, Esther lived in a house trailer located about 100 feet north of our house.

We really enjoyed having Esther so close to us while Franklin was in Germany. During this time, I had the privilege of taking Esther to the hospital for the birth of our first grandchild. An unusual thing happened when I was in the waiting room. When they told a young man that he was the father of a baby boy, he fainted dead away. That reminded me of the story told of the three men who were each waiting for the birth of his first child. The nurse announced that one was the father of twins. He said, "Isn't that odd? I work at Twin Motors." About that time, another nurse announced that the next man was the father of triplets. He said, "Isn't that odd? I work at 3M." The next man groaned and said, "I work at 7-Up," and then he fainted.

We really enjoyed having our first grandchild so close. After Franklin got home from the service, they started to plan their house. They built on the farm we bought from Mr. Yoxheimer about a half-mile from the plant.

When Franklin returned to the cannery in June of 1962, he established a quality control department that checked the quality of the vegetables from the time they entered the cannery until they were delivered to the final consumer. Today, we have a very sophisticated procedure. The two long suits of Furman Foods are quality and service. We are known for our quality throughout the United States, as well as abroad. Recently, we had an order from a buyer in South Africa who was impressed with our quality.

The raw vegetables are bought with detailed specifications as to quality. Anything not meeting these specifications is rejected. We have a system whereby quality control can slow down the flow of a product through the plant if the product is not getting inspected to meet proper standards. The quality control personnel check the product just before it is filled. After filling, they check the fill, weight, etc. at regular intervals. After processing, samples are taken from the line every thirty minutes, and the time is marked on the can. As they are palletized, the time is marked on a card on each pallet, along with the row and the warehouse number in which they are stored. All of that information is automatically fed into the computer as the card is being printed. The samples taken off of the line are graded using government forms and regulations. A different government grading form is used for each product. Since we fill a pallet with canned vegetables about every five minutes, if there are any problems when it is graded, it is easy to locate in the warehouse. All they need is the day and time it was packed, and it can be traced and put on hold if it is not up to grade. When the product is sold, the person in charge of labeling can locate any item he wants on the labeling work order. On this computer generated work order, the products are listed with the oldest showing first. This helps in stock rotation.

In 1962, our Albany broker, an Italian, brought crushed tomatoes to us and asked us to pack them, as the cannery which was packing them went out of business. We made a trial run. He said, "The flavor and texture are fine." I said, "Italians in Albany will not buy crushed tomatoes with a Dutchman's name on them. We need an Italian name and colors."

He said, "That is simple, just add an 'o' to your name; call them Furmano's." That was one of the best sales moves we ever made; Furmano's outsells our Furman brand. If he would have known how much that would benefit us, he would have asked us for a royalty on the name. We have a good name; we could pack Spanish food and call it "Furmandez," or Polish food and call it "Furmanski."

In 1964, a farm south of Selinsgrove on the Isle of Que was offered to us. Mr. John Bittinger had grown vegetables for us for many years. When he wanted to retire in 1964, he gave us the first chance to buy his farm. The farm contained 370 acres, and most of it was flat river-bottom ground, ideal for growing vegetables that were to be harvested by a machine. It took us several weeks to decide. A construction company had a sand and gravel pit on the island. When they heard Mr. Bittinger was retiring, they offered him more money than he had asked for it from us.

Mr. Bittinger said, "I made my money to pay for the farm growing vegetables for Furman's. I want it to remain as farm land. I gave them a price, and I will not go back on my word." My, how we need more businessmen today whose word is as good as their bond!

There is a lot of history with the Isle of Que. Conrad Weiser worked for William Penn and was the go-between with Indian Chief Shikellamy. On one of his trips to negotiate with Chief Shikellamy, Conrad Weiser brought his new musket along for protection and to show it to Chief Shikellamy. He was as proud of that musket as you would be of a new Lincoln. The next morning, Chief Shikellamy said, "I had a dream last night." Conrad Weiser asked him what he dreamed. He said, "I dreamed you gave me that new musket." Conrad Weiser was in a bind. He knew if he was to get favorable answers to some of his problems, the culture dictated he had to give his new musket to the chief. A few days later, he said to Chief Shikellamy, "I had a dream that you gave the Isle of Que to me." Shikellamy thought a few minutes, then said, "Okay, but let's not dream anymore." You must realize the island contains about 1,200 acres. As we look back twenty-eight years, we got a very good buy on the 370 acres we bought.

For a number of years, we had been leasing tractors and trailers from Darrel Whipple who operated under the name of D & H Leasing Company. However, as our business grew into other states, we had to expand and use commercial carriers. Because of Interstate Commerce Commission regulations, it became increasingly difficult to make prompt deliveries at reasonable rates. So, in March of 1964, we bought Whipple's garage and equipment and hired him to run it for us. Owning our own fleet allowed us to make deliveries anywhere we wanted and to pick up return loads. Also, with our own trucks, we could improve service to our customers and tell them the day and hour shipments should arrive. Service is one of the hallmarks of Furman's. We are able to get return loads over 80 percent of the time. Thus, we were able to haul it less expensively and make a little money besides.

For years, we had dreamed of starting profit sharing with our employees. When this dream became a reality in 1965, it was like receiving a gold medal at the Olympics. The big question was how much to give. We found that the wages amounted to about 15 percent of our total costs, so we chose 15 percent of the profits before taxes or owner bonuses. The first year, the total given to our sixteen regular employees was $21,593. Today, that doesn't seem like a great amount, but then it was equal to 15 percent of their wages. They were given about one-third of the bonus in cash for Christmas, and the balance went into a pension fund. In the first ten years, the smallest bonus, $10,063, was in 1972, the year of the June flood in the Susquehanna Valley. The highest was $104,735 in 1974.

At Furman's, we always have been deeply concerned that our employees be treated fairly. One way was to share our profits with them. During the years that we were struggling financially, it did not seem to be practical. What a great day when we announced to our employees that we could give them a percent of the profits. We always believed that if the employees are treated fairly, there is no need for a union. We had one union election among our trailer drivers around 1970. The unions lost that election and have tried several times to interest our employees but could never get enough employees to sign up for an election.

The profit sharing created an attitude among the employees of wanting to do the best they could. Sometimes when an employee who had been with us for a number of years would see a new employee not working, he would go to them and say, "Get to work, buddy, you are taking money out of my pocket."

Another big achievement was making a plan so that our children could become owners by getting stock each year. Franklin had been with the company for over thirty months. His pay was just a little more than our warehouse foreman's, whose job did not require a college degree.

Since Franklin started at a rate about 25 percent below what other companies had offered to him, I told him to trust us that someday his pay would improve. The time had come to make that promise good. The minutes show we had many long meetings in 1964 trying to solve the problem. A motion that our children share in profits of the business failed on April 4, 1964. However, on March 20, 1965, Franklin's twenty-seventh birthday, it passed by a three-to-one vote. Most of the bonus they received was in form of stock. I believe this profit sharing, to a great extent, explains why all of the third generation of boys and some of the girls, as well as three from the fourth generation, are working for the company. Many family businesses break up because one father thinks the children of one of the other men may be getting special treatment. This is especially true unless all of the board members are committed Christians. When I think of the problems we had, I am glad we were all committed Christians.

I quote part of the agreement in which people running a family business may be interested. "Whereas, the business of this corporation has grown through the united efforts of the members of the family of J. W. Furman, the founder of such a business, related by blood or marriage; and whereas, it is the opinion of the directors that the continued growth and strength of this corporation will depend upon a similar united effort devoted to the promotion of the corporation's best interest on the part of the younger members of the family related either by blood or marriage; and whereas, in view of their education, training, and interest, and in view of the lure of competitive fields, it is deemed essential, if their services are to be engaged and their loyalty and best efforts retained in form of wages and ownership of equities in the corporation; now therefore be it resolved, the following bonus plan be adopted." The plan provided for stock to be given based on a percentage of profits.

By the year 1965, the need for water was strangling our growth. Just across the cannery road was a farm of 127 acres that had several good springs on it. We thought we should be able to drill a well on it and get a plentiful supply of water. The owner, Albert Snyder, was blind and in poor health. We offered to buy his whole farm with an agreement that he could live there, rent free, for the rest of his life. He wanted to retain the house and about 27 acres. In April of 1966, we were able to buy the barn and about 100 acres for $16,000.

Since Dr. Parizek had checked all of our other land close to the cannery a few years earlier and picked a fairly good well, we asked him to pick sites on the Snyder property. He chose a number of sites where he thought we would hit a good supply of water. In May, we drilled a well about 360 feet deep. It proved to be an artesian well, overflowing at a rate of about twenty gallons a minute. Our test pump would only pump 584 gallons per minute. After pumping for twenty-four hours, we only drew it down thirty feet from the top. He estimated that, if we only pumped it sixteen hours a day, it would produce about 1,500 gallons a minute, drawing it down 200 feet. It was located about 500 yards from the factory. Boy, what a help and relief to get a plentiful supply of water. However, it contained so much sulphur that we could not use it for brine to put on the vegetables or water for our steam boiler. Nevertheless, it could be used for washing vegetables and cleaning up after a day's work.

In 1966, we bought the Red Cross label which was a major label in the Middle Atlantic states and in some of the Southeastern states for almost 100 years. Their main items were butter beans, tomatoes, golden corn, and white corn. This gave us a good opening in six or seven states along the East coast. When you look at the total picture, it was a good move. It also helped us to reach our one million case goal. However, even though we were sure it was a good buy, we lost money in that division for four years. We really never made the amount of money on Red Cross that we had anticipated, but it was a great help in expanding into those markets. As of 1992, most of that business has been replaced by the Furman or Furmano's label.

In 1966, we realized, if we were to continue to grow, we needed more retort processing capacity. At that time, we had nine retorts and a 100-foot cooling canal. We needed to more than double the number of retorts, double the water supply, and the steam boilers. That would have cost us over $175,000, and we would still have a system that was becoming obsolete. Also, our competitors were putting in automatic, can handling systems which greatly reduced their labor costs. We talked to a lot of people and visited a number of factories. Basically, there was only one American company, one British company, and one French company who manufactured continuous cookers. Our biggest problem was that we wanted to process cans of many different sizes—cans with diameters from 2.02 inches up to 6.03 inches. Also, these cans had many different lengths. The French Carvallo Hydrostatic was the only cooker that would meet our needs. It could process the many can sizes because it carried the cans in tubes.

As I look back on it after twenty-six years, I say, "Boy, oh boy, am I glad the Lord led us to buy this cooker." The cooker stands fifty feet tall and holds 26,000 of the 303 size cans at one time. I believe, even today, it is the most versatile cooker made. With it, vegetables can be processed for as little as thirty minutes and as long as sixty-six minutes and at temperatures of 215 degrees to a high of 250 degrees.

Since this was a relatively new type of machine, the big question was whether it was safe to eliminate all our retorts. If the hydrostatic cooker broke down during the fresh pack season, we could lose thousands of dollars. It took us several years to learn how to do preventative maintenance work and keep chains the right tightness to prevent breakdowns. We had several of them lock up and had to cut tubes out. However, it is running better today than when we first bought it twenty-six years ago. With proper maintenance, it is supposed to run another five to eight years. The main chain needs to be replaced about every four years. We are thankful the four lock-ups always occurred while we were packing dried beans, thus we only lost part of what was in the cooker rather than losing great amounts of fresh vegetables.

A little over a year after we bought the 100 acres from Albert Snyder, he passed away. The balance of the farm (twenty-seven acres of land, a house, and a barn) were sold at a public sale on November 25, 1967. In a board meeting before the sale, we agreed to bid as high as $6,100. However, at the sale, we had to pay $9,700 for it. Since the house was only 200 yards from our factory, we decided at a hastily called board meeting at the sale that we could not afford to let anyone else buy it.

The house was an old-style house with high ceilings. Many of the doors had rat holes through them. Albert Snyder was blind for several years. There were so many rats that he kept his bread, cereal, etc. in lard cans on the table, otherwise, the rats would eat the food. The house had three nice big rooms downstairs and five bedrooms upstairs. Those rooms contained sixteen truckloads of junk. He also kept chickens in several of the rooms. What a mess. What should we do with the house? When consulting with a local contractor, his examination showed it to be structurally sound. He said, "Any house I build today will settle more than this house has."

Our youngest son, Joel, graduated from Penn State with a degree in food technology in 1966, after attending Philadelphia College of the Bible for a year. He then went to the University of Delaware to get his Master's degree in sales and distribution. He was married in June of 1967 to a lovely girl, Margaret Reid, from Allenwood, a town about twenty miles from Northumberland. Joel graduated from the University of Delaware in 1968. Up to this time, I was president, sales manager, and general manager. As we were approaching a million cases in sales, I needed help. When Joel joined Furman's after graduation, it was a great help to me. After a few years of training, he was made vice president in charge of sales. The company sold the Snyder house and one acre of land to Joel and Margaret for about what it would cost to tear the house down. Joel and Margaret had it remodeled with a modern kitchen, electric heat, etc. It made a wonderful large house. Joel and Margaret moved into it in December 1968.

Joel, like all of the third generation, started picking beans when he was about eight years of age. He earned enough money to pay for four of his seven years of college. After he was old enough to work in the factory, he rolled cans, cased cans, palletized labeled cases in the warehouse, and did many other jobs that required manual labor, since we were not mechanized in 1958, as we are today.

David Geise, Elnora and Norman Geise's oldest son, graduated from Penn State with a degree in horticulture in the spring of 1968 and started working for us in May of that year. (Elnora was my sister and Norman was our vice president.) As a result of our growth, the acreage of vegetables and the harvesting of the crops was more than his father, Norman, could oversee. Our acreage of tomatoes was 335 acres; stringless beans, 366 acres; and peas, 388 acres. Our acreage of vegetable crops had almost doubled in the last ten years and would almost double again in the next ten years.

David, like all of the other children of the owners, had started picking beans as soon as he could carry a basket. Since his father was responsible for the picking, David may have started a year or two before the others. David tells me that he has a picture of himself picking beans when the basket was almost as big as he was. During the summer when he was attending Penn State, he worked with his father, checking when peas and string beans were ready to harvest. Sometimes he was in charge of the pea combines and bean harvesters.

New varieties were becoming available every year. Because of mechanical harvesting, it was necessary that each vegetable mature at the same time. That was true of peas and string beans. Hybrid tomatoes were just being introduced, and new insecticides, herbicides, and fungicides were being introduced every year. In order to keep up with these advances, we needed to attend seminars, etc. At that time, we were operating three pea combines and two bean harvesters. Norman and David were responsible to see that these machines were kept running during the harvest season. Sometimes, it was necessary for them to work twenty-four hours a day.

In the summer of 1969, we signed an agreement to buy the Ross property of 122 acres. We paid $110,000 for the barn and land. David married Joyce Moyer on August 3, 1968, and bought the big farm house on this property. The farm was located along the west branch of the Susquehanna

River across from Bucknell University. This was mostly flat, rich, river-bottom land. Just like the Bittinger property we had purchased in 1964, it was ideal for mechanical harvesting of vegetable crops. One problem was that both farms flooded whenever the river reached flood stage.

Many arrowheads were found on both this property and the Isle of Que. On freshly plowed fields, right after a rain, many people found it a good time to look for arrowheads. We do not find as many arrowheads on land half a mile from the river. The river was the Indians' main means of transportation and the most common site for battles, and they used that land more than the other.

Also in 1968, James Franklin Kohl graduated from Penn State with an associate degree in agriculture business. He is the son of my youngest sister, Alice, who was married to K. James Kohl, our corporation secretary.

With the purchase of the Ross property, we owned 600 acres of farmland, in addition to renting another 200 acres. It was obvious that Jim's father needed help. Bigger farm machinery was being introduced. At this time, we owned six or seven farm tractors. I believe our biggest tractor was an 806 International diesel that pulled a five bottom plow that plowed two-and-a-half acres per hour. This was twenty-five times faster than when I plowed with a team of horses twenty-five years earlier. We were also growing 200 acres of tomatoes, 110 acres of beans, and 145 acres of peas on our farms. Vegetable crops require more work to get the seed bed ready to plant than grain crops. New herbicides were being used to control weeds since labor was too expensive to hoe and cultivate the crops. Jim had learned much about the latest in farming and farm management.

Since his father managed the farms, he started driving a tractor almost as soon as he could reach the clutch and brake. Before he could drive the tractor, at eight or ten years of age, he had also, like the other three of his generation, picked beans and worked on the farm in the summer. He knew farming from the ground up. Jim was the fourth of the third generation that the Lord directed to follow in his father's footsteps. Just when the company had a real need, he was ready to step in and help. In no case did family members replace other employees. We never created jobs just to give one of our children work.

William Furman, Jr. joined the company in June of 1969. He was the son of William and Dora Furman. (William was our treasurer.) He graduated from Taylor University with a B.A. in psychology and a minor in business and philosophy. He also took a course in computer programming. That became his first real love. He did a lot of reading and working on computers. We said it seemed he would rather work on that computer than eat.

Like all the others of his generation, Bill started at about eight years of age to pick beans and pull weeds and many other tasks that were not very glamorous. In high school, he was interested in science and built a "demonstration of automation." On this, he won first prize both in the high school science fair and the Susquehanna Valley Science Fair at Bucknell University.

He was the fifth of the third generation to join the company. However, he did not inherit his father's love for mechanical engineering. Since he did not enjoy that type of work and his talents were elsewhere, he did not start working with his father in maintenance. In the summer of 1969, Bill did manual work of many kinds. I well remember talking to him about his future with the company while he was feeding bean nippers.

We needed help in the office in accounting as well as a supervisor. He asked if I thought the company had any interest in computers in the near future. I said, "The day you can show me that it pays, we will go to computers." That winter, Bill started to learn bookkeeping procedures and educated himself in computers and programs as a hobby. The computer revolution was just starting. We purchased a key punch. During the day, Bill programmed, and he and his secretary would key punch. We leased time at night from the Shikellamy School District and used their computer, an IBM 1130. This required transporting hundreds of cards back and forth each night. In June of 1972, we installed a computer just like the one at the school. The line printer cranked out 110 lines a minute.

In 1975, we converted to an IBM System 3, replacing the cards with floppy discs and a printer that ran 150 lines a minute. Our accountant said our conversion from hand bookkeeping to computer was the smoothest he had ever seen. I believe most of that was due to Bill learning our needs and then building a system to meet them. When I would ask if we could do this or that, he would say, "Tell me what you want, and I think we can do it."

For many years, we wanted to have a thirty-minute chapel service on Wednesdays at noon. For speakers, we had good evangelical ministers from local churches. Attendance was voluntary; there was never as large a group as I had hoped. One of the greatest disappointments of my life was the fact that Christians did not support it as well as they should have. I often wondered if it was my fault that more people did not attend. Of course, if the Christians did not support it and bring unsaved persons to the meetings, it was discouraging. We had a few conversions, and it helped to solve some workers' family problems. I am sorry to say we discontinued chapel after about ten years. One problem was the fact that employees complained about not getting in as much time on Wednesdays. Other days, we only took half hour lunches, but on Wednesdays, we took one hour. Also, with continuous production lines, the lunch hour had to be broken up to about three or four different periods.

Father and Mother continued to live in the farmhouse, which was only about fifteen feet from the cannery building that housed the time clock. When we would run double shifts on peas and stringless beans, the plant did not finish until two or three in the morning. The employees' loud talking and laughing interrupted Father's and Mother's sleep. All of us were glad when, in 1959, a little bungalow became available just a few hundred yards from Alice Kohl's home, the youngest daughter. We needed the farm house for office space. We were glad to buy the bungalow for them to live in. Our agreement with them was to provide suitable housing for them without any charge as long as they lived. Buying that house for them was a great help to all of us. It was only about a half-mile from the factory, so we could all go to visit them. Even though Father was eighty-three years old, almost every day, rain or shine, Father walked to the factory until he was ninety-six years of age. He said, "I like to visit it, I think of it as my baby."

Our son-in-law, Frank Severn, remarked that it is dangerous to live close to Furman's if they need a farm or house nearby. It is interesting how the Lord made places available when we needed them. When we needed a house close to us, the neighbor either died or moved. When we needed additional personnel, the Lord provided the third generation with the proper training and skills to fill that need.

On January 1, 1964, Furman Farms was incorporated and took over the farming operation. They bought all the assets and liabilities of J. W. Furman Cannery and the partnership was dissolved. The farm corporation owned all of the canning equipment and land. A lease was drawn up so that Furman Canning could lease the factory and all of the canning equipment from Furman Farms.

Hurrah! Call out the band! Let's celebrate! The Lord gave us good weather and a bountiful harvest. Not only did we reach our goal of a million cases in 1969, but we passed it. I watched Bonnie Blair, the U.S. speed skater, cross the finish line well ahead of her closest competition. I watched the jubilation on her face and her mother's face as they realized she had won the Gold Medal at the 1992 Winter Olympics. I believe it was the first U.S. Gold medal at that Olympics. What a thrill! Just as thrilling was the passing of our million case goal. Father was ninety-three, and Mother was eighty-eight. It was a great day for everyone. Pictures were taken of the four officers and the three generations of sales managers. Father, myself, and Joel Furman were photographed with charts showing our growth. There were news articles in local papers, the Pennsylvania Packer, and national food papers. We praise the Lord the good crops continued for the year 1970. In those two years, production grew by 38 percent. This was real reason to celebrate!

At the beginning of the chapter, I mentioned a number of things that helped us to reach the million case goal. They all played an important role. We could not have reached the goal without all of the things working together. Neither could we have reached it without a lot of hard working, faithful employees. We thank each one of the forty-two full-time employees. A number of them have recently retired with over forty years of service.

The next chapter will tell of the challenge of the third generation becoming board members. It will also tell how we bridged the generation gap.

Chapter 14
Bridging the Generation Gap
Years 1969–1977

I repeat, the only place success comes before work is in the dictionary.

What a challenge! All four of my generation were over fifty and without a college education. Some of us had had a year at Bible school and a few night classes or Saturday classes at Susquehanna University. The five of the third generation all had college degrees, some having spent seven years in college. Of course, it was just as much of a challenge for the younger generation as it was for us. I say that every organization needs some under fifty to give it drive and some over fifty to give it balance. Often the older people are satisfied to continue to work with old equipment and ideas that are out of date. Sometimes those in the younger generation want to make a change just for the sake of change. The old Dutch saying, "If it ain't broke, don't fix it" doesn't always work. Many times if you are going to make progress and be competitive, you must change to keep up with the times. I like this saying better. "Do not be the first to try the new, nor the last to give up the old." In other words, let someone else spend the money to experiment with something new. However, as soon as a machine or idea is proven to work, you need to change or you will be left behind.

We thank the Lord that he gave each of us one or more children. Thus it gave each of us an incentive to work with our children so the business could continue. Having someone to carry on after we were gone also helped to relieve any tension that may have been caused if one of the owners did not have any children to inherit his stock. I have noticed that if one of the owners does not have children, they fail to understand what it means to have someone to carry on the business. They also often fail to realize what the son of one of the other owners is worth. Often, the son of one of the owners is not given a high enough salary to keep him in the business.

Records show that about three out of five college graduates change jobs in the first five years out of college. The reason given by most of them is that they were not given enough responsibility to challenge them. Furman's was fortunate in that all of the older generation had more work than they could do, and they were glad to give their sons sufficient responsibility to challenge them.

We are thankful all of our children wanted to go to college and that they all studied hard. We did not have the trouble one person had. His son just wouldn't apply himself. In order to motivate him, the father said, "When Lincoln was your age, he was a lawyer." The son replied, "Yes, and when he was your age, he was president."

As our children's responsibilities increased, we realized we needed to get more stock into their names. If we failed to do that, the inheritance taxes could cost so much that they may have to sell the business just to pay the taxes. Before 1975, the federal exemption was very low. We hired a consultant from New York City to tell us the best legal way to get enough business assets to the next generation without the taxes killing the business. The idea was that we were to pay a flat fee instead of being obligated to buy insurance from him.

I think the following incident will help to explain why seven children from the third generation are in management positions in the company, and four children from fourth generation are working for the company, with one of the fourth generation on the Board.

The consultant mentioned above spent about one-and-one-half hours with each of the fathers and the children of the third generation. When those interviews were finished, he probably knew more about our goals in life, finances, etc. than our wives knew. Jimmy Kohl, who is now our executive vice president, was the fourth one he interviewed. Jimmy was asked, what is your goal in life? Whom do you work under? Are you happy in your position? Jimmy had started working full-time for the company about five years earlier. After Jimmy said that he was working under his dad, the consultant asked him the second time if he was happy. Jimmy said, "Yes." The consultant said, "You are the fourth one I have interviewed. All of you seem relatively satisfied; I don't understand it. You are the youngest and the lowest on the totem pole, and you are happy. I have never found that in a family business before." Jimmy said, "I think you will find the answer to that is the fact that we all know the Lord, Jesus Christ, as our personal Saviour." I was the eighth one interviewed by the consultant. He said, "I don't understand it. I have never interviewed a family business where all are so well satisfied." My answer was not as good as Jimmy's. I said, "We always open our Board Meetings with Bible reading and prayer. After we have read the Scripture and prayed together, we may disagree, but the arguments seldom get personal or angry."

As the result of what he saw in our family, he was interested in our faith. After I found out he was Jewish, I gave him a Gideon Bible from my desk and asked him to read Isaiah 53 and tell me if there was anything in that chapter that my Messiah did not fulfill. I was able to explain the way of salvation to him. Several months later, he said to me, "Do you mean to say to me that, unless I take Jesus as my Messiah, I will never get to heaven?" Instead of me quoting it to him, it was better for him to read it for himself. I opened the Bible to John

14:6 where Jesus said, "I am the way and the truth and the life. No man comes to the Father except through me." After reading it, he said, "I am not ready to take that step yet." However, before he left, he hugged me and thanked me for talking to him about Jesus. I am sure he would not have even listened to the Scripture if we, as a company, were fighting among ourselves. He did not make a commitment then, but I hope someday to see him in heaven.

Just because we are all Christians does not mean we did not have problems. Before the third generation started working for the company, there was a definite relationship between our ownership and our votes on the board. To maintain that, there was objection to Franklin Furman, a third generation member, being put on the board after working six years. David Geise and Joel Furman were put on the board before Franklin after only working for the company three years whereas Franklin worked for the company fourteen years before he was elected to the board. Sometimes harmony in a company is more important than position or prestige. I thank the Lord that Franklin had a personality that was not offended by this apparent injustice. I thank the Lord that all of us were committed Christians, thus we were able to avoid hard feelings over this issue.

With a pack approaching one and one-half million cases, we needed to install our own computer. We also needed more office space. In February of 1972, we decided to add to the farm house which we had made into offices. The computer, an IBM 1130 system, was put in what used to be the living room of the farm house. The sales offices were located in the new addition. The new building was one story with 1,500 square feet and was attached to the north side of the farm house and contained seven offices. It was constructed so we could add the same amount of floor space on a second story.

Two big events happened in 1972 that cost us more money than anything we had ever had happen before. One event over which we had no control was very traumatic for us but disastrous for other people, especially farmers. On June 21, Hurricane Agnes stalled over the Susquehanna Valley, dumping as much as nineteen inches of rain in about thirty hours. Agnes had built to hurricane force in the Gulf of Mexico, came ashore in the Florida panhandle, and moved up the East coast, leaving eighty dead and thousands homeless.

The Susquehanna River is one of the largest rivers east of the Mississippi. The storm moved the full length of the river. According to Richmond Myers in his book, The Long, Crooked River, the north branch rises from the waters of the Otsego and Canadarago Lakes in New York State. It winds back and forth, passing within a few scant miles of the Delaware river. The Susquehanna dips a few miles into Pennsylvania and then returns to New York, forming a great bend, and then flows west through Binghamton, New York. From there, it returns to Pennsylvania at Waverly, then turns south through Wilkes-Barre. Here, it joins the west branch at Northumberland, just a few miles from our factory. It flows almost 320 miles before it reaches Northumberland.

The west branch starts out in Jefferson County and flows through Williamsport, which is a total of 228 miles, before reaching Northumberland. Together, they form the majestic Susquehanna River that flows south another 130 miles to the Chesapeake Bay. Sixty miles south of Sunbury, the river becomes about a mile wide at Harrisburg. Agnes moved up to the head waters of the north branch, and then made a very unusual turn southwest and moved over the headwaters of the west branch.

Since 90 percent of the fresh vegetables the farmers grow for us are grown in the Susquehanna River basin covered by the storm, it reduced our production more than any other event in our seventy-year history.

Sunbury is located just six miles from our plant and had a disastrous flood in March of 1936, with water flowing ten feet deep down Market Street. They also suffered some minor damage in a smaller flood in 1946. In 1948, the U.S. Army Corps of Engineers built a flood wall to withstand a flood of thirty-six feet, or about a foot higher than the 1936 flood. On June 23, 1972, a forecast went out that the river would crest a foot higher than the flood wall. They expected the west branch and the north branch to crest at Sunbury at noon on June 24. However, at 2:37 p.m. on the twenty-third, the dike broke at Wilkes-Barre, sixty miles upstream on the north branch. Thousands of acres were flooded. That delayed the crest at Sunbury for about twenty-four hours. By that time, the west branch was falling. The river crested at Sunbury on June 24 at noon just inches below the top of the flood wall. Sometimes, the water would slop over the wall. Thus Sunbury was spared another disastrous flood.

The main reason this flood was so devastating to the farmers was that during June farm crops are at a critical stage. Since it continued to rain for about a week after the storm, when the soil finally dried out, it was too late to replant. Since there was so much rain, they could not harvest good hay crops or grain crops. The farmers' losses were much greater than ours, as farming was just a small part of our total operation. We buy the seed we want planted and sell it to the farmers. Since many of the farmers lost their total pea and bean crops, we decided to forgive half of the cost of the seed for the crop they had lost.

If you have ever been in a flood plain and watched the water rise, flow into you home, and wash away your farm crops or garden, then you know how helpless the farmers felt.

We were combining peas. When the field crew heard the weather forecast, they decided to continue until it got too wet to work. When they quit about midnight, they moved the combines to the highest place in the field. The farmer said the water had never covered that place. The next morning, David Geise went to see if water was coming up in the field. We had rented a tractor from Jay Bacon to pull a pea combine. He met

David at the field and said, "You will sleep better tonight if we move those pea combines to higher ground." To get to higher ground, they had to walk through water up to their waist to be sure they could pull the combines through. We were very fortunate that David moved those combines. If they had waited two hours longer, it would have been too late. Before the next morning, the water was so high it would have washed the tractors and combines away. To replace those six combines and tractors would have cost about $600,000.

All of our river bottom land (approximately 500 acres) was under two to twenty feet of water. Most of our vegetable crops were under water. We not only lost the crops, but much of the top soil had washed away as well. The river floods this land about once every fifteen years. However, the 1972 flood was the only time in my memory that the river was so high. Most floods actually deposit rich soil on our farms. It was also the only time we had a bad flood when the ground had been plowed and was loose, and the water washed away much of the top soil. Because of the damage, we got a twenty-year $53,000 loan from the Small Business Administration at 1 percent interest. Also, we received a $5,000 disaster grant that we did not need to pay back.

We are thankful that our facility is several miles from the river. Several of our warehouses are built over a little stream. The storm pipe was not big enough to drain the water, so the water backed up and broke an overhead door. By knocking some blocks out and opening a door on the lower side, the water flowed through the warehouses at about six inches deep. Since the canned vegetables were up on four-inch pallets, only the bottom layer of cans got wet. We were able to run that bottom row through the cooker to sterilize them and were able to sell most of them at the regular price. Several warehouses were higher and did not suffer any flood damage. Our total loss at the cannery was about $30,000. We were able to move most of our customer's labels, so we lost only a few labels. We were sure we would show a loss for the year; however, we did finish with a small profit.

An unusual thing happened one day when our accountant, Jim, and I were returning from signing the loan papers in Lewisburg. About two years before, late one evening after everyone in the office had gone, I had witnessed to Jim. The next day, his wife called me up and thanked me, saying she had been praying for his salvation. His wife, Carol, and I had prayed for Jim many times.

Several times, I asked Jim if he didn't want to decide to accept Christ as his Saviour. He would always say he wasn't ready but would do it someday. When we were about a half mile from the plant, I said, "Jim, you have been putting off accepting Christ for over a year." When we arrived at the office, the Lord led me to press him for a decision as we sat in the car.

After a little time, Jim said, "Well, I guess I better do it now." I suggested that he pray and thank the Lord for his salvation. He prayed, saying, "Lord, thank you for showing me what life is all about." It seem so unusual and casual, I must admit I wondered if he was sincere. A few days later, when he was in my office, he said, "Foster, since I accepted Christ as my Saviour, I understand the Bible so much better." I said, "Jim, now that you know the Author personally, the Bible will mean a lot more to you. First Corinthians 1:18 says, 'For the message of the cross is foolishness to those who are perishing, but to us who are being saved it is the power of God.' " Jim also said, "It used to be if someone did me a dirty trick, I always wanted to get even with them. Now, I can forgive them." I thanked God, for now I knew it was real.

We lost over $100,000 on the farms; also, the value of our stock dropped by that much. Since most of the crops were destroyed, we had very little to can. Our pack was reduced about 35 percent to 475,000 cases. Jim had estimated what our total loss would be for the year. He said to our attorney, Bob

Diehl, who is also a Christian, "I don't understand how Furman's could lose so much and not be upset about it." During the flood, Attorney Diehl's office had burned because the firemen were occupied with the flood. Their office had records going back about 100 years. Jim had said to me, "I don't understand how Diehl could lose so much and not be upset about it." I am sure that Jim saw that a person's relationship with the Lord is much more valuable than material things.

The other costly problem was of our own making. I think it was the most costly mistake I made in my thirty-two years as president. We were trying to find some way to use our waste or what would be called recycling today. We had a lot of vegetable waste that cows could eat. Also, we had about 60 acres of pasture land, so we sprayed waste water on part of it. That grew good pasture grass for beef cattle. I thought this was ideal to grow beef cattle. After one of the other Board members investigated it and did a lot of figuring, we decided it was a good way to recycle our vegetable waste and perhaps make some money. It looked good on paper, but it proved to be a financial disaster.

In 1973, we formed Nature's Acres Farms, Inc. We incorporated under Stock Plan Section 1244 of the International Revenue Code as a small business. This allowed us to be taxed as a partnership. In those days, many professional people were in the beef-raising business as a tax shelter. Instead of making a profit, we lost money every year.

First, we started with thirty-eight beef cattle. We had about ten breeding cows. In April, we hired a manager for the operation who had some experience with managing a breeding herd. We also fattened some steers. In March of 1978, after losing money for three years, we got out of the breeding business. Our experience with fattening beef cattle did not do any better. By 1987, we decided to quit the beef business. We found out that, when beef prices rose enough that we could make money to recover our losses from years when beef prices were down, the government would drop duties and South American countries would flood our markets with cheap beef.

Another problem was feeding them the right amount of supplement, as well the proper nutrients. Waste from peas, beans, tomatoes, as well as different types of dried beans, each had different nutrient contents. Thus, the volume of the mixture and the mixture of supplement were different for each type of waste. If we did not use enough supplement, then the cattle would fill up without getting enough nutrients. Jimmy Kohl compared it to eating watermelon; you fill up with water but get very little food value.

Growing beef is a very exact science. In order to be profitable, we had to weigh some animals every thirty days to know how many pounds they were gaining daily. If I recall, to be profitable, they had to gain close to three pounds per day, and ours were gaining less than two pounds.

When our losses were about $100,000, we decided to get out of the beef business. Of the $90,000 we had spent in fixed assets, the only thing we could use was the beef barn, which we converted to a wagon shed. The cost of the barn was about $12,000. I hope we have learned the lesson that most things cost more than you think and are less profitable than you think. I think experience has taught me that you only gain about half as much profit on new business deals as you think you will. Regardless of these lessons, it seems every generation must learn these things for themselves by experience, instead of taking the advice of the older generation.

In 1961, a neighbor by the name of Mr. Gibbons passed away. Since this farm was only several hundred yards east of the cannery, we were eager to buy it. We asked a real estate agent to bid in our place. A local builder wanted some of the land to make a housing development. We were bidding against each other. When it got too high, we quit bidding; they then started to sell household furniture. When we realized the builder could pay a much higher price then we could, we decided to talk to him. About half of the farm was north of the Gibbons Road. This contained twenty-five acres with the house and barn on it. Much of that land was wet and not suitable for a housing development. That was the part next to our factory. The acreage south of the road was suitable for housing. On a handshake, we agreed to stop bidding if he would sell the part we wanted to us. When they put the farm up for sale after a break, it was knocked down to him. The deal proved very profitable for both of us. Soon after that, William Furman, Jr. bought several acres from Broscious Lumber Company and built a home. Don Geise, son of Norman Geise, bought several acres from us to build his home.

In 1978, a local farmer, Mr. Bob Reitz, wanted to retire. He owned a farm of about 113 acres next to the Ross property which we had purchased earlier. This was rich, river-bottom land that had been pasture for the beef cattle which he raised to supply his restaurant, called The Fence, along the river. He gave the first chance to us to buy the farm and the restaurant. The Fence was very popular in the summer time. People went dressed as they were and stayed in their car. The waitress took their order and brought their food to them on a tray that fit on the car door. Because we would be able to farm the two farms together and the quality of the farm land was good, we were very eager to get the farm land.

We had a serious disagreement in our Board about buying the restaurant. The restaurant did more business on Sunday than any other day. Some of us prayed that the Lord would raise up someone to buy the restaurant as we objected very strongly about being involved in the Sunday business. We believed, as Father did, that Sunday is the Lord's day.

We thank the Lord that He answered our prayer. Mr. Reitz sold the restaurant to someone else, and we bought the farm. Today, we are operating a fresh market stand during the week across the highway from the restaurant. In 1989, the Anspach farm, containing fifty-nine acres, became available. We bought the farm and sold off the house and barn, the same as we did with the Reitz property. That gave us three farms in a row along the river. There was about 254 total acres suitable for farming. Having that much acreage together helps to keep farming costs down.

We also have worked with our growers just like we do with our employees. When we have exceptionally profitable years, we pay the farmers a bonus. The year of 1973 was very profitable. We paid a bonus to our pea growers of $15 per ton; stringless beans, $5 per ton; and tomatoes, $4 per ton. The total bonus paid to our growers in 1973 was $48,048. Because of some canners' questionable practices, some farmers were lobbying in Harrisburg for a marketing agreement with the canner which would force everyone into a straight jacket, and the state would set the price which we would have to pay for our vegetables. We argued that, if they set the price higher than neighboring states, we would face competition which we could not meet and would be forced out of business. Thus, it would leave the farmers of Pennsylvania without a market for their vegetables. The farmers who grew vegetables for us, and had received bonuses from us, were not in favor of such a law. In our testimony before the Agriculture Committee, the fact that we paid a bonus to our growers above the contract price really impressed the legislature. Also, we were able to show those canners causing the trouble that it was to everyone's advantage to treat their growers fairly. Thus, we were able to defeat a serious threat to the canning industry of Pennsylvania.

Don Geise, who is the youngest son of our Vice President, Norman Geise, joined the company in 1974. He, like the others of the third generation before him, started working by weeding beets and tomatoes even before he was allowed to pick beans. By the time he was old enough to pick beans, we had gone to mechanical harvesting of beans. The first bean harvester delivered the beans into pallet boxes. Don rode in the box and picked out stones and bean leaves. During his high school years, he loaded trucks at the dock and worked at manual labor jobs.

Don went to Williamsport Area Community College and studied electrical engineering. After graduating from college, he joined the Air Force for four years where he worked in electrical communications. After leaving the Air Force, he worked for us as a supervisor of building and electrical maintenance for three years. When his brother, David, was elected president, there was a vacancy left in the Field Fepartment. Don then transferred to the Field Department as he had worked with his dad in that department while in high school and really liked that better than electrical maintenance. Don Geise was elected to the board in 1987. He was the seventh member of the third generation to become a Board member.

Bill Furman, Sr. was both Personnel Manager and Plant Engineer. By 1962, our pack was over 600,000 cases. We had forty year-round employees plus over 100 employees who worked in the summer during the perishable vegetable season. We needed a full-time plant engineer, and that was the type of work Bill really liked.

Paul Geise was put in charge of Personnel. In addition, Paul ordered cans and did some purchasing. You who have been responsible for taking care of employees know there are usually a few unhappy employees. I had held every position in our company, and I knew how difficult it was to keep everyone happy. I have said, of all the positions I have held, dealing with employees is the hardest job I know.

Purchasing was divided between me and others. When Kermit Kohl became Personnel Manager, we consolidated purchasing under Paul Geise. This relieved the pressure on several of us who were doing part of the purchasing.

Kermit Kohl, the oldest son of our secretary, K. James Kohl, joined the company in 1975. Since his father was Farm Manager, he started driving a tractor almost as soon as he could

reach the clutch and brake. He, like the others of the third generation, harvested tomatoes and removed stones from the farmland and had many other tasks that were not very glamorous.
In the summer, he helped on the farm until he went to college.
Kermit attended Lancaster Bible College and continued his
studies at Calvary Bible College in Kansas City, Missouri. He
graduated with both a Bachelor of Arts and a Master of Arts
degree. His major was Bible with a minor in Pastoral Ministry.

When Kermit graduated from college, he started working
for Youth for Christ. As that was part-time for him, he started
his own excavating and trucking business. He also sold life
insurance for two years.

When he came to work for the company, we were not
sure in which department his education would make the biggest
contribution to our company. Since his father needed help on
the farm in the spring of that year, he operated a farm tractor
for several months. As we reviewed our need and his training, it was decided that he could fill a need as head of our
Personnel Department. Before this, we had not had a full-time
person in personnel. By the year 1975, our year-round employees had grown to ninety with over 150 summer employees. Thus, Kermit joining the company was another example of
how the Lord provided one of the children to fill an important
job just when we needed him. Kermit was elected to the board
in 1983 as the sixth member of the third generation.

That first summer, Kermit worked as a trainee with Paul
Geise. Also, Kermit worked in many different departments to
prepare him to take over the Personnel Department (later
named the Human Resource Department). Paul Geise had
been with us for thirty-five years and was well qualified to take
over as our purchasing agent.

I was approaching sixty-five, and someone else would
soon take over. Four of the junior executives were interested
in becoming president. On May 28, the decision was made that
each of them was to give a five-minute talk on why they were

qualified to be president. The junior executives who spoke were Franklin Furman, Joel Furman, Dave Geise, and William Furman, Jr. Following the talks, a straw vote was taken, and Franklin Furman received the most votes. It was also decided the official vote would take place between December 1, 1976, and June 1, 1977.

We were packing two million cases per year and growing at the rate of about 20 percent a year. I was hopelessly overloaded. Since we did not know what positions the junior executives would fill after the election, I made the mistake of not splitting my workload up as much as I should have. As a result, I starting getting chest pains. Several times before when I was under stress, I had chest pains, but when I took a little time off, they would go away. However, these chest pains continued. My doctor sent me to Geisinger Hospital for a detailed physical. After giving me an E.K.G., the doctor said, "Why are you here, I don't find any problems." I insisted my chest pains were severe, so he put me on the treadmill. After the treadmill test, he said, "We must catheterize the heart; you do have problems." The catheterization of my heart would show just where the problem was and possibly lead to a heart operation. After the catheterization, he said, "Your heart is better than mine, you should live to be a hundred." I asked who could explain the severe chest pains to me. He sent me to a different department. They said a lot of nerves are connected in the chest. This is a warning; cut your hours from ten to less than nine and take thirty minutes of rest at noon. I did that, and it took care of the problem. Thus the Lord gave me a caution flag and, as long as I pay attention to it, I am not likely to have serious heart problems. As I look back, it would have been better for the company if I had delegated more of my responsibilities earlier.

All of us had been praying for over a year that the Lord would guide in the election of a new president. The oldest of the third generation was my oldest son, Franklin. The straw vote indicated he would probably be elected. Also, Franklin was, by far, the most popular owner among all of the employees.

The day before the election, I considered talking to my two sons and some of the other Board Members to ask them to vote for Franklin. The Lord said to me, "You have asked Me to guide this election; you better keep quiet and do not muddy the waters. Trust Me, I know the future, and you do not." The election was conducted by our attorney. Much to my surprise, David Geise got a two-thirds vote on the first ballot. I must confess I was greatly disappointed.

Following the official vote on December 29, Franklin Furman made a motion, K. James Kohl seconded it, and it carried to make a motion by acclamation to have Dave Geise declared President of the Corporations as of January 1, 1977, and Foster Furman to be Chairman of the Board. However, this shows just how the Lord—who knows the future—works. Within two years, Franklin would develop cancer. Esther, his wife, is a registered nurse; her devotion to him may be the reason he is alive today. I thank the Lord that He guided the election. If Franklin would have been President, it would have been a burden for him. Also, it would have paralyzed our organization for several months, just when we were in the middle of a big expansion program.

We have missionary friends around the world praying for Franklin. Today, his short term memory is not very good. He can read some, and he walks with two arm canes and gets to church three times a week. We do not understand it, but we believe that everything that happens to a committed Christian is filtered through God's love.

In August of 1976, my younger brother, Bill, bumped his head on an overhead garage door. His neck became so stiff, the pain was unbearable. He went to Geisinger Hospital (which is called the Mayo Clinic of the East), where they discovered he had a brain tumor. For several years, we had not been able to understand why he backed his car into things. The doctors said his side vision was very limited which was caused by the brain tumor. They operated and, for about a week, he seemed to be doing well, but in less than thirty days, he was with the Lord. I'll never forget that week. His wife, Dora, called me around one o'clock in the morning and said he might not live through the night. He passed away before morning. We also had a prayer chain going for Bill. Why the Lord saw fit to let my granddaughter, Ruth (who had contracted "H" fever), and my son, Franklin, live and take Bill, we will not know this side of heaven.

This was a very trying time for all of us. Not only did we miss Bill as a person, but this was in the middle of our packing of fresh vegetables. We had a good group of employees, and they all worked a little harder to fill in the gap left by Bill's sudden death. We had a memorial service at 7:00 a.m. at the plant so that the employees could attend. Our pastor, Reverend Dave Clark, was a young man in his late twenties. He preached a gospel sermon at the memorial service. Only the family went to the cemetery for the committal.

On October 4, 1977, William Furman, Jr. was elected to the Board of Directors and also treasurer for both companies, thus replacing his father.

The next morning after Bill passed away, at about 2:00 a.m., our daughter, Jane, who was a missionary in the Philippines, called to say her oldest daughter, Ruth, had "H" fever and only had a 50 percent chance to live. As early as possible, we called people on different prayer chains. People all over the United States, and also many missionaries around the world, prayed for Ruth. In the Philippines, monitoring equipment is not available in the hospitals like we have in the United States. An intern checked her vital signs. Her heartbeat was going from 50 to 150 before they finally found a drug to control it. They only had enough for six hours. After many telephone calls, the Seventh Day Adventist Hospital said they had the drug. When our son-in-law, Frank Severn, went to the desk to pick it up, the lady said, "I am sorry, but we only have one vial, and regulations say we must keep it." Frank said, "I walked to the door and then turned around and went back to her and said, 'Lady, without that drug, my daughter has only four hours to live.' " She said, "I am sorry, but we must keep at least one vial here all of the time." Frank said, "I couldn't help myself. I just broke down and cried."

When he got back to the hospital, Jane and he got on their knees at Ruth's bedside and prayed, "Lord, Ruth is Yours, but would You please spare her?" Before they were done praying, the phone rang. It was the hospital saying they had found four more vials. By that time, curfew was in effect, and he had to get a permit from the police to be on the street. Also, there was a severe typhoon, and Frank had to make many detours. However, he got the medicine on time. They said the "H" fever had left her with a weak heart.

We praise the Lord that He healed her, and she was able to play basketball in high school. Ruth is a registered nurse today and was married the summer of 1993. It brings tears to my eyes every time I tell this story.

Another big problem the company faced was to find a way for my generation to retire and get a reasonable income. In order to finance our fast growing business, the Board required that most of our salary be reinvested to buy stock. Thus, we had very little invested anywhere else. Since it was a closely held corporation, it was almost impossible to get money out of it without hurting the company. Also, we did not want to sell to outsiders since our children wanted control of the company. We did not have sufficient funds for retirement. Our net take-home pay was only a little more than that of our employees. Thus, when we retired, we were allowed to set up a deferred compensation payment plan. This plan was allowed because our salaries had only been a fraction of what other corporation officers were paid.

We adopted a pension plan on January 13, 1976, which would pay a set figure to us for eight years. It was specified in the agreement that each of us would work 260 hours per year as a consultant. If we were requested to work any hours beyond that, we would be paid an hourly rate. After eight years, or upon the death of the husband, it was to be reduced by 15 percent to be paid as long as either spouse lived. The amount was to be adjusted for inflation by 70 percent of the cost of living. With the cost of living going up 13.3 percent in 1979, it would have been disastrous for the retired people if inflation would not have been included. This policy for retirement was set for all of the second generation. We were thankful this deferred compensation was set up before my brother, Bill, passed away, or we may have had trouble with the Internal Revenue Service in making payments to his wife. I was concerned that, after retirement, my income would not be enough to continue my support of missionaries around the world. I am thankful the deferred compensation makes it possible for me to give 50 percent of my taxable income to the Lord's work.

About ten years before my retirement, I had invested approxiamtely $10,000 of my retirement funds in a Bible camp. Due to a change in the interpretation of the tax law for that area, the Bible camp was assessed for thousands of dollars of taxes, which forced the camp to close. It seemed that would make it impossible for them to pay me or the other investors. I told my wife that I may as well kiss that money goodbye. However, I said if I ever get it back, I will give it all to the Lord's work. The invested money of $10,000 plus interest amounted to almost $15,000. Praise the Lord, they paid us all off in full, and I was able to keep my promise. I told a Christian doctor about this and another case of bad debt. He said that he had a lot of people who owed money to him; maybe he should try that. Perhaps some people owe money to you; maybe you should promise all of it to the Lord.

It is very difficult to set salaries in a family organization. We struggled with that for eighteen years, with all of us receiving the same salary regardless of our responsibilities. As president, sales manager, and general manager, both our accountant and attorney said that was unfair to me. However, in 1941, if I would have insisted on a higher salary than the other partners, it could have caused dissension and may have broken up the partnership. Because of my heavy responsibility as president and sales manager, I thought it was unfair that I was not paid for the extra responsibility. However, I believe one must have harmony among the officers if a business is to succeed.

Effective May 1, 1962, after 18 years, the salary of the president was set at 16 percent higher than that of the secretary and the treasurer. The vice president's salary was set about 4 percent above the secretary and treasurer. Peace and harmony are often worth more than several thousand dollars. The sands of time are littered with shipwrecks of family businesses that could not work out their salary problems. I am thankful that all on the Board are committed Christians, and thus, we were able to work out our problems.

Of course, I will never forget the retirement party that was given to me by the Board. The occasion was in connection with the annual employee banquet. The party was a complete surprise. I wish I had a video of it; however, this was before the days of the video. I thank the Lord for the great memories I have of that night. It was held at the Country Cupboard on Route 15 in Lewisburg. Part of the program was a special group of singers with a patriotic program. Then a tribute was paid to me for the thirty-four years that I was president of the company. They gave a portable television set to me which traveled with us in our motor home wherever we went. That television lasted for seventeen years. When we were not traveling, it was in our kitchen so we could watch the news while we ate. Many times, I think of that banquet and thank the Lord for those who gave us that gift. The other gift will outlast the television; it was a rocking chair. Frankly, I thank the Lord that He has given good enough health to me that I use the rocking chair very little. However, it has added a lot to our living room. I suppose when I reach ninety, I will use the rocking chair more than I have in the past. They say you are growing old when you cannot make the rocking chair go anymore. Both gifts are very useful and were deeply appreciated.

Some retired people say they get up in the morning with nothing to do and go to bed with it half done. However, in my case, especially while writing this book, I get up in the morning with a lot to do and go to bed with it half done.

The next chapter will tell of the many challenges the third generation overcame.

Chapter 15
The Third Generation in Command
Years 1977–1983

The officers elected on May 25, 1977, were:

President...David Geise
Vice President ....Norman Geise
Treasurer ....William Furman, Jr.
Secretary..K. James Kohl
Chairman of the Board...................F. Foster Furman

At this same Board meeting, James Franklin Kohl was elected to the Board. The Board consisted of a total of eight members, three of the second generation and five of the third generation.

David Geise, the new president, assumed his duties as president in January 1977. He had worked full-time at Furman Foods since he had graduated from Penn State in 1968. He was thirty years of age, a few years younger than I was when I became president. Many things were different. In 1944, the financial condition was only fair. By 1976, Furman Foods had a current ratio of over two-to-one, which was the best financial rating of any family-owned vegetable cannery in Pennsylvania. Banks were bidding for our business. Our pack in 1944 was 60,000 cases; by 1976, it was two million cases.

In 1944, the number of full-time employees was fifteen, by 1976, the number was 130 full-time employees and 250 part-time employees.

One of the many challenges facing the new president was the sudden death, in August 1976, of Bill Furman because of a brain tumor. Thirty days after the day he learned he had a brain tumor, he was with the Lord. Bill had been plant engineer for over thirty years, and there was no opportunity to train someone to take his place. Since Bill was my brother in the flesh and a Christian brother in the Lord, as well as an important business partner, his death was very painful. Franklin, who was in charge of quality control as well as being plant manager, was off a lot of the time taking cobalt treatments for cancer. When two key employees are taken out of a small organization, it is traumatic.

One of the biggest problems was that we were in the middle of negotiations with the Department of Environmental Resources (D.E.R.) about our waste water. We have always been concerned about clean streams. In 1945, we were one of the first vegetable processors to build lagoons for our waste water.

The Lord was good to us in that our neighbor who owned land on the west side of the road about 200 yards from our plant was willing to sell five acres to us. Since this was about 100 feet lower than our plant, our waste water flowed by gravity into the waste lagoon. From January 1970, to May 1972, the disposal of our waste water was inspected eight times and approved every time. In July 1972, without any warning, we received a violation notice. Bill Furman, Sr. had numerous meetings with the D.E.R. in an effort to work out something we could afford. On May 30, 1973, a five-man team from the D.E.R. made a complete survey about the possibility of expanding our spray irrigation. One of the specialists on spray fields told Bill it was one of the best spray fields he had seen. However, on August 16, 1973, we received notice that the D.E.R. was fining us $4,000. Bill and Attorney

Diehl went to Williamsport to meet with the D.E.R. On September 6, 1973, after the D.E.R. was shown that we did everything they had asked, they realized the problem was in their department, so the fine was abated and not charged.

The D.E.R. told us to get a registered engineer and have him draw up a plan for them to approve. On May 5, 1975, we signed an agreement to have a plan in effect and operating within a year. For ten months, they approved our monthly reports to them. At the end of ten months, they said our plan would not be approved, but we had to have an approved plan in operation within two months or they would shut us down. Since they could not tell us what they would approve, it was impossible to have an approved waste disposal plan operating within sixty days. Frankly, the D.E.R. had hired a lot of engineers as they graduated from college, and they really did not know what the law was or how to comply with it. Also, they said it was a violation of the law to have the warm water from our continuous cooker entering what they called a stream. They finally recognized that it was a dry weather ditch and not a stream. Therefore, it was not a violation of the law.

Since they would not listen to reason, we went to our state senator for help. On April 13, 1976, Senator Franklin Kury went to lunch with me. I will always remember that he would not let me pay for his lunch. He said, "I don't want to be obligated to anyone." What a difference today! About seven D.E.R. officials met with us that afternoon. Senator Kury asked them if we were killing any fish. They said, "No." He said, "What are they doing?" They said, "They are killing aquatic life." The little stream didn't even have a name; it was a dry weather ditch not even registered by the Army Corp of Engineers. Around 1936, we applied for a permit to discharge waste water into it, but they returned our $100, saying, "It is not a stream." When Senator Kury asked the D.E.R. what our employees would do if the D.E.R. shut us down, and what about the farmers who grew vegetables for us, their attorney said, "The employees can get jobs some place else, and the farmers can grow another crop." Senator Kury said, "I am an environmentalist, and I wrote the law. You are going beyond the law. It was never intended to do what you are doing." After he spoke, they listened to us and talked common sense. We were able to work out a reasonable solution to our problem. They agreed to let us continue to operate beyond the May 5 deadline. A later date of August 31 was set for filing a new application. They agreed to allow us to spray our waste water on the field. We had to run tests to see how much the soil would absorb without run-off. We also had to drill wells at a number of locations to find out if the spray irrigation was polluting the underground streams.

Experience has taught me that most elected officials are reasonable if they understand your problems. We appreciated that the D.E.R. allowed us some extra time because of Bill's sudden death. On August 25, 1976, we were given almost an extra year to complete compliance.

Anytime there is a death in a closely-held family corporation, there are many legal problems. We had followed the advice of our attorney and accountant very closely. Some of the things we had done that made it relatively easy to settle Bill's estate were that each year we had an appraisal of all our real estate and equipment, and we set a dollar value on any stock we would sell. If you do not do this, the I.R.S. usually puts a much higher value on it, which increases the estate tax. Stock in a closely held corporation is often hard to sell. No one wants to buy a minor interest. Our minutes showed that the actual value should be discounted 10 to 20 percent. After negotiating about two years, we settled for a discount of about 10 percent below our book value. However, that was about 10 percent below what the I.R.S. wanted to value it. This saved thousands of dollars in inheritance tax. In a former chapter, I mentioned the estate planner had suggested we give much of the stock to our children. Bill did that in 1975. Since it was less than three years previous to Bill's death, the I.R.S. wanted to include those gifts in his estate, saying he did it in anticipation of death. The Geisinger Medical Center records showed Bill only knew about the tumor less than thirty days before he died.

Another thing that helped in settling the estate was that Bill's interest in the company was covered by life insurance. Thus, settling his estate did not create a financial hardship on the company.

On March 8, 1977, we hired Tom Fitzgerald as our plant engineer. Tom did a good job installing a waste treatment system to fit D.E.R. requirements. We are still using that system today for part of our waste water.

I was on the Board of Pennsylvania Food Processors for about twenty-five years. During those twenty-five years, we had grown from one of the smallest packers to the fourth largest vegetable packer in the state. Maybe I am vain, but I dreamed of the day I would be elected president. However, I thought that would never happen. I think the main reason I was by-passed several times was that I did not join in the dirty stories and drinking parties. However, the Lord had it all planned. In 1975, an official of H. J. Heinz was elected vice president. Soon after the election, he was suddenly moved to a branch outside of the state. At a special meeting of the Board, they asked me to serve out his term. Then, in November 1976, at the sixty-second annual meeting of Pennsylvania Food Processors, I was elected president. Since I was retired, the Lord knew I could give it the time it deserved, which would have been impossible before retirement.

I note from the minutes of 1976 that the main areas of concern were legislative, the same as today. The main problem facing the industry was over-regulation by O.S.H.A. and the D.E.R.

For many years, the food processing industry was listed as a seasonable industry, allowing us to utilize up to thirteen weeks a year of unlimited hours without paying overtime to can perishable vegetables. The reason for this exemption is that when packing perishable vegetables, two to three times as many people are required for short periods of time. Thus, it is often necessary for people to work overtime since it is difficult to get enough people for only a month or two in the summer. In addition to that, weather conditions, such as high temperatures, can mature almost twice as many vegetables at one time than was expected. Since the vegetables are perishable, they cannot be held to process at a later time. About this time, the exemption was reduced to six weeks. A few years later, it was eliminated. That, together with higher wages, forced all of us to automate as much as possible to save labor. The minimum wage was increased in 1976 by twenty cents per hour to $2.30. By 1992, it was $4.25 per hour. In the short run, it looks like higher wages helps the working man. However, since prices go up based on the things that the working man buys, and the government takes more of the laborer's wages as you move to a higher income bracket, many people believe it does not really put more money in the working man's pocket.

At that time, Pennsylvania had the largest mushroom production of any place in the world. Half of the members of the Pennsylvania Food Processors Association were mushroom packers. About half of the finances to run the association were provided by mushroom growers and packers. Their biggest competition was Taiwan. The mushroom packers visited Washington and contacted Congressmen, the White House, and Cabinet members. The International Trade Commission gave them some short-term relief. Today, imports account for more than half the mushrooms consumed in the United States. Imports have been devastating to the mushroom packers. Only a few mushroom packers survived, and today's production in the United States is less that half of what it was in 1976. Today, we are having the same battle on tomato imports.

An opening for someone from Pennsylvania to be elected to the Board of Directors of the National Canners Association (known today as the National Food Processors Association) occurred about 1970. Mr. Allen Wareheim of Hanover Canning approached me about proposing my name for that position. I really wanted to serve on the Board. If I allowed my name as a candidate, my election was almost guaranteed as Mr. Wareheim was on the Board. The Board met about once a quarter. After much prayer and talking it over with my business partners, I told Mr. Wareheim I deeply appreciated his recommending me. However, because the Board usually held their business meetings on Sunday, I didn't feel it would be fair to canners of Pennsylvania if I didn't attend the Sunday Board Meetings. I said, "I have more important things to do on Sunday than attend board meetings of the National Canners Association." Also, one of our board members thought it would take too much time away from my responsibilities as president of our two corporations. Being a committed Christian sometimes costs position, prestige, and, yes, in some cases, money. However, the Lord's blessings far outweigh the problems.

We, as a company, have always been concerned with the welfare of our employees. We believe if we make money, they should share in it. The profit sharing put into effect in 1965 was a dream come true. New laws made Employee Stock Ownership Plan, or what is known as E.S.O.P., a better plan than we had. In 1978, David Geise suggested that we convert our plan to E.S.O.P. The employees owning stock in the company helps them to realize that what is good for the company is good for them. E.S.O.P. also helps provide cash for the company. Instead of taking the cash out of the company and investing it elsewhere, it buys company stock. So the company gets a tax deduction, and the employees get stock. We also think the employees like it so well they will never form a union that is harmful to the company. The first year, we were able to put $230,505 in E.S.O.P. for our 130 full-time employees. Now many of our employees say, "I own part of Furman Foods."

Owning our own trucks contributed a lot to the service we could give to our customers. By 1978, our fleet consisted of eight over-the-road tractors and twenty trailers. We also had eight straight trucks, used mostly on the farms. To properly service the fleet, we needed a larger garage. Also, the can companies were putting more cans on a pallet. This required what is called "high cube" trailers. The door of the old garage was not high enough to accommodate high cube trailers.

We were able to buy four acres from the Whipples next to our old trailer garage, which is located about one-half mile from the plant. This is the corner property on Ridge Road and Cannery Road directly across from the Point Township Municipal Building. On this lot, we built a steel building 65-by-100 feet. It has two bays with drive-through doors. The other two bays only have a door on one end.

Today, in this modern garage, we do all of the maintenance on our equipment except machine work on the blocks. We have three full-time mechanics and one part-time mechanic. They service all of the trucking equipment for both Furman Farms and Furman Foods. That includes twelve over-the-road tractors, twenty-five trailers, and twelve straight trucks.

We were desparately in need of a farm workshop, so it worked out really well to move our farm repair shop into the old garage. Since the two buildings are only about 400 yards apart, it is easy for the two shops to work together.

In the spring of 1979, Kent Kohl, the youngest son of K. James Kohl, was the eighth member of the third generation to join the company. As a teenager, like all of the other sons of the owners, he worked hoeing tomatoes, picking rocks, irrigating, and doing other manual labor jobs. He continued doing that type of work as well as driving a tractor on the farm in the summer during his high school years. After graduating from high school in 1974, he attended Williamsport Area Community College and graduated in 1976 with a degree in diesel technology. Then he enrolled in an agri-business program at Penn State, graduating in 1979.

Upon graduating, he worked on the farms, later joining the Canning Crop Specialist Department. In 1986, the job opened up as fleet manager for our trucking operation. His training in both diesel technology and agri-business made him ideal for the job. Here again, as the need developed in the company, the Lord had one of the third generation prepared for the job.

A dramatic shift in tomato production took place from 1950 to 1980. In the early fifties, the east coast was producing about 30 percent of processed tomatoes in the United States. By 1980, that dropped to about 4 percent. That meant that about fifty tomato canneries on the east coast went out of business during that time. It also meant that most of the tomatoes consumed on the east coast were shipped in from California. Today, California processes about 90 percent of all tomatoes processed in the United States. Factors causing this shift to California are ideal weather conditions and soil for growing tomatoes. Most of their water is controlled by the farmer through irrigation; they only water the tomatoes when they need water. Thus, they can control just when the tomatoes will be harvested. They do not usually have any rain during harvest season. California was able to convert to mechanical harvesting in the sixties. The yields in California in 1980 were double what they were on the east coast. The average price the processor pays for tomatoes in California is about 20 percent less than our cost. Thus, they could undersell us.

We could not use the same varieties of tomatoes that California did, because they split when it rained. A common joke was that if a cloud passed between the sun and the field, the California tomatoes would split. In mechanical harvesting, the machine cuts the stock off and elevates it up to where the machine shakes the tomatoes off of the vines. It requires a "jointless" stem that does not drop off with the tomatoes. After the tomatoes are separated from the vine, they drop on a conveyor belt where two to four sorters pick out stones and trash. From there, they go through electric eyes that drop out the green tomatoes, as well as balls of mud and small stones. After passing through the electronic sorters, they drop onto a belt where sorters pick out things the electric eyes have missed. Harvesters without electronic eyes need twice as many people as ones with electronic eyes. With good tomatoes, about a ton could be harvested every two minutes with a total of eight to ten people. Not only must the tomatoes all ripen at the same time, they also must be solid enough to withstand the rough handling when they drop several feet from the harvester to the bed of the truck that will transport them to the cannery. The varieties we have now do not split when it rains. This took years of special breeding. However, heavy rains make it impossible for the harvester and truck to get through the fields.

By the eighties, the East had developed new varieties that were suitable for mechanical harvesting. This helped us to overcome some of the advantages California had. Also, as freight rates increased from California, we were able to be more competitive in price.

Because of this, we saw a golden opportunity to get a greater share of the market. We needed more tomato processing capacity. The big question was if we should expand our present site or purchase another plant. In 1979, the tomato processing plant of Conte & Sons was up for sale. It was located on Route 100 at Palm, Pennsylvania, about 110 miles from Northumberland. As we studied the situation, we felt it would be cheaper to acquire another plant, with additional customers, than it would be to expand our facilities at Northumberland. This reduced our risk of bad weather at just one location. Also, it was close to all of the markets on the eastern seaboard.

Conte's biggest volume items were various kinds of crushed tomatoes the same as ours. They also had a lot of customers we did not have, thus, we were able to expand our markets. For years, the Conte brand of tomatoes were recognized as top quality. However, because of family problems, their quality had deteriorated over the last few years. The plant was relatively modern; it was automated, and labor costs were well controlled. The plant had 65,000 square feet of production area and 50,000 square feet of warehouse. The Conte property contained 185 acres. Some of it was used for waste disposal and about eighty acres were used for farming. We had many legal problems to solve as they had gone through a bankruptcy and owed a number of farmers a lot of money. We bought the inventory and real estate but not the corporation. Some of the farmers and other creditors tried to collect from us. It caused some hard feelings, but we had made the purchase legally and above board. On May 10, 1980, we signed the final papers; we had paid $455,000 for it.

Their normal pack of tomatoes was about the same as ours, but they were only using about 70 percent of their capacity. We moved some of our tomato production to the cannery in Palm and concentrated on packing some specialty items at Northumberland that had a better margin of profit than crushed tomatoes. It also provided us with extra production space in which we installed a pepper line with modern coring equipment. Peppers also have proved to be more profitable than tomatoes. Financially, we made very little money in the Conte operation. However, one thing that helped to make it profitable was that one of the can companies was giving Conte special can discounts which they did not give to us even though we paid our bill promptly, and Conte did not. The law required that we get the same discount. After we threatened the can company with a lawsuit, we got a credit of several hundred thousand dollars from them to use on new purchases.

The year we purchased Conte, over-production forced tomato markets down. Also, we soon learned that absentee ownership is greatly different from the way we operated. After operating four seasons with very little profit, we decided to expand at Northumberland and consolidate our production.

The year 1980 yielded a poor crop of tomatoes. We followed the practice of sharing our profits with our growers by paying them a bonus of three dollars per ton above our contract price. We were glad we had the Conte plant, thus we were able to supply our customers needs.

The purchase of the Conte plant provided the necessary facilities to increase our tomato production. However, our production facilities at Northumberland had grown like crazy. We had many different floor levels. Back in the days when they were built, earth moving equipment was not available like it is today. A lot of the ground was moved with hard, hand labor. Our facilities at Northumberland were not big enough to handle our production. We had machinery everywhere and no place to put new, labor saving equipment. The plant was built to process about two million cases. It was very difficult to produce our needs of about three million cases. The production facilities included:

Year Built	Description	Size	Square Feet
1947	Factory	65 X 100	6,500
1958	Factory addition	70 X 70	4,900
1963	Can building	50 X 150	7,500
1966	Cooker & boiler rooms		4,200
1974	Steel strain building	50 X 100	5,000
1974	Dry bean storage	50 X 200	1,000
	Misc. production		5,000
	Total production space		34,100
	Total warehouse space		120,910

To meet our growing needs, we built a warehouse about every five years. We completed warehouse number eleven in

1980. The fresh-pack vegetables of peas, stringless beans, tomatoes, and peppers can only be packed in the summer time. We needed warehouse space for an eleven-month supply as customers want a processor who supplies them throughout the whole year. We process dry pack from October 1 to June 15, so we get more turns per year on dry pack items.

Now, we faced another challenge as the macadam road off Route 147, which was a little over a mile long, was not built to withstand the heavy trailers traveling to and from our plant. Ridge Road and Cannery Road, which were macadam, were owned by the State, and they wanted to put a ten ton limit on it and fine us for everything heavier than that. The fines would bankrupt us. One of the suggestions was that we pay the extra maintenance on the road. Since we were already paying taxes, we argued that this was double taxation. It looked like a hopeless obstacle as Penn DOT said they did not have the money to improve the road. The cost to improve the road to carry the heavy trucks was over $655,000. We thank everyone for working together. Without a good road, we would not be able to expand. The following groups put together the amounts listed:

SEDA-COG agreed to fund (80%)	$524,400
Penn D.O.T. (10%)	65,500
Northumberland County Commissioners	20,000
Penna. Dept. of Commerce	20,000
Point Twp. Road Supervisor	12,000
Furman Canning Co.	13,500

After the State improved the road and brought it up to specification to carry this heavy traffic, they turned ownership over to the Township.

One day, David Geise got a telephone call asking if we could arrange for a ground-breaking ceremony for the road in a few days, if a state official would be in the area. Later, we were advised that Governor Thornburgh would be coming. He was running for re-election. We took a flat bed trailer and fixed it up for a platform. Margaret Furman, Joel's wife, took a

199

four-by-eight-foot piece of plyboard and, with finishing nails, made a sign, "WELCOME GOVERNOR THORNBURGH," and placed tomatoes on it. Governor Thornburgh said, "This is the first time I was ever welcomed with a sign made out of tomatoes, and woe to anyone who takes one off to throw at me!" David Geise was the master of ceremonies and spoke, welcoming the Governor. Of course, all of the local officials and many state politicians were there. It was a great event. One thing that stands out in my mind was that the governor arrived a little early. When no one stepped over to welcome him as he got out of a state police car, I went over and shook hands with him and welcomed him. Guess whose picture was on the front page of the local paper shaking hands with the governor?

Did you ever try to project where you would be in five years? What a challenge! We needed to try to figure our needs for the next five years, and since it would take two years from planning until completion, we really needed a ten-year projection. So you can visualize the challenge we faced since the projections needed to be made for thirteen different canned pea items, thirty different green and wax beans, twenty-five different tomato items, forty-four different dried bean items, four different bean salads, four different juice items, or a total of 116 different projections. That required more wisdom than we had. Only God knows the future. Since we always opened our Board meeting with prayer, we asked Him to guide us in our decisions.

As we talked and planned for expansion, we also considered the possibility of doing things other than canning. Of course, we would be putting our name on the new building. In March 1983, we decided to change the name to Furman Foods, Inc., which would be suitable for any type of food we packed.

During the years of 1981 and 1982, we drew graphs that showed our growth of each item over the last ten years and then tried to project what our needs would be for the next five years and for the next ten years. Our records showed that, in ten years, our total pack of dried items should more than double. Of that increase, 28 percent was new items. During that same ten-year period, our fresh pack should more than triple. The acquisition of the Conte plant was responsible for tomatoes which would represent 79 percent of that increase. Also, new items should represent 42 percent of that increase. I personally spent many hours and drew many different rough plans of buildings. Then I drew pictures of machines according to scale and cut them out like you cut out paper dolls. I would place the machines in the rough drawing of buildings. Of course, the cheapest way would be to add to our present factory. All was under the direction of David Geise, our president, and Tom Fitzgerald, our engineer.

In December 1981, we applied for a loan from the Northumberland County Industrial Development Authority for three million dollars. Of this amount, $300,000 was for waste treatment, and the balance was to expand our processing facilities. In March 1982, our accountant worked up a statement as to how that would affect our cash position.

It is impossible to find words to describe the number of meetings and the amount of work and time it took to plan for the new plant. Unless you have helped to plan a major expansion, it would be difficult to understand how much work it took or to understand the joy of seeing a new plant being built. By late 1981, it became apparent that we could not just add to the old plant. It also became very apparent that three million dollars would not be enough money. Finally, the decision was made to sell the Conte plant and move everything to Northumberland. The cost of a new facility in the summer of 1982 was estimated at seven million dollars. Anyone who has built a new home or has overseen a major expansion knows how new things increase expenses. Of course, picking a proper architect is time-consuming and of utmost importance. By the time the architect got done with the plans, the price tag had jumped to nine million dollars. In January 1983, we committed one million dollars to cover interim interest, loan commitment fees, architect, engineering fees, etc.

We decided to move the whole operation to Northumberland for several reasons. Absentee ownership seldom works as well as having everything where you can supervise it. Moving everything to Northumberland eliminated dual administration and speeded up customer service and delivery. We needed large volumes to pay for the best and latest technology. The biggest need was for modern evaporators; the cost for two was one-and-one-half million dollars. We later found out that, for our products, we needed only one evaporator to produce 18 percent evaporation. The second one was to produce tomato paste at 31 percent specific gravity. Since we could usually buy 31 percent paste from California cheaper than we could produce it, we later sold the one evaporator. The freight rate from California on 31 percent paste was about half of what it was on 15 percent paste. To pack most of our tomato products, we needed to evaporate a little more than half of the water out of the tomatoes. The evaporator we installed uses the principle of high vacuum and evaporates at a much lower temperature than the atmospheric method of 212 degrees. This produces a better flavored and better colored product. In order to operate efficiently, evaporators also require more volume than we had at either plant. Another great advantage was that evaporators use only about 70 percent as much steam, thus saving fuel and water. Estimates showed that it cost $4.50 per ton to concentrate tomatoes with the method we were using. With the evaporators, the cost would be $1.44 per ton, or a cost savings of about $.18 per case. This amounted to about $300,000 per year. In today's competitive market, we would not be in the tomato business very long using the old atmospheric method.

The next chapter will tell of the challenges of how we spent nine million dollars and where we found the money to finance the expansion.

Chapter 16
Nine Million Dollar Expansion
Years 1983–1991

What a tremendous challenge! If you have never organized a plant expansion, I doubt whether you can appreciate the almost impossible task that faced us. Many of you have moved from one location to another. You know the planning and trauma that may be involved. Take that experience and multiply it by ten, and you will have an idea of the challenge we faced. I guess you could compare our planning sessions to the strategy meeting sportsmen have when getting ready for a championship game in sports. Just as there must be a game plan, we had to have a goal. Our goal was to build the cleanest, safest, and most efficient plant possible. If you visit our plant, I hope you will be impressed by our cleanliness. Also everything is automatic. Most things are never picked up by hand.

We had purchased the Conte plant in March of 1980. At the end of the second tomato season, we reviewed our costs. We found wages were 20 percent higher and electricity was much higher. Administrative and other overhead costs were $.35 per case higher. Total costs at Conte were $.70 per case higher than at Northumberland. We had expected to find costs $.15 to $.20 per case higher, but thought that, when we increased production, we would have about the same cost as we had at Northumberland.

At the annual meeting of the Board of Directors on May 27, 1981, a discussion was held concluding that we could not compete with such high costs and the fact that, in two years, our production facilities at Northumberland would be operating at full capacity. If we were to continue our growth of about 10 percent a year, we needed to make some definite plans for expansion. In January 1982, the following people were appointed to check out all options and make a recommendation to the Board: David Geise, Foster Furman, Franklin Furman, Barney Stahler, Kenneth Dunkleberger, Tom Fitzgerald, and Kermit Kohl. The following options were explored and presented to the board on May 26, 1982:

1. Expand production facilities at both Northumberland and Conte.
2. Sell Conte; consolidate and expand production facilities at Northumberland.
3. Sell Conte; consolidate tomato production from Conte and Northumberland at a new location near present Northumberland plant where processing of other products could continue.
4. Retain present production levels at Conte and expand production facilities at Northumberland.

During the process of these meetings, a list of advantages and disadvantages for each option was compiled. Dollar values or rankings were assigned to each one and put onto a performance statement. The performance statements indicated that option number two was the most economical and was unanimously approved by the board.

As we planned, we found that to get financing, it was necessary to have the land on which the factory was to be built surveyed and then purchased by Furman Foods from Furman Farms. The amount of land required was 41.86 acres.

There was a tremendous amount of figuring to be done, so we hired our first in-house accountant, Paul Dubendorf.

Of course, all dreams and plans for a new plant would not amount to anything unless we could get the money to build. Many business executives dream about new plants and offices without adequate knowledge of how they will pay for them. The sands of time are littered with shipwrecks of businesses expanding too fast and eventually losing the plant of which they dreamed. This problem can be avoided by doing two things. First, do not finance an expansion with cash needed to operate. Second, keep some financial reserves, as many expansions or acquisitions operate without a profit for a year or two. This happened to us in both our acquisition of Conte and our plant expansion at Northumberland.

I realize that many reading this will never run a business. May I also give a little advice to young couples just starting out. Do not build or buy a house that you cannot pay for with one person's income. You may get sick or babies may come sooner than you plan. Many couples end up with so many financial problems it wrecks their marriage. You can avoid having your marriage become a shipwreck by living within your income. Stop and think which is more important to you—a lot of new household appliances, a new car, and a big house or time spent together enjoying life. How can you enjoy each other and your children if both husband and wife work or the husband must work two jobs to pay the bills?

Where do you go to borrow nine million dollars at a reasonable interest rate, as prime was over 12 percent in 1983? We were told by the local Chamber of Commerce this was impossible. However, our president, David Geise, was sure it could be done. With the help of God, we accomplished what seemed to be an impossible task.

Several things were a great help in getting the loans. Over the years, we had always met our obligations. That tradition goes back to my father, J. W. Furman, when he started the business seventy-two years before. During the years when our current ratio was less than one-to-one, a man who sold us fertilizer said to Father, "You don't need to worry about paying me." Father said, "If I am not concerned about paying you on time, you will end up being the one that worries!"

For many years, while the second generation was in charge, we had been improving our current ratio. By 1983, our current ratio was at an all-time high of 2.40, and our overall ratio was 1.88. Our sales were $24,400,000. Our cash flow was good the year around, and our increase in working capital was $1,131,293 in 1983. One of the things that helped our increase in working capital was the funds from our E.S.O.P. that would add $893,000 over the next four years.

Northumberland Borough (the closest town) met the depressed income and age requirements, so we were eligible for a two million dollar loan from the Urban Development Authority Grant known as UDAG. That loan was for twenty years. We did not start paying interest or principle for four years. In the fifth year, we paid $870,671, which were the payments for previous years. That was a great help in our cash flow as it allowed us to get our plant operating on a profitable basis. Instead of paying it back to the federal government, we pay it to Northumberland Borough, and they use it for capital improvements. If you should travel through Northumberland, you will note they have put in new sidewalks, new parking meters, planted shade trees, put all the utilities underground, and put in new sewer and water lines. One million dollars was used to build high-rise apartments for low income people, build Pineknotters' Park, improve the streets, etc. It also helped businesses on the main street to modernize their buildings. The money to do that came from the payments we made to them. The total they will receive in interest and principal is over three million dollars.

Because we would hire forty-five additional full-time employees and 100 part-time employees, as well as require a large number of farmers to supply our needs, we were able to get low-rate interest loans from PIDA (Pennsylvania Industrial Development Authority), SEDA-COG (Susquehanna Economic Development Authority-Council of Government), and IDA (Northumberland County Industrial Development Authority). We only had to go to commercial banks for $2,475,000. Our average interest rate was 9.5 percent. To service our debt, it took $1,119,425 which included interest and payment on principal. Of course, the accelerated depreciation and investment credit were a great help.

I guess the biggest challenge was not the size of the building but how to continue to operate while constructing the new plant. The problem was that much of the new plant had to be built on the site of the old plant. Much of the equipment we were using had to be set up in the new plant. We were operating fifty-two weeks a year and could not shut down any part of the plant more than three weeks. We had to build in phases and had to set target dates as to when each part would be finished.

If you are thinking of expanding your business, remember, it will cost you a lot more than your first estimate, just as ours turned out to cost three times more than we originally talked about. The same is true when you remodel a house. There are always some other things that need to be repaired. Ask anyone who has done it, and they will tell you it normally costs about twice the amount of their first estimate. There were many challenges to decide where the spending of nine million dollars would be most effective. I mentioned before that we felt there was a real opportunity to fill a need for a food processor in the East that packed a full line of tomato products.

By far, the largest expense for any vegetable was for tomato processing equipment.

Tomato equipment	$3,320,000
Production equipment for other vegetables	790,358
Warehouses #1 and #12	1,405,432
Production building	1,178,242
Can storage building	661,269
Quality control in can building	69,005
Miscellaneous equipment & other costs	<u>1,600,000</u>
Grand total	$9,024,306

The first phase was to tear down a lot of old buildings which had been built thirty to forty years earlier and to move other buildings. All of our labeling facilities were in old buildings with wooden posts every sixteen feet. The forklifts were constantly knocking them off their footers. These were the buildings that my generation had built by cutting the logs out of our woods to make the rafters. We also had made the block on a hand machine and helped to build them. All of us partners have memories of tired backs from cutting logs with a hand crosscut saw.

As I sit at the breakfast table this morning, instead of looking out over the barn and wagon shed, I see a modern canning building. Frankly, the new buildings look a lot nicer. However, there are a lot of boyhood memories with the old buildings. I played hide-and-seek in the barn with my three brothers and three sisters. We had many good times in the haymow. When neighboring boys visited us, and we would start wrestling in the kitchen, mother would get the broom and say, "Boys, the barn is the place to wrestle." Our whole family, as well as my business partners, had milked cows, curried horses, etc. We also liked to go horseback riding. I have a picture of our youngest son, Joel, standing up on one of the steers. All of our children have many pleasant memories of playing in the barn. Some of the things I remember happened twenty years ago and some seventy years ago, but the memories are still very fresh. I guess I don't want the good old days back, but I wish I could relive some of those pleasant boyhood memories.

Our plant is built on ground with a gentle slope, with the entrance of the raw product about thirty feet above the cooker. This elevation is of great help as the product drops from one machine to another by gravity. This is less expensive and more trouble free than elevators. We also use this elevation to float peas and tomatoes into the plant.

From the closing machines, the cans are conveyed by cable to the warehouse where they go to an automatic bright stacker (if they are to be stored without labels). At the bright stacker, the cans are picked up by a 40" by 48" magnet and automatically stacked on the pallet. When the pallet is full, it rolls to a place where plastic is automatically wrapped around it so the cans do not fall off and get damaged. While the pallet is being wrapped, the operator feeds into the computer the date, code, item, time, warehouse number, and the row where it will be stored. This is automatically printed on a card which is then placed on the pallet. This information in the computer makes it very easy to locate any item in the warehouse. After it is wrapped, the pallet automatically rolls out to be picked up by the forklift and stored in one of our thirteen warehouses.

Some items are labeled immediately off of the production line. The cans come from the cooker and roll into the labeling machines, then they are cased and automatically palletized. The first time they are picked up by hand is when the store clerk puts them on the shelf. I think we have about every labor-saving device available on the market.

We had one line used for labeling #2 cans, 303 cans, and 2.5 cans. Another line labeled the 40 oz., 46 oz., and #10 cans. Labeling so many sizes on one line was very expensive as we spent a lot of time changing over from one size to another.

About half of our production was #10s, so we needed a line dedicated to #10s only and another line for 303 and 300, and another for 2.5, 40 oz., and 46 oz. A long straight line always works the best. We found we needed a building 200 feet long. In the winter of 1982, we took the end out of warehouse #5 and added thirty-two feet. Then we moved a lot of the old labeling equipment into that building. Of course, we bought some new equipment, so we had three labeling lines. It was quite a challenge to place twenty-seven machines in the new building and get them operating in time to supply all of our customers' needs. We appreciated the way our customers gave us orders a month in advance so they did not run out of stock while we were changing our labeling lines. Our engineer was busy planning the factory; with the help of the people who did the labeling I laid out the labeling line, which was approved by the engineer.

We planned for our label capacity to be sufficient for ten years of growth. They have put in faster labelers and made a few minor changes, but basically the labeling lines ten years later are sufficient to meet our needs. Jim Boyer, our warehouse manager, gives us monthly reports that show, by running three shifts, we are using an average of about 82 percent of our capacity. In 1983, as soon as we got the labeling line moved, we demolished the old warehouses. These buildings were 14,000 square feet. In their place, we built a modern fireproof building of about 28,000 square feet.

In this warehouse, we put rest rooms in two locations and a print shop of 2,000 square feet. The print shop has a dark room, electronic typesetter, five letter presses, and two off-set presses. We do not print any consumer size labels as that requires a four-color picture of the product. However, we are printing the labels for consumer sizes which we are exporting to Saudi Arabia, the Cayman Islands, Haiti, South Africa, Liberia, Panama, Puerto Rico, Poland, Kuwait, Oman, Canada, and Europe. Most of the labels for the Middle East are printed in Arabic. We must imprint the date packed and shelf life.

On the large, foodservice cans that are only packed six to a case, we get labels in from many customers with just the brand name and logo, and we imprint the vegetable and weight.

Having our own print shop makes it possible for us to give our "buyer label" customer very prompt service. It would take a lot of extra work and time to haul the labels to another print shop. Our top quality and prompt delivery service gives us an advantage over most of our competition. In 1991, for export alone, we imprinted over fourteen million labels in addition to the seven million we imprinted for use in the United States.

It would have been difficult and expensive to move our steam boilers with a total of over 3,000 HP. Other things that we could not move were our warehouses and hydrostatic cooker. The new plant needed to be located close enough so that it would be economically feasible to convey the cans to the cooker and warehouses and pipe the steam to the factory. It was a big job to move over 100 pieces of machinery. I believe one of the biggest challenges was to build the new plant on the site of the old can storage and can unscrambler and move the equipment so we were not down more than thirty days. We moved one 50-by-100 foot can storage building that was built thirteen years earlier and was still in good condition. The total production area moved was 12,500 square feet, and the total area demolished was 6,000 square feet. We demolished part of the old can building and built the new building over part of it while the can unscrambler was in operation.

We started pouring the foundation for the new factory in early October of 1983. The reason we could not start earlier was because we were using stringless bean equipment located in the buildings that were to be moved or demolished. By Christmas, most of the walls were up. I remember the extremely cold and windy weather (just as cold and windy as the winter of 1994) we had the day of the Furman Christmas party. A small part of the wall was not finished. They had put up plastic to keep the wall from freezing, and the wind ripped the plastic off. We called the contractor, and they came and put up stronger plastic. Did you ever try laying a block wall with temperatures down in the teens every night and some days never getting above freezing? It was a real challenge. I had lunch recently with Tom Fitzgerald who was plant engineer at that time. He told me about heating the sand and using chemicals in the mortar to prevent freezing. Of course, the higher the wall, the more trouble you have. The can building and part of the factory wall is thirty feet high. The extremely cold weather delayed the building completion and would cost us hundreds of thousands of dollars in August because we would not be ready to operate at full capacity early enough for tomatoes.

In spite of the fact that both December and January were much colder than normal, the walls were finished in February. The Robert A. Feaster Corporation, the general contractor, worked through all kinds of weather and did a good job; we thank them for it. They set steel in March, and we were ready to put on the Carlisle roof. Of course, we needed warmer weather for the roof. We needed to get the concrete floor poured as it had to cure a definite number of days before we could put on the special acid-resistant coating needed. Because of the many floor drains, this took more time than a flat floor. Our experience from visiting other canneries, as well as our own problems, told us we needed to do something to keep the floors dry. Since so much water is used in cleaning and canning vegetables, many floor drains are needed. We placed floor drains every twenty feet with the floor sloping toward the drain from both sides. That actually made the maximum distance about ten feet that water could be on the floor. We had to pour the floor at the same time that about fifteen men were putting on the roof. On April 29, the engineer wrote a note to David Geise that the cement floor was not drying because of the wet weather, and we could not get the equipment installed to run dry beans by April 30.

The main building of the new processing plant was 175-by-200 with 35,000 square feet. On the south end of the plant was a mezzanine which was 50-by-175 feet. It is known as the brine room in which we put thirteen stainless steel mixing and holding tanks. Each vegetable takes a different brine formula. Ingredients are carefully weighed on an electronic scale and mixed with hot water. The brine tanks are located above the fillers and closing machines, and the brine flows by gravity to the fillers.

On the west side of the main building is an adjoining can storage building, 76-by-240 feet or 18,240 square feet. This is thirty feet high so we can store cans four pallets high. Part of this was completed first and several can depalletizers were installed. A temporary can track was put in to convey the cans to the fillers in the old factory so we could continue to run while the first dry bean line was being installed in the new building. After the new can depalletizers were in operation, we could finish tearing down the old building. It was a real challenge for the plant engineer and the contractor to coordinate the construction and keep the plant running.

Attached to the main building, on the north side, is a building 75-by-175 or 13,125 square feet. This building is not enclosed as it is only used in the summertime for receiving all of our fresh vegetables. The fresh vegetables are given a preliminary grading before entering the production area. They also are all washed and cleaned in this building. The tomato receiving and grading areas are north of this building where there are three flume troughs with a sloping concrete pad on each side. That gives us room to unload three trailers at the same time. Also, we can be moving three more trailers to the flumes for unloading. The forty-foot trailers have two eighteen by eighteen inch doors on the side. A four-inch water hose is used to wash the tomatoes out of the trailer.

Now the race began to move equipment and install over 150 machines. We had to meet deadlines for peas by June 14, stringless beans by July 14, and tomatoes by August 1. We met the deadlines on peas and beans. The plant was designed to process four tons of peas per hour, seven to eight tons of stringless beans per hour, and about 80 tons of tomatoes per hour or almost one-and-a-half tons per minute. The old plant built just forty years before was a two-line plant—we could run many different items in it but could only process two vegetables at a time. The new plant has six closing machines and is a five-line plant. If the product was all packed in consumer size cans, it would be equal to 2,000 cans a minute, about four times as fast as in the old plant. Many of the tomato items are hot fill which do not need to be processed. However, we did need to buy a rotary F.M.C. cooker for #10 cans so we could process all the different vegetables in #10s at the same time as running smaller size cans.

The can storage building also had a mezzanine. Part of it was built to receive ingredients on pallets for making brine. Handling the ingredients by forklift sure was a big improvement over lifting them by hand. The balance of the mezzanine was built to house five-can depalletizers. That way, the cans are able to flow by gravity to the filler, thus eliminating a lot of can elevators which can be a source of trouble. Under the mezzanine, we have rest rooms and showers and two offices for the production supervisors. There is also a Quality Control laboratory of about 1,400 square feet, as well as a refrigerator and walk-in freezer. We can put pallets in both of these with a forklift.

The original plan called for the Quality Control laboratory to be in the old factory building which was about twelve feet lower than the new production area and about 100 feet from the inspection belts. The construction was greatly handicapped because Franklin had spent several years planning the location of different machines. He had made rough drawings but, due to his problems with cancer, the drawings were not complete. During this time, Greg Kratzer, who was in charge of Quality Control, was moved up to Production Manager because Franklin was only able to work part-time. I'll never forget the day Greg Kratzer said to me while we were discussing the site for the Quality Control Department, "We should have the Production Manager's office and the Quality Control laboratory close to production." We asked our engineer if there was any possible space available next to the production area. He said there was a space of twenty-five-by-fifty-five feet available under the can unscramblers. Greg said, "That spot is ideal." I believe the Lord guided that decision. The outside of the building was already built, and the engineer said if we would have waited until the following week, it may have been too late. It would have been a grave mistake not to have the Quality Control Department right beside the production area. The closer the quality control is to production, the better control there is.

From his office, Greg can see the filling operations and the closing machines. The office of the quality controller is right next to Greg's. The fillers and closing machines are only a few steps away. The Quality Control Department checks the quality of the raw product before it enters the plant and must check the picking table and sorting operations often. They are also responsible to check the fill level and can seams regularly. Everything being so close really saves hours of walking, and it gives the best quality control possible. "Quality you can taste" is one of the hallmarks of Furman Foods.

Most of the equipment used for the first dry bean line was new, so we could install it while the old plant was operating. Thus, we were able to make the switch from the old plant to the new in about a week, an incredibly short time considering all of the changes. Only an electrician knows how much work it took to install new heavy service wire for over 225 motors. They had to install new can lines to convey the cans to the six fillers. Several hundred feet of cableway were needed in a number of can sizes to convey the filled cans from the closing machine to the cookers. We want to express a special thanks to our maintenance people who accomplished what seemed to be an impossible task.

Strike up the band! Let us celebrate! How do you describe the feeling, the emotions, and the victory of seeing the first can of dried beans go through the closing machine on May 23, 1984? It was like making your first touchdown after months of practice, or moving into a new house, or playing the piano at your first concert, or buying your first car, or passing your driver's test. Just as these great events in your life required hours of preparation, so it took over three years of planning to make this great accomplishment possible.

It was easy to meet the deadline on peas as much of the equipment was the same as we used on dry beans. We purchased six large stainless tanks to soak the dried beans, each with a capacity of 10,000 pounds of dried beans. Since they were new, they could be installed while we were using the old tanks in the old factory. These tanks are also used as storage tanks for peas. We needed to get the stringless bean line ready for some early beans we were getting from the south to make up for a short crop the year before. That required a lot more work than the pea line. It required the installation of over fifty machines used only for beans. To snip the ends off the beans, and then cut and grade them is a very complicated procedure.

We had real problems with the tomato line. Three of our greatest problems were caused by the weather. However, our own mistakes were responsible for about half our losses. The first problem with the weather had occurred the previous summer. Because of dry weather, we were so short of beans that we decided to can some in October. The bean machinery was in a building that had to be moved before we could finish excavating for the new building. Excavation was delayed for about a month. That made it impossible to complete the new building before winter arrived. Then the severe winter mentioned before further delayed the completion of the building. By spring, we were about two weeks behind schedule.

216

We may have been ready for tomatoes if the weather had not further complicated the matter by doing two things. First, tomatoes were ready July 31; this was the earliest date ever and about ten days earlier than normal. This was further complicated by a crop 10 percent larger than normal. So, within days after we started, we were behind and lost raw tomatoes throughout the whole season. Secondly, during the five weeks when we can tomatoes, we usually have some rain almost every week, which prevents the farmers from harvesting. During that time, if we were behind we would usually catch up. However, we had unusually nice weather in 1984, and the farmers could harvest every day.

We also made some engineering mistakes. The target date for start-up was not set early enough to compensate for adjustments and problems. I mentioned earlier that Franklin's sickness complicated ordering and installing the equipment. This may have delayed the delivery dates of some of the machines. The type of evaporator we needed was not manufactured in the United States; we ordered it from Italy. The blue prints they gave us for installation were not correct, and we had to pour additional concrete at the last minute for setting the evaporator. Trying to communicate in Italian caused some problems and delays. Some of the equipment did not perform up to our expectations. We finished the season by losing $600,000 of raw tomatoes. Pretty expensive mistakes! However, these mistakes complicated other matters. Our waste treatment plant could not handle the extra load put on it because of spoiled tomatoes, so the Department of Environmental Resources fined us. Since we could not unload the tomatoes promptly and had to put quotas on the farmers, they were very unhappy; we lost some very good growers. To make matters worse, the tomato yield was below normal the next year.

If we could have processed the tomatoes in 1984, the farmers would have made more money than average. However, most of the farmers only broke even. When they had a poor crop in 1985 and did not make any money two years in a row, we had to raise our price exceptionally high to get them to grow tomatoes in 1986. Thus, our cost was so high we had trouble meeting competition. The problems we experienced in 1984 affected us for several years.

Why do I mention our mistakes? I hope someone reading this book may avoid making the same mistakes we did. At the age of eighty-three, I try to learn from other peoples' mistakes, as I realize I will not live long enough to make them all myself. One other mistake we made was overloading our engineer. When we discussed the need for a clerk of the works, Tom, our engineer, thought he could save about $10,000 by doing it himself. But he was hopelessly overloaded during the construction. I believe a clerk of the works could have saved us thousands of dollars.

The Lord has blessed us more than He has most companies. On September 14, 1984, the monthly luncheon meeting of Susquehanna Valley Chamber of Commerce was held in warehouse #1 next to the print shop. Following the luncheon at 2:30 we had the formal dedication. The list of people invited included all local government officials, state officials, our U.S. representative and U.S. Senators. We invited Governor Thornburgh, but he sent Secretary James Pickard, Pennsylvania Department of Commerce who gave the Keynote Address. Over one hundred business people attended. After the meeting, plant tours were conducted.

The program of the formal dedication was:

Welcoming remarks	David Geise
National Anthem	Terry Hoffman
Invocation	Rev. Sinclair Reid
Scripture, Psalm 127	Foster Furman
Dedication	David Geise
Recognition of Financial Leaders	
Financing "A Cooperative Effort"	Robert Postal

Keynote Address ....James Pickard
Contractors...Tom Fitzgerald
Suppliers...Franklin Furman
Customers ....Joel Furman
Agri-Business: Number 1 in Pennsylvania ......Gary Babin,
                                    Penna. Dept. of Agriculture.

David Geise dedicated the new facility to the "Big Four" (the four members of the second generation) in appreciation of the solid foundation they laid for the company's continued growth. The first verse of Psalm 127 was my father's favorite verse, "Unless the Lord builds the house, it's builders labor in vain. Unless the Lord watches over the city, the watchmen stand guard in vain."

Following the dedication, we conducted plant tours after which we had a buffet in the same warehouse in which we had lunch.

Previous to the dedication, we had an open house, which included tours and light refreshments, for the following groups:

August 6 & 7 ....Employees and families
August 9 ....Farmers who grow vegetables (lunch)
August 9 (evening)...........Special invitation to all neighbors
September 13 ....60 of our food brokers and salesmen
      (We have 28 different brokers, covering about 20 states.)

To close our celebration, we advertised open house for the public for Saturday, September 15. We estimated that over 1,400 people attended these meetings.

Norman Geise was born on March 9, 1918. Recently, he reminded me that was the same year that the Furmans moved to Point Township. We had a retirement banquet for him at St. John's Lutheran Church in connection with our annual banquet in the fall of 1983. In addition to other entertainment, Dave Betts, one of our regional sales managers, took a number of videos sometime before the banquet. He interviewed

Norman's son, David, and many others regarding the things they remembered about Norman. One of the questions asked of K. James Kohl was, "Do you really think Norman will retire?" Jim's answer was, "I think Norman will be like Foster and come to the office almost every day." Elnora, his wife, said the same thing, but added, "I know we want to do some traveling." Some of the other statements were that he was a good boss and worked just as hard as everyone else. His brothers, Paul and Ira, who worked at the cannery, also mentioned that Norman was a good brother.

For retirement, he received a large suitcase which was very useful for the traveling they wanted to do. He had been in charge of harvesting peas, so they also gave him a big sign which had been signed by the president, Dave Geise, saying he had the use of the pea mower as long as he lived. He used a pitchfork a lot during the pea mowing, so they gave him a pitchfork. He also gassed up the tractors with a five-gallon gas can, so they gave him one of them to remember the work he did at the cannery.

At the 1984 Board Meeting, Norman Geise, having reached the age of sixty-five, was elected Vice President of Operations, and Franklin Furman was elected Executive Vice President and Assistant Chief Executive Officer. At the annual Board Meeting on May 29, 1985, Franklin was re-elected. In July, it was realized that Franklin's inoperative brain tumor would make it impossible for him to continue to serve. On September 11, James Franklin Kohl was elected to replace him.

To supply water for increased production, we drilled several more wells. A few years previous to 1984, a number of new homes were built within one-and-one-half miles of our plant. Our new wells may have affected a total of forty-seven homes over the next two years. Dr. Parizek from Penn State, who picked the sites for us to drill, designated the homes that were in the same aquafer from which we were pumping water. Then others charged us with their water problems. They failed to realize that every home built draws water and may affect their wells. We felt we had a responsibility to the forty-seven homes to the cost of about $200,000. It was the right thing to do; we have good relationships with our neighbors. It proved to be a good Christian testimony. Rather than going to court, we paid for some wells that may not have been our responsibility.

We passed another major milestone in company history when Franklin George Furman, the first of the fourth generation, joined the company. He goes by the name of Frank. New labor laws would not allow him to start working for the company as young as those of the second and third generation. At the age of thirteen, he started hoeing, planting tomatoes by hand, and picking stones. He attended Philadelphia College of the Bible for one year, then transferred to Penn State. During the summer months, he worked on the farm until he went back to school. At the age of eighteen, he worked in the cannery in the summer as a laborer until he was a junior in college, then he worked in Quality Control. Frank graduated from Penn State in 1985 with a degree in food science. He started working full-time for the company in January of 1986, in product development and assisted in Quality Control.

In 1989, our customer service manager resigned to take a position with another company. This gave Frank early advancement as he was the best qualified person for that position. In 1991, he also became the export manager. Our export business almost doubled this past year as we now export to thirteen countries.

In July of 1984, David Geise brought to the attention of the Board that, on numerous occasions, company business was being conducted on Sunday. Since Furman's has always claimed that they don't operate on Sunday, a policy on this needed to be established. It was decided that work on Sunday should be curbed as much as practical and to try to uphold the past policy. During the discussion, it was mentioned that we believed the Lord has blessed us for taking the stand that Sunday is the Lord's day.

In April of 1984, David reported to the Board concerning a wood-fired co-generation plant. Since these plants require high pressure steam to run the electric turbines, and we used steam pressure of about 125 pounds, Viking Energy would sell the steam to us at 80 percent of what it would cost us to produce this steam with oil or gas, whichever was the cheapest. At that time, energy prices were very high, and it looked like they would go higher. It was estimated that it could possibly save us about $200,000 per year. However, we only realized savings of about 75 percent of that amount.

The plant was to be located above the firehouse about 200 yards from Joel's home. In July, Joel opposed it, and Franklin and I did not vote. We were concerned about the noise. I had visited several co-generating plants to check the noise level, and the noise level seemed to be acceptable. In August of 1984, I made a motion that the noise level outside Joel's house was not to exceed fifty decibels. The co-generating plant objected to that clause, and we made the mistake of replacing it with another clause that was too liberal, making it impossible to hold the co-generating plant accountable for the noise and trouble the noise caused. As far as I am concerned, it was a bad deal all the way around.

Construction was to start in 1986 and be completed in 1987. Joel vigorously protested putting the plant there in the meetings and by letter. My, how I wish we had listened to him. The co-generation plant created so much noise and vibration both during and after start up that in 1992 Joel desired to move because he and his family could not sleep at night. This plant caused more tension and trouble in our family business than anything we have had in recent years. After several years, the co-generating plant spent a lot of money reducing the noise level. To try to help solve the problem, in 1994, Furman Farms bought the house and converted the downstairs into a meeting room and the upstairs into offices for our field department and farm operations.

Joel's home was only about 200 yards from our house. Whenever I needed help, I could always get it from one of them. Joel's family moved to a farm behind Sunbury about seventeen miles from here. I really miss the walks with my grandson, Reid. We often walked several miles through the local woods. It was always a delight to see several deer on some of those walks. Since both Hazel and I are over eighty, we miss their help.

Joel and Margaret hated to move from this large house where they had room for large family Christmas parties, extra bedrooms for missionaries and guests, etc. They could walk to work and, until Viking Energy was built, they thought they could live there the rest of their lives. They had lived there twenty-five years, had a fine garden, a large orchard, and all of their children were born while they lived there.

Profits in the food industry go in cycles of about seven years. By the time we got our plant in full operation, importers from Israel and the Mediterranean basin countries were flooding the Eastern seaboard with tomatoes below our cost. Imports rose over 600 percent from 1980 to 1984, and tomato prices dropped drastically. Our largest volume item, crushed tomatoes, went from a profit of $1.11 per case to a loss of $1.51 per case. Imported catsup sold at $2.69 below our cost. For the first time in fifty years, we lost money to the tune of $1,300,000 in 1985. Because of investment credit and fast depreciation, part of this was a paper loss.

The loss was 13.2 percent on investment. If markets would not have been overloaded and profits would have been normal, we may have broken even. Of course, the low prices because of surpluses were beyond our control. Everyone reduced their acreage a little and, by the year 1989, most surpluses had been used up. Then the Lord allowed a poor crop year and shortages developed. In 1989, we made the most money we had ever made. With the new plant, we were able to increase production.

In 1985, a loss of this amount demanded drastic action. Most expansion projects were put on hold. Budgets for capital projects was held to only those things necessary to continue present efficient production, or $383,500, compared to one million dollars in normal years. Of course, no money went into bonuses or pension plans for either the employees or management. We eliminated the annual banquet. On March 12, 1986, a motion passed, with only one dissenting vote, to eliminate family member management's bonuses. This was done in spite of fact that many of their salaries were less than half of that which officers were getting in other companies of our size. Everyone worked together, and we thank the Lord that, in a few years, profits returned to normal.

On May 19, 1986, we bought additional irrigation equipment as there was no measurable rainfall for five weeks.

On August 27, 1986, a motion was made that, at the end of the year when a Board member turns seventy, they discontinue serving on the Board. Also, anyone who is disabled and inactive for over a year must discontinue serving on the Board. Since I was seventy-five, I was not reelected as Chairman of the Board but was appointed Vice President of Legislative Affairs. Because Norman Geise was seventy, he was not reelected to the Board. In May 1988, the number of Board members dropped to eight.

When a company is small, everyone in management knows the company goals. In January of 1988, it seemed best to put our goals in writing. We spent half a day with a consultant trying to tell us what we should put in our mission statement. Most wanted a mission statement that reflected our strong religious convictions. Some of us were very upset that the consultant tried to tell us it would be very detrimental for us to mention God or the Bible in our statement. He tried to tell us it would almost be illegal to do that. I talked to our attorney about it. As a Christian, Robert Diehl was surprised at the attitude of the consultant. At the annual Board Meeting in 1988, the following mission statement was adopted as well as definition of ownership:

CORPORATE MISSION STATEMENT
Furman Foods is a growth-oriented producer and processor of high quality food products and services. Furman Foods is a family-and-employee-owned corporation that seeks to follow the highest ethical and moral standards as set forth in the Bible with a sense of community responsibility.

OWNERSHIP
Ownership should remain with active family members (descendants of J. W. Furman past the second generation). All voting stock should be held only by active J. W. Furman descendants who are board members, management, or staff who have been approved by the Board after 36 months of employment. A plan should be devised for retirees and disabled to transfer all voting stock to the above. It is acceptable for nonactive family members to hold nonvoting stock provided it never becomes a majority holding.

I think the above ownership decision is the only way to fulfill our mission statement. Many family-owned companies go public for a variety of reasons. Often, if they want to expand, they must go public to raise capital. However, when a company goes public, they start losing control. Many a company started by godly owners goes public, and the godly principles are discarded. The Lord has been good to us. He gave each of the four original partners children who are interested in the business.

All of us gave stock to our children to break down our estates. We would rather give it to our children than to pay inheritance taxes. With children and grandchildren owning stock, we have a total of fifty-three stockholders. Since we do not pay dividends, it does not provide any cash for the stockholders.

225

Our stock increases in value by about 14 percent a year. Some of the grandchildren wanted to cash in their stock to pay for their college education. It was decided that we would redeem about $75,000 worth of stock per year on a first-come basis. After much discussion, it was decided we would discount the stock 25 percent. If the owner died, the discount would only be 15 percent. The above discounts are in accordance with government regulation and best accounting principles.

In December 1985, a retirement banquet was held at Stuck's Restaurant for K. James Kohl. His wife, Alice, his daughter, Darlene, and about sixty-five employees attended. Darlene lives in Texas and was home for the holidays. After a delicious meal, Dave Geise, who was master of ceremonies, presented him with a CB set for his motor home as well as some other presents. Each employee was asked to tell of something they remembered from by-gone days.

At the time Jim and Alice were married, he milked the five or six cows we had. He never really liked to milk cows. Several recalled the days when Jim drove the team of mules. Also, when they were sowing peas on the four-acre field which was about three blocks from the barn, they needed some more pea seed and, rather than unhitch the team from the drill and hook them up to the wagon, they carried a bag of pea seed on their shoulders. I believe it weighed a hundred pounds. Of course, today that would have been gotten with a pickup truck.

Jim plowed with a team at the rate of one acre per ten hour day and, before he retired, he plowed with a four-wheel 2470 CASE tractor with eight eighteen-inch plows at the rate of fifty acres per ten hour day. That cut a twelve foot wide swath down through the field. During his lifetime, hybrids were introduced in many grain and vegetable crops which increased the yield five to seven times per acre. We all had a good time recalling many funny things that had happened during the more than forty years he worked as manager for Furman Farms.

When writing about the tremendous gain in yields of farm crops, I think of the Texas rancher who was touring Australia. You have all heard about everything in Texas always being bigger than any place else. As an Australian rancher was showing the Texan his ranch, they passed a nice flock of sheep. The Australian said, "Isn't that a beautiful flock of sheep?" The Texan said, "You should see our sheep in Texas; they will give almost twice as much wool as your sheep." As they came to a corn field, the Australian asked, "What do you think of our corn? Those ears are almost shoulder high." The Texan said, "You should see our corn in Texas. Why, I can hardly reach the last ear." Then they came to a dairy herd, and the Australian said, "Look at that beautiful herd of cows. They will average sixty quarts of milk a day." The Texan said, "You should come to Texas. We have cows that will produce up to seventy-five quarts a day." As they drove on, a kangaroo hopped across the road in front of them. The Texan asked, "What was that?" The Australian replied, "Don't you have grasshoppers back in Texas?"

The next chapter tells how to make your presence felt in Washington and Harrisburg. We won many victories at both the state and federal level.

Chapter 17
Influencing Washington and Harrisburg

Most unjust laws that affect either private citizens or businesses are made because we, as individuals, fail in our responsibility of keeping our government officials properly informed. The average person or business executive is so busy making a living and meeting his family's needs that he neglects to express his views to local, state, and federal officials. Worse yet is the fact that many Christians are not registered and do not vote. If this book would stir up enough people to vote and become active in government affairs, it will have served a very useful purpose.

We are in danger of losing our religious freedom and moral decency because many Christians were not active in voting. For too long, Christians have been silent. Even now, police are arresting children for praying silently in the classroom. Recently, several men were arrested for getting down on their knees and praying silently in a courtroom. You may think one vote will not make any difference. Did you know that the location of our state capital at Harrisburg was decided by one vote? Do you realize that literally hundreds of officials have been elected by just one vote per precinct? In Pennsylvania, one vote per precinct amounts to over 9,500 votes!

I think of a member of the Governor's cabinet who died very suddenly. At the funeral, a man, who was very anxious for the job of the man who had died, said to the Governor, "Could I exchange places with Mr. Jones?" The Governor said, "If it is alright with the undertaker, it is alright with me."

I feel a Christian should be as nonpartisan as possible. There are good, godly men on both sides of the aisle. I remember attending a fund-raising banquet for a Democratic state senator in Harrisburg. I was the only businessman at my table. As we got acquainted, I asked each one of the other four where they were from, where they had gone to school, and what they did before coming to work at Harrisburg. One of the young men was the chief legislative assistant to the president of the Senate. Each one, without exception, had come to work in Harrisburg as soon as they graduated from college. The last one asked, "Why did you ask what we did when we graduated from college?" I said, "You are not going to like the answer, but since you asked, I will be glad to tell you. You do not know what the real world is like. There is no way that you can properly advise your Senators, if you have had no actual experience earning a living in the real world. There should be a requirement that, before you can advise our lawmakers, you should have to face the real world for at least five years. Now I understand why so many foolish laws are proposed."

We, as Christian citizens, have a duty and privilege to pray for all government officials as commanded in 1 Timothy 2:1, 2: "I urge, then, first of all, that requests, prayers, intercessions and thanksgiving be made for everyone—for kings and all those in authority, that we may live peaceful and quiet lives in all godliness and holiness."

We should not only pray for them, but also attend their rallies and fund raisers. We need to know them on a first-name basis. Then, when you call them on the phone, they have a mental picture of you. They know you vote in their district and probably influence a number of people, as well as your family. We need to be in constant contact with them on moral issues. They need your support. If you fail to advise them, a small but vocal minority will get laws passed that are entirely contrary to the Bible.

I write to Washington so often on so many different issues that Senator Arlen Specter, the late Senator John Heinz, and Representative Gekas have sometimes referred to me as their pen pal.

I had been active in limited ways in trade organizations before I retired. I am fortunate that the Lord gives me good health, and our company sees the need for us to be more actively involved with our legislators.

We became active on the Governmental Affairs, Education, and Transportation committees of the Susquehanna Valley Chamber of Commerce. In addition to the monthly meetings of the full Chamber, the Governmental Affairs Committee meets twice a month. We often have county, state, and federal officials at these meetings.

As the result of our company activities in the Chamber of Commerce, I was given the Special Achievement Award of the Central Susquehanna Valley Chamber of Commerce in 1988. As Joe McGranaghan described the achievement of the person to receive the award, I thought it was going to our state representative, Merrill Phillips. I certainly was surprised when he mentioned the things that could only apply to me.

I was the fourth one to receive this prestigious award. The Central Susquehanna Valley Chamber of Commerce has about 400 active members of the business community. The award is given at the Annual Meeting and Business Awards Dinner. In accepting the award, I thanked the people of our organization and family who made those achievements possible.

Our committees were influential enough to get a bridge built over the Susquehanna River at Sunbury in a little over half the time it usually takes from the time they are proposed. We also helped get the main road north and south through the Susquehanna Valley, Route 15, put on early schedule; it is under construction now. Of course, we worked very closely with our Representatives Merle Philips, Russ Fairchild, and Senator Ed Helfrick. Without their help, we could not have accomplished what we did.

At one of the Governmental Affairs meetings, right after Jim and Tammy Baker had disgraced the Christian television ministry, someone called out, "Foster, how are you and Jim and Tammy getting along?" I said, "Hazel and I watched a few of their programs and decided they were more interested in Jim and Tammy than they were in the Lord's work. We never sent them a penny." For six weeks, they kept ribbing me about this. Then when Jimmy Swaggart went bad, I knew they would roast me again, so I asked the Lord for a special Scripture to answer them with. The executive secretary with a loud voice said, "How are you and Jimmy Swaggart doing?" The Lord gave the Scripture to me. "Let him that thinketh he standeth take heed lest he fall," and "Let him that is without sin cast the first stone." Someone said, "Bill, you have enough sin of your own, you better keep quiet." That was the last I heard about that.

Hearings and legislation regarding tomato imports took almost half of my time. When I know I will be appearing before six to ten people and every word is being recorded, I must be careful of what I say. I must be able to document everything I say. Because I may be questioned and cross-examined, a lot of research is necessary. Many times, I am given only three to ten minutes to speak, so I must condense what is said to the most important and essential things. Prior to the hearing, I prepare a written statement with graphs and figures which is given to the committee I am appearing before; they have the testimony in front of them during the hearing. Normally, an amended testimony can be sent in writing within a limited number of days. Sometimes they ask questions to which I do not know the answers. In that case, it is better to admit it and ask to send it to them later rather than try to bluff my way through.

Tomatoes and tomato products are our principal business and represent 72 percent of our seasonable pack and 42 percent of our year-round production. Since they often account for 50 percent of our profit, it is understandable why they are so important to us. In fact, without a profit on tomatoes, it would be very difficult for us to survive.

I believe it was about 1967 that the flood of imported tomatoes became a real problem for our industry. In July of 1968, hearings were held before the House Ways and Means Committee. In 1967, imports of canned tomatoes reached 133 million pounds, an all-time high. To make matters worse, in April, 1967, at the Kennedy rounds of General Agreement of Tariff and Trade, as a special concession to European Community countries, the United States negotiators reduced the tariff on tomatoes in spite of the fact they had earlier guaranteed that they would not be reduced.

Trade negotiation and import regulations are very, very complicated. I have been involved in literally dozens of hearings over the past sixteen years, but I feel I am just beginning to learn something about it. We must realize that we are in a global economy. Our business decisions must take into account what is happening on the other side of the globe. Even though the United States has the lowest tariff of any tomato producing country, other countries apply every three years (as often as the law allows) to eliminate tariffs.

In 1980, the Common Market countries were the main source of trouble. Before the Tokyo rounds of GATT negotiations, the paragraph about subsidies said, "If the United States could prove damage because of subsidies, we could assess countervailing duties to offset the subsidies." Our negotiator allowed a paragraph change to read, "If we could prove substantial damage because of European Community country subsidies, the United States could put on countervailing duties."

The European Community countries realized they could pay whatever subsidies they pleased, and the United States was not likely to be able to prove that subsidies were the main reason for damage they did to the United States tomato industry. As a result of adding the words "substantial damage" to the agreement, they increased their subsidy to cover over half of their cost. To illustrate, #10-size crushed tomatoes cost us $9.26. The European Community governments paid their tomato packers a $5.77 subsidy.

The tomato processors of the United States can and will compete if they have a level playing field. In comparing this to a 100-yard dash, the European Community countries were starting on the fifty-yard line, whereas we were starting at the beginning. If they would have been on the ten-yard line, we could have caught them, but there is no way we could run 100 yards while they ran only fifty yards.

During my many trips to Washington, I became friendly with the people in the Agriculture Department. One of the negotiators in the Tokyo rounds said, "The European Community countries really took us across on that issue, as they interpreted it differently than we did. We had no idea of the impact that would have on the United States tomato industry." Thus, tomato imports in 1984 were six times what they were in 1980. That increase in imports put almost half of the small tomato packers in the United States out of business. Of course, those subsidies almost bankrupted the European Community country governments, so in a few years, they greatly reduced the subsidy. Imports in 1992 from those countries have shrunk to only a fraction of what they were in 1984.

Imports are a continuing problem. Even though there is a duty of about $1.50 per case, imports sometimes sell below our cost. In 1983, most of the 100 tomato processors in the United States formed NAGPFT, the National Association of Growers and Processors for Fair Trade. I was elected to the executive board to represent all of the tomato packers east of

Ohio. About 90 percent of all the tomatoes processed in the United States are processed in California. The office of the organization and most of the meetings are held in California. Since we are only about three hours from Washington, I testified more often than any other canner. For several years, it seemed most of my time was occupied preparing to testify in Washington and traveling to Washington. There were numerous trips to California. When the thruway collapsed in Oakland, California, during the earthquake, I said to my wife, "About a year ago, I traveled that thruway six times in a week. I am glad I am home and not in Oakland."

In April of 1984, the tomato industry was faced with a challenge that everyone said we would lose. Israel applied for General Service Preference on tomatoes. This would have removed all duties on tomatoes from Israel. They have a very strong lobby in Washington and are very powerful. Israel used the same evaporators for tomatoes they were using for citrus juice. They had the plans and potential to produce and replace all of the tomatoes grown in nineteen states in the United States. In fact, they could replace all the tomatoes except for those processed in California and Ohio. In addition, if duties were removed from Israeli tomatoes, we faced the possibility they would tranship tomatoes from other countries. We have laws that are supposed to prevent that; however, they are very difficult to enforce. Records show that many years, Israel exports more citrus juice than they pack. We were afraid the same would happen on tomatoes.

We helped to organize a lobbying campaign that will go down in history. We wrote letters to 140 of our growers, many of our customers, fifty of our suppliers, forty Granges, many farm organizations, four banks, and twenty-five of our brokers. We also explained to our employees that their jobs were at risk; we told them this was almost life and death for us. We asked them to write to their Senators, their Representatives, and about six government agencies that were involved.

The California tomato growers and California Canners' Association also sent letters to their members, asking them to write to the same people mentioned above. Since I represented the east coast, we sent letters to about sixty canners in the Midwest and on the east coast asking them to contact the same people we did.

Our employees, farmers, and suppliers, realizing how important this was to them, mailed hundreds of letters. I would like to say thanks to each one of them. Without their support, we could not have won. The Department of Agriculture got so many letters, they sought me out at a hearing and said, "Please don't have anymore people write to us. We are getting so many letters, we don't have time to answer them." The senators, representatives, and government agencies told us the letters and calls from their voters gave us victory. Tomatoes were one of only a few items on which the tariff was unchanged for five years.

We had the same battle all over again in 1989 when the five years were up. Again, there were numerous hearings in front of about three congressional committees and three or four government agencies. Five government agencies were involved in making a recommendation to the Congress and the President. Several times, they scheduled the meeting, only to cancel it at the last minute. I will never forget, one afternoon about two o'clock, I got a call from a friend in the Department of Agriculture asking if I knew a special meeting was called on short notice for the following day to decide if they would extend the tariff.

Knowing how Washington works, I believed the short notice was a trick to catch us off guard. The Department of Agriculture tried to reach Leonard Lobred, our consultant, but could not reach him. Our friend said, "I want you to know we will fight to protect you, but it doesn't look good. Do not be surprised if you lose." In other words, she was preparing us for a loss. I immediately called the head of our association in California, Dave Zollinger. He did not know about the meeting. We discussed as to whether we had contacted all the agencies involved in making the decision.

The Department of Commerce had not been contacted. It was agreed that Mr. Zollinger would contact friends in the International Trade Office. I was to try to reach someone in the Department of Commerce. Time was running out. After a number of calls, I finally reached someone in authority. They asked for facts to substantiate our position that the tariff should remain for five more years. It was close to four o'clock; however, they assured me if I transmitted the facts to them at once by facsimile, they would examine them before the meeting the next morning. In addition to a number of statistics supporting our position, I also transmitted copies of a letter Representative Gekas and eight congressmen from Pennsylvania had signed plus a similar letter signed by four congressmen from New York state.

The next afternoon, we received a call saying the whole attitude of the committee changed from the day before, and duties would remain on five more years. Since having the duties removed could mean up to one million dollars per year to us, this was equivalent to Penn State (or your favorite team) winning the national championship in football. Knowing how Washington works, it was nothing short of a miracle that we won. God saw to it that we had friends in the various departments so that we got a fair hearing. I am persuaded that God prompted that telephone call from the Department of Agriculture. We have had many things happen over the years that prove to us God takes care of His own. As Romans 8:28 says, "And we know that in all things God works for the good of those who love him, who have been called according to his purpose."

May I suggest, if church members would put as much time in calling, writing to, and going to see their congressmen as the tomato growers and processors did, laws like the Gay Bill of Rights and Freedom of Choice would be defeated by a large margin. Of course, that applies to many laws affecting morality.

I spent days walking the halls of Congress, visiting not only my senators and representatives but the senators and representatives of our tomato growers in four states. Many times, we could not see the senators or representatives themselves, but I got to know many of the legislative assistants on a friendly basis. You must remember, to have a real impact in Washington, you must know someone that votes in the congressional district of the congressman you go to see. At first it was fun, but after a dozen trips to Washington, it became real work as I approached eighty years of age.

On one of my trips to Washington, I had an appointment with our Representative, George Gekas, who was very helpful. When the receptionist took my card, I said, "Today is my seventy-fifth birthday." Representative Gekas came off the floor to keep our appointment. About ten minutes later, the receptionist walked in with ice cream and a cake with two candles on it, and the office staff sang "Happy Birthday." Representative Gekas' birthday was that same week; he was just twenty years younger than I was. The next year, they had a fund raiser for him. The fee was one dollar for every year of his age. At his birthday party, I reminded him of the year before. He said, "Yes, that cost me some money." I said, "Your birthday cost me $56, a lot more than you spent on me!" He said, "Oh, I should have kept quiet."

To have your representative take time out of his busy schedule to appear at hearings on your behalf sends a message to the committees that this issue is of real importance. Of course, the fact that they depend on Congress for their pay has a lot to do with it. Representative Gekas appeared at several of the hearings to testify on our behalf as well as for the farmers who grow tomatoes for us. Of the hundred tomato canners, only one other canner was able to get his representative to testify at the hearings. At one of those hearings, Representative Gekas could not attend because an important vote was coming up. He sent his chief legislative assistant with his testimony. After the hearing, three national news services asked to interview me. I couldn't understand it because there were men there from the West coast and men much more prominent than I. It was almost a day later when I figured out that Representative Gekas's aids had asked the press to be there to cover a story for him to send back to his voters. Since he wasn't there, I got the press. They gave me a really good write-up, saying, among other things, that I was dressed in a dapper olive green suit!

Recently, because of the reduction of subsidies in the European Community countries and a 100 percent tariff imposed because of trade problems on meat, imports of tomatoes are only a trickle from those countries. However, tomato imports from Chile and Mexico have more than replaced the imports from Israel and European Community countries.

At this same time, we had hearings about the Uruguay rounds of GATT who proposes that the United States will reduce tariffs on things coming into the United States if Japan and European Community countries will reduce subsidies on farm products. In the United States, the vegetable growers and the processors do not receive, or want, any subsidies like they get in the other countries. However, we do have subsidies on grain crops. Negotiations are still continuing, and no one can predict the outcome. At this point, it looks like our negotiators are not giving the store away like they have at other times. Of course, we have appeared at several hearings on the Uruguay Rounds of GATT.

In 1989, Chile and several other South American countries asked to be given G. S. P. treatment. That petition was denied on July 23, 1990. Later, when President Bush was in Colombia, South America, and asked for their cooperation in the war on drugs by stopping the growing of plants that produce drugs, they wanted to know what they could grow and how we would help them. The Andean Trade Preference Act of 1991 was presented which would have removed duties on tomatoes from 140 countries. This represented 77 percent of all tomatoes imported into the United States. If it would have affected only Colombia, we would have supported the President to help reduce drugs, but the law was too broad. After many hearings and work by tomato processors, the act was defeated.

On September 26, 1990, President Bush proposed the Free Trade Agreement with Mexico. As of 1992, this agreement will not be acted upon until after the presidential election. We attended hearings in front of two congressional committees and three government agencies. We asked for five years before any reduction of tarrifs and then phase them out at one percent per year. This would take twenty years before all duties were removed. I understand the terms presented to Congress will suggest only a ten year phase-out. The threat from Mexico is greater than any of the other countries. Mexico is so close to our markets that some of our customers can call Mexico on Friday and have canned tomatoes at their dock the following Tuesday. It takes three or four weeks from all of the other countries. Our employees are paid more per hour than Mexican workers are paid per week. Our fringe benefits amount to more than they receive per day; they do not have any fringe benefits.

One of the last hearings I attended was in 1991, on Free Trade with Mexico. A friend introduced me to Representative Sam Gibbons, Chairman of the House Ways and Means Committee. Senator Gibbons said, "Oh, I remember him being here for other hearings." I said, "Yes, I was here on my seventy-fifth birthday, five years ago." When I was called on for my testimony, he said, "Mr. Furman was here on his seventy-fifth birthday, and now he is eighty. Are you going to be here when you are ninety?"

Another unfair thing about imports from other countries is that we have very rigid restrictions on the types of insecticides, fungicides, and pesticides we can use. Every grower must keep a record. Many times, the approved spray costs two or three times as much as sprays we used several years ago. All of these other countries are allowed to use sprays which have been banned in the United States. We are opposed to using any sprays that cause health problems, but we would like a level playing field with other countries. The import inspection finds only a fraction of the illegal sprays that we dare not use. If the trade agreement passed in its present form, the tomato growers and processors are in for some very tough times. In the next chapter, David Geise will mention some of the things we are doing to reduce our dependence on tomatoes for such a large portion of our profits.

One highlight of my legislative work was being a delegate to the White House Conference on Small Business held in Washington in 1986. To be eligible, you needed to be the owner or a corporate officer of a small business. Anyone employing less than 500 full-time employees is classed as a small business. Pennsylvania was entitled to fifty elected delegates; 450 delegates applied. We made up a list of those things that should qualify us for being a delegate. These were circulated among the delegates. My paper was on Furman's stationery. I listed:

- My attendance at the Pennsylvania Conference on Small Business in 1980.
- How the business grew from employing three people the year I graduated from high school to 220 employees in 1986.
- How the business grew from a pack of 3,000 cases in 1928 to 3,000,000 cases in 1986.
- Past state chaplain of Pennsylvania Gideons.
- Offices I held in my church.
- My activities in the local Chamber of Commerce and Trade Associations.

I described myself as a progressive conservative. I listed my favorite Scripture verse as Psalm 127:1, "Unless the Lord builds the house, its builders labor in vain. Unless the Lord watches over the city, the watchmen stand guard in vain." One of the men I was consulting with told me to take the Scripture out, that it would be my defeat. I said, "The Scripture stays in, win or lose." I think the fact that so many recognized me as part of Furman Foods helped me to be elected. The National Federation of Independent Businesses (of which Furman Foods is a member) listed me as one of the top ten vote-getters in Pennsylvania. In addition to the fifty elected delegates, twenty-five were appointed by Senators and Representatives.

Nationwide, there were about 2,500 delegates. The convention was held in the Holden and Sheraton Hotels. With consultants, newsmen, and foreign observers, about 4,000 attended the conference. It was quite a thrill to be part of a group composed of people from every state in the Union. As we discussed issues, we found they all had the same problems. Before the conference, each delegate was asked to list, in order of importance, the three most important out of the eleven issues to be discussed. We could attend any session. The conference lasted five days.

Some days after the various sessions closed, the Pennsylvania delegation would caucus to discuss the position we wanted to take on various issues at the final general session. One night, we did not get out of the caucus until after eleven o'clock. Needless to say, at seventy-five years of age, I was tired. I pressed the wrong number on the elevator and got off and went to what I thought was my room. Every floor was alike. When my digital card did not open the door the first time, I tried again. Imagine my embarrassment when a lady came up behind me to ask why I was trying to get into her room. Then I discovered I was on the wrong floor!

We made sixty recommendations to President Reagan. Senator Robert Dole accepted them on behalf of the President. They were listed in order of the number of votes they received. It is interesting that the problem that got the most votes was tort reform of liability laws. In September, 1992, a bill was before the Congress to try to correct some of those problems. The number two issue opposed any bill endorsing mandated parental leave. That bill passed the Congress in February of 1993. The fourth item was to pass a balanced budget amendment and line item veto. I was glad that our most pressing problem–imports–was listed as fifth.

We had many fine speakers such as Secretary of Labor, William Brock; Secretary of Education, William Bennett; Secretary of Transportation, Elizabeth Dole; Congressman Jack Kemp; Tom Peters, author of *A Passion for Excellence*; and many others.

One amusing incident was when a man from Germany, who wanted to learn about the food business, was introduced to me as one who could help him. We ate three or four meals together as he could speak good English. About the second meal, I said, "I will not ask you how old you are, but I will ask you what year you were born." He said, "1911." I said, "Oh, both of us are seventy-five, the same age as Ronald Reagan, our President, only we are not as popular." With a grin, he said, "Not yet!" I said, "My, you are optimistic."

In 1988, when Governor Casey called for a Pennsylvania Governor's Conference on Small Businesses, the state was divided into six regions with Northumberland County being in region four which was composed of the sixteen central counties. I was chosen as one of the forty-five delegates from our region. The format followed the former presidential conference. There were about 500 delegates there. We met at the Hershey Lodge and Convention Center for three days. We had about three previous meetings in our region to organize. The fifteen issues receiving the highest number of votes were presented to the Governor. I found it very helpful and educational. Some time after the conference, Governor Casey hosted the delegates at the Governor's Mansion on Second Street. I think both conferences did a lot of good and probably saved businesses many unwise regulations. However, I guess I would say their value was more in preventing laws that would hurt business, rather than getting laws passed that we proposed that never were enacted.

Chapter 18
Seventy Years Young and
Still Growing
Written by: Mr. David Geise,
President & CEO, Furman Foods, Inc.

As the eight members of the third generation (myself, Jim Kohl, Joel Furman, Bill Furman, Kermit Kohl, Kent Kohl, Don Geise, and Franklin Furman) became involved in the leadership of the company, it was something taken very seriously. After all, we were all reminded many times that "the first generation starts the company, the second generation builds it, and the third generation blows it." Statistics prove that to be the case the majority of the time; 85 percent of family businesses do not make it past the third generation.

But to our advantage, the eight of us were exposed to a lot of positive influences through Grandpa Furman who walked the mile walk spring, summer, and fall with several of his grandchildren every Sunday morning to Sunday school and church. It was on those walks that he shared his philosophies of commitment; stick-to-it-iveness of faith in God, our family, our work; and the value of thanksgiving. These values were reinforced by our parents who lived them by example.

We were given many opportunities to work at a very young age, developing a strong work ethic within each of us. Most of our early work exposure was in the field—planting tomatoes, hoeing weeds, picking rocks, and picking beans.

I particularly remember that we were paid two-and-one-half cents per pound for picking beans, and when anyone picked 100 pounds or more in a day, that person received a fifty-cent bonus. But if you were caught throwing beans, you had your bonus taken away. I learned at an early age that being the boss's kid did not afford special treatment but meant added responsibility. One day while picking beans, I was caught throwing a bean and had my bonus taken away. That wasn't the end of it, either; when I got home, my father, who had been informed of my bean throwing, gave me a paddling and a lecture that I was to set a good example as the boss's son.

As we got older, we were exposed to many different jobs which gave us a broad understanding of the business and exposed us to several different bosses. We loaded trucks at the warehouse after school and worked in the production area when we became sixteen years old. We also operated harvesting equipment in the fields and made deliveries to our customers. This exposure allowed us to understand the variety of responsibilities in the business and to determine which career path we wanted to pursue.

After college, all eight of the third generation that entered the family business pursued a different aspect of the business's operations. Helping us work together to this day is the fact that we were geographically close (within a half mile of each other) and only a ten-year spread existed in our ages. As a result, we played and worked together for many years before assuming the leadership of the company. This helped us to develop a bond that has continued into our leadership of the company.

The area of the business in which I chose to become involved was raw product procurement, the primary area of my dad's responsibility. This included dealing with the growers and managing the harvesting of the vegetables.

A real growing experience for me occurred during the summer after I had graduated from college. I was asked to go to upper New York state to meet with several growers that were supplying us with carrots, celery, and onions for our mixed vegetable and carrot pack. The broker whom we had been dealing with for years had passed away, and we now needed to appoint a new buyer. I'll never forget the challenge of finding these growers who were working out in their muck fields. I learned that I needed the help of many other people in this task, but most of all, I learned that I had a very supportive new bride, Joyce Ann Moyer, who accompanied me on this less-than-glamorous venture. After visiting with the growers, I decided that they were all very capable, trustworthy farmers; that we could save the brokerage and deal with them directly.

My dad taught me a very important management philosophy, an approach that focuses on being a servant and meeting the needs of the people with whom we work. Dad did not ask them to do all the dirty work that he didn't want to do, but worked with them and helped them as they worked to accomplish their job. In Matthew 20:25–28, Jesus describes the difference between the world's philosophy of management and that of Christ, which my dad exemplified:

> You know that the rulers of the Gentiles lord it over them, and their high officials exercise authority over them. Not so with you. Instead, whoever wants to become great among you must be your servant, and whoever wants to be first must be your slave—just as the Son of man did not come to be served, but to serve, and to give his life as a ransom for many.

As the second generation retired and the third generation took on the leadership of the company, we realized the need to spend more time and effort in communicating and planning. As we grew from 75 to over 200 full-time people, we worked hard to continue the family philosophy that we are all on the same team, and that we can get a lot more done working together. In order to encourage more ownership in what the people did, we developed an Employee Stock Ownership Plan (ESOP) which gave company stock to full-time people. This stock is held in trust until an individual retires.

Along with the ESOP, we started communicating all financial information to everyone and keeping people informed concerning all aspects of the business. This improved the understanding of our people and boosted moral. Additionally, a weekly newsletter is made available to all our people which includes the minutes from the weekly staff meetings. These minutes provide comprehensive information of what's happening and what's planned to happen in the upcoming weeks and months.

In an effort to keep our most important resource (people) productive, we have developed a Quality Life Program which encourages our people to deal with problems which may develop in their lives. This program offers help in four basic areas—mental and emotional, family and spiritual, financial, and physical. The program is designed to help and encourage everyone to maintain a quality of life that will positively affect their life and work and the lives and work of those around them.

Our planning process has reaped many benefits over the years. As we involved more and more people in the process, it has stimulated action, innovation, and creativity. Planning is an essential process which takes considerable time and effort. In our weather-dependent business, we found it was also valuable to consider "what if" scenarios and to develop contingency plans.

In 1983 and 1984, we went through a major expansion of our physical plant and equipment. As we struggled to get everything up and running, we were quickly reminded that our most valuable resource is our people. While we had invested millions of dollars in modern equipment, it was the ingenuity of our people that fine-tuned the equipment and made it work efficiently.

Our years were not without emotional pain and anguish. It was during the struggle of getting the new plant started that we lost the help of one of our most valuable resources, Franklin Furman, our Vice President of Manufacturing, who became disabled with cancer. Franklin exemplified Grandpa Furman's stick-to-it-iveness as he kept fighting for his life. He always kept a positive attitude and was a continuous witness for Christ. He sure helped me to get things in proper perspective when I was worried about the future of the company as we struggled with the problems of the new plant and depressed market conditions due to oversupply. I'll always remember his words to me, "It doesn't really matter what happens to the company, you still have the most important thing in your life, your salvation through Christ."

Through a lot of help from God and the efforts of our people working in unity, we ended the eighties with the best years in the company's history.

As we embarked on the decade of the nineties, we realized that the planning and changes which had taken us through the eighties needed to continue if we were to grow through the nineties. In Grandpa's days, a good business idea could begin a company and last for fifty years. When I was a child, a good business idea would last twenty-five years. Today, the life expectancy of most good business ideas is less than five years. We need to be constantly looking for new ideas and be receptive to change.

In our strategy for the nineties, we focused on four main directives: (1) to lessen the impact on our business from the cyclical nature of the vegetable markets, (2) to seek to more completely satisfy our customers by working with them to pack to their needs, (3) to improve our corporate philosophy to focus on developing our people through empowerment, and (4) to encourage the stability of our family business by encouraging the next generation of family members to become involved in the company.

We developed a strategy that included additional value-added products in our product line that would be less sensitive to the ups and downs of the market due to the supply of the raw vegetables. Included in this new product line was a cooperative venture to pack a nutrient drink (complete diet supplement for individuals limited to a liquid diet). This product has had a fast growth and is not impacted by the weather elements which cause our vegetable markets to take drastic swings.

Many vegetable products are considered commodity items, like peas, snap beans, and crushed tomatoes. That means they are basically all the same. So when the weather is good for growing, there is a surplus and the price drops dramatically. If weather conditions are poor, there may be a shortage, creating higher prices which result in better profits. But the weather and any profits generated by commodity type items is outside of our control.

We realized that another way to lessen the impact of the commodity vegetable markets was to be more sensitive to our customers' needs. We put a greater emphasis on custom packing to meet our customers' recipes. We extended our product line to create more value-added specialty products. And we challenged ourselves to break out of our baseline paradigm and extended our processing capabilities by adding a pouch packaging line.

The pouch line helped to meet our customers' need to reduce solid waste removal cost. The pouch is convenient and efficient, but has other advantages that make it a revolutionary method of food processing and handling. Pouches are almost 10 percent lighter than traditional packagings, giving the potential to save thousands on annual shipping costs for the customer. Products packed in pouches require 15 percent less storage space, are easy and safe to open, don't create any sharp edges, lie flat so they occupy virtually no space in the trash container, and can cut the amount and cost of refuse by as much as 85 percent. Also, pouches avoid waste since they are clear. Employees can see how much product is left in them, and with a simple squeeze, they can make sure the pouch is completely empty. Pouches have a shelf life of eighteen months, and our hot-fill packaging process guarantees freshness without freezing. And, pouches are durable. It would take a force of nearly thirty pounds per square inch to break one of our pouches. With all these advantages, we feel the pouch provides real benefits for our customers. We broke our paradigm on cans being the only way to preserve freshness.

The pouch line offered us one of our best opportunities to leave a mark on the nineties. Working with several different customers and with the developer of the pouch filling machine, we developed a process to combine tomato and kidney beans to form a pouch packed base for chili mixes. Not only has this put the advantages of the pouch to work for us, but it was also the direct result of working to give the customer what they wanted. It also gave us some great opportunities to let our people really challenge themselves.

The eighties had confirmed for us the value of our people as our most important resource. Through our Quality Life Program, we had tried to show our employees we valued them as people. To move into the nineties, we need to further learn to let our people reach their full potential.

Machines and computers were made to be run; people were not created that way. Too often, we have treated people as something to be controlled, not as someone to be enabled. Our people don't need someone to manage them, like you would a bunch of schoolboys who are out of control. Our people need someone to lead them. Sometimes, to be a good leader, I had to learn to just get out of the way.

I'm really fortunate to live in a time where I can learn about serving others in the business world by people like Max

DePree or Stephen Covey. God has blessed us with many gifted individuals. As businesses grow over time, they tend to become institutions. They tend to develop barriers which keep people from using all of their gifts and reaching their potential. I don't want Furman's to be like that. We're trying to remove barriers which keep our people from growing and thereby keeps us from growing. As we become servants as leaders and enable our people to do their best, we will create an attitude of continuous improvement towards customer satisfaction.

In the past decade of business mergers and acquisitions, many career employees of publicly traded companies have found themselves transferred, replaced, or simply let go. At times like these, employees of closely held businesses can find security in their family ownership.

Family ownership can provide two key stabilizing influences. One is that ownership of the company cannot change overnight by stock buy-outs and "unfriendly take-overs." As long as the family takes pride and has involvement in their company, they will want to preserve the company for their future generations. Their interest is not in stock market evaluations. Their interest will be in maintaining the family commitment to a philosophy of quality and the value of people. That gives assurance to our community, our people, and our customers that they will never become disposable assets of some giant conglomerate.

During the eighties, Franklin's son, Franklin G. Furman, became the first of the fourth generation to join Furman's. As the company has grown and needed more personnel, the Lord has continued to provide family members to carry on the Furman tradition.

Jeffrey A. Stuck, son of Lois Geise Stuck and Wendel Stuck, was the second of the fourth generation to join Furman Foods. His mother is the daughter of Elnora Furman Geise. Jeff's family lived in Erie most of his teenage years.

When he was seventeen, Jeff stayed with his grandmother, Elnora Furman Geise, in the summer months and started helping in the fields harvesting the crops, driving pea combine and bean harvesting equipment. He also checked peas and snap bean fields to help determine when they were ready to be harvested.

After graduating from Erie High School, he attended Penn State University graduating with a B.S. in Horticulture in May of 1991. As soon as he graduated, he joined the company as a field representative. He works under his uncle, Don Geise, who contracts with the farmer as to what acreage of each vegetable they will grow. He also keeps them advised as to what spray program they are to follow. Don and Jeff order the seed for the different varieties of vegetables that produce top quality for canning. They also tell the farmer when to plant and harvest their crops.

The explosion in personal computers created a need for a specialist in that field at Furman Foods. The Lord was getting someone in the family ready to meet that need. David Wesley Furman, son of Franklin Furman and grandson of Foster Furman, joined the company in May of 1992. He was the third one of the fourth generation to join Furman Foods.

As a little boy, David started hand shelling peas to be tested for tenderness to determine when they were to be harvested. His first summer job was helping his Uncle Bud (Mary Furman James's husband) oversee strawberry pickers. Our "You pick" strawberry patch was on Route 405 along the Susquehanna river. During harvesting season, they worked from seven in the morning until dark.

After graduating from Northumberland Christian School, Dave went to Philadelphia College of the Bible for one year. In his second year of college, he transferred many of his credits to Bloomsburg University, from where he graduated with a B.S. in Computer Information System Business. His work at Furman Foods is called Micro Systems Support. It is in maintaining and supporting personal computers including programming for them. At the present time, we have about fourteen personal computers, and the numbers grow every year.

It seems there is no end to new programs and Micro equipment. Our first computer, which we bought in 1972, printed fifty-five lines per minute. Today, we have one printing 600 lines per minute and another that prints 1,300 lines per minute on both sides of the paper. They are installing a terminal on each sales person's desk so that when a customer calls on the phone and wants to order, instead of looking up his record on a print-out that is twenty-four to forty-eight hours old, they call up the customer's record on their terminal. It tells them, as of that hour, what is labeled, what the customer's last order was, and if they pay their bill promptly.

Sharon Furman Chivalette joined the Furman Foods management team in June of 1992. She is the daughter of William Furman, Sr. (who is deceased) and the ninth person of the third generation. As a child, Sharon worked at Furman's during the summer, rolling cans, hoeing red beets, planting tomatoes, and picking beans. Later, as a teenager, she worked in quality control, called people advising them when peas for freezing were available, and did other office jobs.

After attending Messiah College for three years, she was hired as a Home Economist for Pennsylvania Gas and Water Company. While working for them, she married Frank Chivalette. He wanted to finish his degree at Philadelphia College of the Bible. It was during that time she finished her education, getting a B.S. from Drexel University in Home Economics and Education.

From Philadelphia, Frank and Sharon moved to New York and then back to Northumberland, during which time they had two children, Andre and Yvonne.

Frank once again decided to pursue his schooling. So, while he went for his master's at Wheaton College in Illinois, Sharon went to work for McDonald's in marketing and public relations. She said, "Little did I realize how working at these jobs would prepare me for the position I would take a Furman Foods fifteen years later."

She later got a job at Shikellamy High School where she taught a course called Quantity Foods. It was basically directing and supervising students while running a restaurant and hospitality center for those students who were planning to go on to Culinary School. She taught there for thirteen years.

Sharon became a Foodservice Sales Specialist for Furman Foods. Furman's is entering a new field of packing tomato products and other products in plastic pouches. As evidenced by her education and experience, the Lord prepared one of our family members to be ready to fill this important sales position for a new product.

As we continue to automate and update our equipment, the need was created for more maintenance people. Kurt Kohl's training in the Navy helped to prepare him to fill that need. Kermit Kurt Kohl is the son of Kermit Kohl, the grandson of Alice Furman Kohl, and the fourth of the fourth generation to join the company. Kurt worked on the farms as a teenager, changing irrigation pipe (which was very hard work carrying the pipe through mud to a new location), shelling pea samples, driving trucks, and hauling out cannery waste.

In September of 1988, Kurt joined the Navy soon after graduating from Shikellamy High School. He enlisted in a three-year program. Kurt took welding in program A-school. He was stationed at Philadelphia for about two months. From there, he was transferred to Charleston, South Carolina, where he was assigned to U.S.S. *Frank Cable*. The job of this ship is to repair submarines. In addition to welding, he did all types of metal work. Most of the work was done in port. He finished his three years in the Navy in September of 1991 and was honorably discharged as E 5, Second Class.

While in Charleston, he visited and took pictures of the First Baptist Church in Charleston founded in 1692. Richard

Furman had moved from New York and was pastor there from 1725 to 1825. In the history of Furman University, they credit Richard Furman with having the evangelistic fervor that formed the Baptist convention in 1821 for the purpose of establishing such a school. Details of our relationship to Reverend Richard Furman will be found in Chapter 20, "The Furman Legend."

In 1992, Kurt started working at Furman Foods as a fork-lift operator. In 1993, he became the hydro-static cooker operator. Whenever someone is needed in the maintenance department, Kurt is able to help out there, too, using the training he received in the Navy.

As we approach our seventy-fifth anniversary in 1996, our mission remains the same as Grandpa Furman's—to be a growth-oriented producer and processor of high quality food products and services; to follow the highest ethical and moral standards as set forth in the Bible, along with a sense of community responsibility; to be a team which collectively exceeds our individual efforts; to be a team able to combine our unique individual skills, communicate openly and honestly, and to contribute to the common good of the organization.

Furman Foods will continue on its successful course if the leadership seeks to do God's will and follows His Word, as we are instructed in Philippians 2:1–7:

> If you have any encouragement from being united with Christ, if any comfort from his love, if any fellowship with the Spirit, if any tenderness and compassion, then make my joy complete by being like-minded, having the same love, being one in spirit and purpose. Do nothing out of selfish ambition or vain conceit, but in humility consider others better than yourselves. Each of you should look not only to your own interests, but also to the interests of others. Your attitude should be the same as that of Christ Jesus: Who being in very nature God, did not consider equality with God something to be grasped, but made himself nothing, taking the very nature of a servant.

John Wesley Furman, age 24, and Emma Elnora Eister, age 19, the year they were married; 1900.

Mary, age 4; Andrew, age 7; and Foster, age 1; 1912.

J. W. Furman Family; 1926.

J. W. Furman Family; 1929.

J. W. Furman
Family; 1935.

Partnership Officers; 1945.

Father and Mother and ten of the grandchildren; 1946.

Partnership Officers; 1960.

Chart showing growth to our one million case pack. Picture shows J. W. Furman, Foster Furman, and Joel Furman.

J. W. Furman's sons and grandsons in the business;
1972.

J. W. Furman Family; 1945.

Father and Mother and extended family, a total of 29; 1945.

Father and Mother,
50th wedding
anniversary; 1950.

261

Father, age 94, and
Mother, age 89,
70th wedding
anniversary; 1970.

Sixteen family members involved in business; 1991.

262

Foster Furman
Family at Foster's
and Hazel's
55th wedding
anniversary.

Shed-type factory; ten full-time employees; 1940.

Factory built in 1947 and first fireproof warehouse; 25 full-time employees; 1955.

Factory with #7 warehouse; 50 full-time employees; 1966.

Nine million dollar expansion; 180 full-time employees; 1985.

Factory; 250 full-time employees; 1991.

Carvalle Hydrostatic continuous cooker; processes 26,000 303-size cans at one time; 1966.

Tomato harvester picks 20 tons in less than one hour; 1985

ADDENDUM

Chapter 19
The Women in My Life

How can I describe Hazel, with whom I have shared fifty-seven of the best years of my life. Hazel has been a true wife as the Lord intended, a true lover, a helpmeet, one whose talents and personality helped to balance my life. Many times, her good advice tempered my tendency to put my mouth in gear before my mind. That saved me a lot of trouble! The Lord blessed us with a son, Franklin; a daughter, Jane; a son, Joel; and a daughter, Sara. We are also blessed with seven granddaughters, six grandsons, two great granddaughters, and two great grandsons. The fact that Hazel was thirty-four years old when our first son was born really demonstrates how good the Lord was to us.

I must confess I thought it would be easy to write this chapter, but I actually find it quite difficult. It is especially difficult since right now Hazel is in a nursing home. I am also facing the fact that she will never again live in the house where we spent so many happy hours together.

On December 29, 1992, while leaving the family Christmas party, I was on her right side supporting her as we walked on smooth payment when, without any warning, she fell away from me. It was just as if someone knocked her left leg from under her. Her brother, George, who was right behind her said, "Her hip broke, and that is what caused her to fall."

We took her by ambulance to the emergency room at the Geisinger Hospital. I begged them to admit her, but the x-rays did not show any broken bones. The laws are so strict; a doctor cannot use his common sense. The hospital would have been fined if they had admitted her. The ambulance drivers laid her on the bed at home at 3:30 in the morning. A young woman, who does some house work for us, came the next morning, but together we could not get Hazel to the bathroom. Because of four collapsed vertebrae caused by a severe case of osteoporosis, together with the broken hip, she screamed with pain every time we moved her.

The Lord was good to us as a bed had opened up at Nottingham Nursing Home, which is only three miles from our home. Two days later, I visited her about four o'clock in the afternoon and could not wake her up. Her blood pressure was very low and still dropping. They had given her another pain killer to which she was having a reaction. The paramedics stabilized her and took her to the emergency room of the hospital. Again, she was x-rayed, but they still would not admit her even though she screamed with pain about her hip.

At the nursing home five days later, they tried to get her to walk. They called me, saying, "We think she must have a broken hip." So we took her to the Sunbury Community Hospital. There, the x-ray showed a broken hip. The walking had probably opened it up. She had to go back to Geisinger for surgery to put a plate on her hip bone. After about a week, we took her back to the nursing home. For about two weeks, she made good progress at the nursing home where they gave her physical therapy. We thought that, in about four weeks, she would walk again. However, her problems with collapsed vertebrae hurt her so much, she will never walk again.

I believe that everything that happens to a committed Christian is filtered through God's love. I know I have had some blessed times witnessing that would not have happened any place else except in the nursing home. On March 4, 1993, the

Lord used me to witness to three people. (I read the third chapter of John to a ninety-seven-year-old man who died a few hours later.) I was rejoicing so much that the Lord had used me, I didn't really comprehend what it meant when, soon after that, the doctor said Hazel would probably never get to come home again. Three days later, on Sunday morning while I was eating breakfast alone, it really hit me that Hazel would probably never eat another meal in our kitchen. When I called our daughter, Jane, her husband, Frank, answered the phone and said, "How are you doing, Dad?" I choked up and couldn't talk. He was scared, thinking perhaps Hazel had passed away. After a few minutes, I told him that the truth just hit me that, unless the Lord intervened, Hazel would spend the rest of her life in a nursing home. As I write this, tears come to my eyes.

Pardon me for not telling you about the wonderful times we had together before I told you about the sorrow. I am reminded of the Episcopal minister from England. While visiting in the United States, he attended a church where the pastor would usually tell a joke in the middle of his sermon to waken up his people. The preacher knew it was the last Sunday the Episcopal minister would be there, so he thought, "I will really give him something to take back home." When he saw his congregation was going to sleep on him, he said, "The happiest days of my life were spent in the arms of another man's wife—my mother." After arriving home, the Episcopal minister, when he saw his congregation getting sleepy, said, "The happiest days of my life were spent in the arms of another man's wife." Then he choked, coughed, sputtered, and said, "By Jove, I forgot her name."

Chapter six is a tribute to my mother. I spent many happy hours in the arms of both my mother and my wife. One way to describe my wife is Proverbs 18:22, "He who finds a wife finds what is good and receives favor from the Lord."

Hazel was the only daughter of George Epler and Sara Larue Miller Epler. Hazel had three brothers, which probably accounted for the fact she could play ball better than most girls. She grew up on a farm about three miles from our home. We went to the same church and also to the Northumberland Grange. Our families knew each other for eighteen years before we were married. Hazel's mother was a godly woman—like someone you would want to be the mother of your children. To the young men reading this book, please remember when you look for someone to share your dreams with, the first thing to look for is a born-again Christian. Please note, I did not say a church member. You also need to look past her present beauty to see what her mother looks like. It is almost certain that twenty or thirty years later, she will look and act like her mother. Remember, if you marry the devil's daughter, you end up having the devil as your mother-in-law. They say behind any successful Christian business man is a wife who prays for him and helps him. Some also say there is a surprised mother-in-law. I must say that Hazel's mother was a great encouragement to us.

One Sunday in June of 1935, Hazel and I attended a Christian camp named Kanesatake near State College. We had a wonderful time and took a number of pictures. When showing those pictures at our fifty-fifth wedding anniversary dinner, I said, "I will always remember that evening on the swing on the back porch of her home when I asked her to marry me. After she demurred a little while, she said, 'Yes.' "

I jokingly remarked that after she said "yes," I did not say anything for a long time. Finally she said, "Foster, why don't you say something?" I answered, "I said too much already."

We were too poor to have a public wedding. We only told our parents and some of my sisters we were getting married. Reverend Sassaman, our former pastor who now pastored at Williamsport, drove us to Eagles Mere for the wedding on June 18, 1936. (One thing I will always regret, we did not get any good wedding pictures.) The factory was running peas, so we did not have the time or money to go on a honeymoon.

The day Hazel and I were married was also the birthday of my youngest brother's girlfriend, Dora Propst. I promised him I would get the car home in time for him to take a birthday present to her. I really regretted that promise. How do you kiss your bride that first night and hurry home with the car? (Can you imagine a family with five drivers and only one car? What a scramble for a car!)

We were married on Thursday. Hazel's cousin, Dorcas Epler, and my closest friend, Carl Riggs, had invited us to their wedding on Saturday. This was held at her home. After the reception, before they left for their honeymoon, Hazel and I asked to see them in private. In Dorcas's bedroom, she asked us when we were going to get married. They were really surprised when we said we were married on Thursday! The next day in Sunday School, when my younger sister, Elnora, who was the Sunday School Secretary, read the names of the teachers, she read Mrs. Foster Furman. Some people thought she made a mistake as they did not know we were married. But when the truth sank in and the shock wore off, they all gave us their best wishes.

Hazel had graduated from Bloomsburg State Teachers' College in 1928 and taught school for eight years. She was making more money than I was! In those days, a lady had to quit teaching as soon as she got married. It was really quite a sacrifice on her part to marry a young man whose success in business was uncertain. To help with the finances, she worked at the factory two summers before our oldest son, Franklin, was born in 1938.

Since I was assistant to my father, it would be very helpful if I lived close to the cannery. Cars were not as dependable then as they are now. At that time, Northumberland had the closest housing available. We decided to build a house close to the factory. The site was in a wheat field along the public road about 270 feet north of the factory. (It was far enough away then, but in 1984, the nine million dollar plant expansion was built within sixty-five feet of our house. Now I wish we had built at least several hundred yards away.) As soon as the wheat was harvested in July, we started to dig the cellar. The backhoe and other earth moving equipment were not yet invented. We dug the cellar with a team of horses and a scoop. The corners had to be dug out by hand. It was in what we call "hardpan" and very difficult to dig.

The house would be very small by today's standards. It was a wooden frame bungalow with a bedroom and three other small rooms downstairs and two small rooms upstairs, plus a bathroom. The total living space is about 1,200 square feet. We had to get a mortgage from the local bank. Even today, I would not build a big house.

We got the lumber from Hazel's uncle (who owed money to Mother Epler) to build a twenty-by-twenty foot garage. Thus he paid part of his debt off by providing lumber for us.

Halloween eve in 1936 was a great day for Hazel and me. It was a thrilling and romantic moment for us. For over four months, we had lived with Hazel's widowed mother. She was good to us, but there is nothing like living in your own home. To make it even more romantic, it was under a full harvest moon. I remember standing on our back porch steps, looking romantically at that beautiful harvest moon as we kissed and entered our new home to sleep in it for the first time. I think the moon was bigger and more beautiful that night than I have ever seen it. Even today, fifty-seven years later, I can still see that beautiful harvest moon.

We attended household sales to get enough furniture to start housekeeping. We bought an oak table with enough extension boards to seat eight people for the huge sum of six dollars. We also bought a few chairs for one dollar each. That was fifty-seven years ago; yet, until she broke her hip, Hazel and I still ate three meals a day using the same table and chairs. They are still in useable condition. We will always be thankful for the wonderful kitchen shower friends gave to us, providing most of our dishes. Hazel often mentioned which dishes were given by many friends; how much we have appreciated them as we are still using many of them.

At first, we cooked on a three burner oil stove. After a few years, we bought one of the first electric ranges in the community. For heat, we had a heatrola in the living room. Also, we bought a used washing machine with a wringer on it. It would be several years before we could afford any new furniture. We had a mortgage which we paid off in a few years. After paying off the mortgage, we put in a furnace for central heating. Also we bought some new bedroom and living room furniture.

Jim Elliot, a pioneer missionary who lost his life taking the Gospel to the Acua Indians, wrote in his journal, "He is no fool who gives up something he cannot keep to gain that which he cannot lose." As Bob LeTourneau said, "It is not how much of my money I give to the Lord; it is how much of the Lord's money I keep for myself." Stop and think for a moment how that would affect your lifestyle.

As a committed Christian, I believe everything we own is a gift from God which he allows us to manage for a few years. Perhaps an interview with a local radio reporter illustrates that fact. The interview was for a program that featured successful businessmen of the Susquehanna Valley. The reporter was new in the area, and I had never met him. I was very much surprised by his first question. "Is it true you are a millionaire?" I said "It is not true, but I could have been." He said, "May I put that on the air?" I said, "No, but you may say that, with so many starving people in the world and millions that have never heard the good news that Jesus died for their sins, it is more important for me to give money to those causes than for me to be a millionaire."

Not only were all of the brothers and sisters involved in helping make our business a successful family business, but some of the daughters-in-law were also involved. One of those was Mercy James. She started working at the cannery about

1930. My oldest brother, Andrew, a school teacher, spent most of his summers supervising work crews weeding vegetables. He couldn't help but be attracted to this industrious brunette. They were married in 1934.

After a few years off to raise her family, Mercy James Furman returned to work at the cannery. She was a very compassionate and a very conscientious person. She was respected and loved by our employees. We asked her to serve as floor lady in 1952, a position she held until she had a cancer operation in 1967. (The floor lady oversees all of the ladies, assigns each their position, tells them what to do, and checks their work. She also decides how many workers are needed for each particular job.) After several years off, she again returned as floor lady. She passed away in 1976 after working for the cannery about forty years.

In 1958, we added 4,900 square feet to the factory. That expanded our work force during tomato season to about seventy women. Anyone who has hired and supervised women knows a good floor lady is a very responsible position. A poor supervisor at this important position can break a company. We were thankful the Lord provided family members for floor ladies from 1935 through 1971. It is always a relief to management to have someone they know will take the responsibility to get a difficult job done.

My sister, Mary, was the second child of Emma and J. W. Furman. She remembers that Mother was very patient and easy to get along with. Mother worked hand in hand with Papa; we never heard them argue. Papa was head of the house, yet he was always considerate of her. He didn't want her to make a big Sunday dinner; he said, "It is to be a day of rest." Going to Sunday school and church was more important than big Sunday dinners. As children, we always had the privilege of bringing friends home for dinner. However, company was always expected to go to church with us. If we were expecting guests for Sunday dinner, we usually prepared most of it on Saturday.

Mary says, "As we were growing up, Mother and Father always kept in contact with our teachers and had them in our home frequently for a meal and an evening." Ministers and missionaries were always welcome, especially after Foster went to Bible School in Philadelphia. Those meals were always big events. These were the days before refrigerators, thus we had many trips to the cool cellar where we stored all kinds of goodies and pies.

Each Saturday, when Mary was about ten years of age, Mother would wash Mary's hair and put it up in rags so she would have curls for Sunday. Mary was referred to as the little girl with curls. She says, "I don't know when mother had the time, for she had five children to get ready for church." Mary felt she was the big girl since she had to take care of a baby sister, Elnora.

Mary had injured her knee while walking to high school and missed five years of school. Thus she did not graduate from high school until she was twenty-two years of age, after which she attended Bloomsburg State Teacher's College. When she graduated, she taught the primary grades at Montandon for eleven years.

When both Elnora and Alice were raising their families, we were left without a floor lady. To fill that need, Mary resigned from teaching school the year of 1944 and started working at the cannery. She says Papa and the boys felt she was needed as a floor lady. It was a very difficult decision to make because she loved her children. Finally, she decided to work at the cannery with the understanding she could return to college to finish her B.S. degree.

As the cannery grew and we added another shift, it was felt we needed a lunch room. (These were the days before the vending machines.) Mary was asked to set that up. They decided on a one-dish meal. That was a big job. The lunch room grew until it was necessary to hire a regular cook, but Mary was responsible for the evening clean-up. There was a certain fine young man with beautiful brown eyes who felt she needed help. That made her work a pleasure. The canning season ended, but their interest in each other did not end. Soon after that, they became engaged.

In February, 1947, Bud James and Mary took his parents with them to Boswel, Pennsylvania. Our bother, James, with his wife, Edna, was pastor of the Baptist church. James had married Edna Beck in 1942 soon after graduating from Eastern Baptist Seminary. They met while attending Juniata College in Huntington, Pennsylvania. After Edna graduated, she taught school. James performed the marriage ceremony for Bud and Mary on February 12. They went by car to see Mother and Father in Florida. Soon after their honeymoon, they moved to Elmira, New York, where Bud worked for the railroad. Later, Bud worked at Celotex until retirement. Then he managed Furman's strawberry you-pick patch.

Bud had cancer for two years before passing away in 1985. Now Mary spends a lot of time helping her brothers and sisters, nieces and nephews. When we need some extra help, we all call on Aunt Mary, as she does not have a family of her own. She is very compassionate and helpful.

Elnora Amelia was the fifth child and the second daughter of Emma and J. W. Furman. She was born while we lived in Delaware. When Mother and I were in the hospital with typhoid fever, Elnora was about two years old. Aunt Lou from Elysburg offered to keep her. When Mother came home from the hospital, Aunt Lou wanted to adopt Elnora, but Father and Mother said they wanted to raise all of their children. Elnora says she was very thankful that Father and Mother wanted her back home. She was the middle one of three girls. She says she was usually the one that went with Mother to the woods to pick huckleberries. At that time, we grew lima beans used in packing mixed vegetables. Elnora says she remembers the many hours she talked with Mother while picking lima beans.

While she was in high school, Elnora did the payroll for the cannery. We grew tomato plants in the greenhouse in the spring, and she helped to transplant them. We also canned soups in the winter. You will note that our business was a family affair from the beginning.

Elnora graduated from high school in 1935. She worked full time at the cannery in the summer time. She became our first full time floor lady. (Previous to 1935, Mother and I often acted as a "floor lady.") During the winter of 1938, Elnora went to Philadelphia College of the Bible. She said that was time well spent as she learned so much about the Bible.

In the spring of 1940, Elnora married Norman Geise, who became vice president when we formed the partnership in 1944. She now says that after fifty-three years, he is still a wonderful husband. She continued to work at the cannery doing payroll and acting as floor lady until their first child Lois was born. She now keeps in touch with the cannery through Norman, her two sons, and now a grandson who work at the cannery. All of Elnora's four children worked at the cannery in the summer.

Dora Propst was a beautiful girl with long black curls. (I mentioned the day I was married, I promised my brother, Bill, I would get the car back so he could take a birthday present to Dora.) They were married in August of 1940 and moved into the house on the adjoining farm. Dora worked at the cannery about two years before and about a year after they were married.

I learned a great spiritual lesson when looking at the house into which they moved. The first part that was built was a log house. Later, they added several rooms. When looking where the two weather boards joined, the dividing strip is about eight inches wide at the bottom and only three inches wide at the top. That means that the log house was about five inches bigger at the top than at the bottom. The owner said that, when they built the log house, they did not use one log for a pattern but used the number two log to measure the third log, and number three log to measure the fourth one, etc. So they ended up with the top of the house about five inches bigger at the top than at the bottom. You know if they would have built the house high enough, it would have fallen apart. That is an example of the Christian church. The Sunday school superintendent looks at the pastor, the teacher looks at the superintendent, the pupil looks at the teacher. None are perfect; they all are off several lines. Every person you look at gets a little farther from Christ when they use men as a pattern. One reason the Christian church is in so much trouble today is they fail to take Christ as a pattern or example but justify what they do by what some other Christian does.

Dora says she remembers in those days we cut the sweet corn off of the cob and scraped them by hand. This was very hard work, and their hands would get very tired. Also, we put the tomatoes in the can by hand, and she was one of the packers. The Lord gave them three girls and one boy. The son, William, Jr., was elected treasurer after his father passed away. Sharon, their second daughter, joined the sales force of the company in 1992. I asked Dora what made their marriage a success. She said, "Considering each other's views and lots of love."

Our youngest sister, Alice, was born on May 31, 1924, causing Mother to miss her oldest son, Andrew's, high school graduation. He said Alice's birth was the best graduation gift he could have had. Alice's first official event was at four years of age, when our father held her up high enough to pull the chain for our first electric light. She remembers that even though it was sixty-five years ago. (Those days, many switches were chains on the light in the ceiling.) Recently, when talking about it, her husband, Jim, said, "Boy, I wouldn't want to try to lift her up to do that today." Alice says we never got a day off for her birthday (May 31, Memorial Day) as we were always planting tomatoes in the field. She helped to load the wooden boxes on the wagon to take the plants to the field. She remembers as a girl she wanted to surprise Father who was in the greenhouse shoveling ground. When she slipped up behind him as he brought the shovel back to get another shovel full, the handle hit her in the face and gave her a black eye.

She says she was the "official can roller." She would take eight cans out of the case and put them on the track at one time. After graduating from high school, she was Floor Lady for a number of years. She also figured payroll and did a lot of office work. She reminded me that, one day, I wanted an urgent letter typed at once. Our office was in part of the house, and the first year they were married, Alice and Jim lived there while Mother and Father were in Florida. She was cooking something that needed to be stirred constantly. She said, "If you stir this food, I will type your letter."

In December, 1943, Alice married K. James Kohl (who became the secretary of the partnership formed in 1944). When I asked her today what date they were married, she reminded me they will celebrate their fiftieth wedding anniversary in December, 1993. My father and mother and three of their children celebrated their fiftieth wedding anniversaries. The other four children's spouses died before reaching that milestone. Alice and Jim had two girls and three boys. All of their children worked on the farm during their high school years. The three boys still work at the cannery.

How do you describe our two lovely and wonderful daughters-in-law. One day when our whole family was in the living room, I said, "You know, I couldn't have had better daughters-in-law or sons-in-law if I had picked them myself." Jane said, "We wouldn't have let you pick them."

Esther, Franklin's wife, has been very helpful and compassionate with Franklin. Her devotion to him probably saved his life. She was a registered nurse who worked at the Geisinger Hospital in Danville while Franklin was courting her. She really took her marriage vows "in sickness and in health" seriously. Franklin's first cancer attack was in 1978. They used radium for the first two attacks, but the third, an inoperative brain tumor, they treated with chemotherapy. Franklin was almost helpless while receiving those treatments in 1983 and 1984. Many times, I heard him ask her the same question three or four times in a half hour. She is so patient with him; I never heard her answer him sharply nor complain about him. When he had chemotherapy, sometimes he didn't even recognize his own family. Many times, she spent twenty-four hours a day at his bedside. We were told if she would not have been a registered nurse, he probably would not be alive today. We thank the Lord for her compassion and patience. Those treatments left him with neurological problems. Also, to make things worse, he fell in the spring of 1993 and broke his hip. Today, he can walk only short distances with two arm canes.

Jane, our oldest daughter, was born on May 9, 1940. In those days, the doctor came to the home. I remember how we waited for the doctor. When I saw him arrive, I ran to the door and said, "Hurry up or you will be too late!"

From high school, Jane went to Philadelphia College of the Bible for a year and then to West Suburban Hospital School of Nursing. She often heard me pray that the Lord would call one of our children to the mission field. She thought nursing was good for a start to the mission field. West Suburban Hospital was affiliated with Wheaton College, which is known worldwide for its Christian teaching.

While at Philadelphia College of the Bible, she met Frank Severn, and they dated for five months. While she was in nurses' training, the letters became more frequent. They saw each other about four times a year. The romance deepened. One evening a missionary spoke about the Philippines. Jane felt that was where the Lord wanted her. That evening, she wrote to Frank that the Lord called her to the Philippines. If the Lord was leading him in another direction, they had better break up.

That same evening, about six hundred miles away, the Lord was working in Frank's heart. A missionary spoke in Frank's home church, and Frank felt a call to the Philippines. So he went home and wrote the same type of letter to Jane. Their letters crossed in the mail. It didn't take them long to get engaged after that direction from the Lord.

They were married on August 18, 1962. Jane was so happy to have her Mother at the wedding, even though she was walking with a cane. (This was a miracle since the doctors had said she may never walk again because of her osteoporosis and several fractured vertebrae.)

After the wedding, Frank took a position with Youth for Christ, and Jane went back to Philadelphia College of the Bible for more Bible training. They began their missionary career in the Philippines in 1967. They spent a total of fifteen years in the Philippines in church planting and evangelism with Send International (formally Far Eastern Gospel Crusade). We thank the Lord that He made it possible for Hazel and me to visit them twice for a month at a time in Manila.

In 1980, Frank was elected as General Director of Send International. They came home from the Philippines and moved to the Detroit area. Send International has missionaries in Alaska, the Philippines, Taiwan, Japan, Spain, Hong Kong, and is beginning mission work in many of the former Soviet Union countries and Eastern Europe. Pray for Frank and Jane as their responsibilities as head of the mission are very heavy. Pray for their safety as they travel all over the world.

I asked Jane to list a few of her childhood memories. She tells about Franklin (when he was five years old and she was three) being taken to Grandma Furman's house overnight during the birth of our third child, Joel. (Grandma's house was about a half block from our home.) Grandma tells the story of Jane crying for her mother, of big brother Franklin trying to comfort his sister, reaching over, patting her, and saying, "Don't cry Jane, I'm here." Grandma Furman would always tell this story with a grin on her face and a ready laugh.

Grandma Furman loved to tell about her grandchildren. She often told how Jane and Franklin came to see her. They would walk into the kitchen, and Jane would say (here Grandma would imitate her high pitched voice), "May I have a cook-kie." Of course, Hazel was very unhappy with that repeated story because she had drilled into her children to never ask for things at someone else's house because it was impolite. But to Grandma it was not impolite. The love of her grandchildren for her and her cookies was important to her.

In 1950, when Grandma (Emma) and J. W. Furman celebrated their fiftieth wedding anniversary, their ten-year-old granddaughter, Jane, asked her grandfather what it was like to married for fifty years. With a twinkle in his eye, he replied, "It's a long time to look at one women's face across the breakfast table."

When I think about golden wedding anniversaries, I think of the seventy-year-old man who was in very good health. After examining him, the doctor said, "Jim, you are in wonderful health. To what do you credit your good health?" The man answered, "Doctor, when we were married, we agreed whenever we had an argument, I would go outside to cool off. It's amazing what living out in fresh air for fifty years will do for your health."

Marg, Joel's wife, has been a help to all of us. Margaret is the youngest daughter of a highly respected Presbyterian Minister, Sinclair Reid, who was born in Scotland. Reverend Reid was pastor of the Presbyterian church at Allenwood for over fifty years. As Margaret grew up, she learned many deep spiritual lessons from her father and mother.

Joel met her at a spaghetti dinner which Margaret's sister, Heather, held for Penn State students at her home in State College. At that time, Margaret was a student at Lock Haven University, which is only about thirty miles from State College. It seemed that after dinner, they both lost interest in anyone else.

Margaret graduated with a degree in physical education in 1967. They were married that June. The first summer of their marriage, Joel was doing research for the National Restaurant Association and traveled to restaurants in Seattle, San Francisco, Boston, and many restaurants between those points. This traveling was their honeymoon. While he finished his final year at the University of Delaware, Margaret taught school in Delaware.

Eighteen months after their marriage, they moved within 200 yards of our home, just one month before their first child was born. We have many precious memories of those twenty-five years.

Sara, our youngest daughter, went to Philadelphia College of the Bible for two years after graduating from high school. At that time, they could not give a degree for nursing. She went two years to King's College in Briar Cliff Manor, New York, to get the necessary credits to enter Columbia Presbyterian Hospital for nursing where she graduated with a Bachelor of Science in Nursing and a Bachelor of Science in Bible from Philadelphia College of the Bible.

Following graduation from nurses' training, she worked at Albert Einstein Hospital for three years. While going to Calvary Baptist Church in New York City, she went on a double date with Andy Cilderman. After several months, they started to get serious. She realized that to marry Andy, who was a nominal Christian but never really accepted Christ as his Saviour, would be against God's will. So one evening, she said, "Andy, the Bible forbids me to marry anyone who is not a Christian; we will have to break up." Andy said, "What's wrong with me? I attend church." Sara said, "That is not the same as being a born-again Christian." She came home the next day. I well remember the tears she shed.

We took her along with us to a Zone Gideon meeting at Carlisle, Pennsylvania. You would have thought the speaker prepared his messages especially for a person with a broken heart. She came away from that meeting at peace with herself and the Lord. About a year later, Andy came to the Lord. About a year after that, they were married. They have been happily married for twenty years and have two sons, Christopher, fifteen, and Matthew, twelve. If any young person reading this book is dating anyone who does not know the Lord, discontinue that relationship or you will suffer for it the rest of your life.

Sara's tribute to Hazel on our fifty-fifth wedding anniversary in June of 1991 tells many things about her childhood. She also describes Hazel's virtues better than I can.

Dear Mom,

Recently, a book was published entitled, *All I Ever Needed to Know I Learned in Kindergarten*. The author goes on to explain that all of life is based on those simple, important ideas of kindness, sharing, etc. My school records don't reflect completion of kindergarten—in fact, I never went, but what I learned at your side has well equipped me for my life.

When you were my age, Mom, you had a nine-year-old, a seven-year-old, and a four-year-old. I would not be born for another year. That pregnancy was very difficult for you. Many so called "modern" women would have had an abortion. But you believed in life, and you wanted Jane to have a sister. I'm so glad you did—you taught me the sanctity of life.

You left your career when you married and became a full-time wife and mother. You were always home and available to meet my needs—you taught me the true meaning of "mother."

When I was growing up, there were always others around our table—elderly relatives were included at holidays and other occasions, missionaries were welcomed at a moment's notice, missionary kids spent several summers with us. But by far, the most memorable and frequent visitor to our table was Albert. Albert was the modern equivalent of a homeless person. Oh, he had a house, but not a home. He smelled like he didn't have a home, and he had no manners. He always 'just happened' to arrive at meal time several times a week. Somehow, you found it in your heart to patiently listen to hours of his talk and graciously share your food—you taught me compassion.

286

One thing you were very particular about was how the clothes were hung on the clothes line—you know, like items together, biggest to smallest. That was one lesson I chaffed at. "What did it matter?" However, it became ingrained. When we moved into our first home, my elderly neighbor looked across the fence approvingly at my wash line and said, "You know, you can tell a lot about a person by how they hang up the clothes." You taught me the importance of orderliness.

When I was twelve years old, you became debilitated with agonizing back pain. The doctor was baffled for months. It was a little known disease process then, but now everyone has heard about osteoporosis. You were told you would never walk again. I was told that I would have to do the cooking and cleaning. I despaired, but you never did. You suffered patiently but wouldn't accept the verdict. Slowly, you walked again—you taught me what faith and sheer determination can do.

One of the most remarkable things about you, Mom, is your love for singing or whistling while you work. For as long as I can remember, you would sit in the kitchen peeling apples, or making apple pie, or making apple crisp, or making apple jack, whistling and singing the whole time—you taught me the value of music to lift the spirits.

The four of us kids used to ask permission to do things just hoping you would say, "yes" without checking with Daddy. But it never worked! You always replied, "What does Daddy think?" and then you followed through by asking him!—you taught me the value of good communication in marriage.

I remember most vividly your "afternoon rest" which you began taking daily after your back problems began. You always took your Bible and a devotional book with you. You spent time mediating in God's word and praying before you rested—you taught me the importance of a daily, vital relationship with God.

Today, we celebrate your 55th wedding anniversary. You have stood by your man—for better or for worse, for richer or poorer, in joy and in sorrow, in sickness and in health. This is a rare accomplishment in this day of throw-away marriages— you have taught me the strength of love, the perseverance of faithfulness.

287

Mom, you have taught me many lessons. But have I learned them? Perhaps my own children are the best judges of that. I hope some future day on a similar occasion, my sons will recall lessons they've learned from me. And I will smile, remembering everything I know I learned from you, Mom.

In fact, to borrow a phrase, everything I ever needed to know I learned from my mother.

Love, Sara (June 1991).

The following saying will help many marriages and friendships:

Always remember to forget the things that make you sad.
Never forget to remember the things that make you glad.
Always forget to remember the friends that prove untrue.
Never forget to remember the friends that stood by you.
Always forget to remember the trouble that passed away.
But never forget to remember the blessing of God.

(Author unknown)

The next chapter tells of the Furman heritage and how we came from England.

Chapter 20
The Furman Heritage

What a surprise to find out you are of English descent rather than Pennsylvania Dutch! For over seventy years, I thought we were Dutch. Both my father and grandfather thought we were Pennsylvania Dutch.

How do you mistake an Englishman for a Dutchman? We even have the Dutch accent instead of English. However, the Dutch accent came from my mother, Emma Elnora Eister Furman, who could speak Dutch before she could speak English. It was also exciting to find out that our ancestors were Puritans; if they were German or Dutch, our forebears would probably have been Lutherans. To those not interested in Furman lineage, I am writing several pages on what history says about the Puritans. Also, since we came over with John Winthrop in 1630, I have written several pages about him.

I am sure all of my Furman relatives will find this chapter exciting as we trace our roots back to England and back to 1400. The very name of Firmin denotes the firm character and the STICK-TO-IT-IVENESS that inspired this book.

I believe it was the summer of 1988 that Terry Furman of Sunbury and Stuart Furman of Virginia contacted me about helping to erect a new gravestone on William Furman's grave. I would like to thank and acknowledge Stuart J. Furman of Woodbridge, Virginia, for doing almost all of the historical work.

I am quoting in full the article that appeared in the Sunbury *Daily Item*, January 15, 1989.

In the Deibler Station Bible Church cemetery, not far from Snydertown, are two simple headstones recently placed there, marking the resting places of William and Rachel Furman. The two are part of a family that is among the oldest in Northumberland County. The Furmans arrived in Northumberland County in 1794, settling in Shamokin Township. Their influence extends to the present day, as many families that descended from William and Rachel Furman still live in the area.

The Furman ancestors were part of a group of Puritans who sailed from England, and others who took part in the Revolutionary War and the War of 1812, according to Stuart Furman. Stuart Furman, William's great, great, great, great, great grandson, recently researched the family past.

The first member of the family to come to the United States arrived even before the United States existed. John Firmin sailed from England with the Puritans in 1630 and was one of the founding citizens of Watertown, Massachusetts. He sailed with John Winthrop, who later became governor of the new colony, Stuart Furman said.

Two of the Furman's sons moved to Long Island, New York, in 1652, where they changed the name to its current spelling. Stuart Furman speculated the name was changed because, at that time, Long Island was under Dutch control and Furman more closely resembled the Dutch spelling.

From Long Island, members of the family migrated to New Jersey. It was there that William was born. William and his brother, Daniel, served in the Gloucester County militia during the Revolutionary War. Stuart Furman said they may have been quartered at Valley Forge.

After the war, William resumed farming and married Rachel Woolverton. In 1794, William and Rachel moved, along with many other Baptists, to Pennsylvania, where they settled to homestead on 306 acres along Shamokin Creek near Snydertown. (Later research shows it was along little Shamokin Creek in Irish Valley on what is now called Chestnut road.)

William died in 1826, and Rachel in 1819. Of their sons, Isaac and Daniel continued to farm the land until their deaths in the 1840s, Stuart Furman said.

Another brother, Jonathan, served in the War of 1812 and then moved to northwestern Pennsylvania.

Stuart Furman, who lives in Virginia, said much of this information was uncovered during the last several years as he looked into his family's past. He used documents from the archives and the Library of Congress in Washington, D. C., and the Northumberland County Historical Society.

After learning about his family history, he visited the Deibler Station cemetery in May. He found the original aged and worn headstones from 1819 that marked the graves of William and Rachel. They were lying horizontal and were partially covered by dirt and grass, he said. He decided to contact other relatives to see if they would be interested in contributing money for new headstones. Recently, about 25 descendants of Isaac, Jonathan, and Daniel bought a new marker for their distant relatives. For the entire Furman family, it was a rediscovery of their past.

Here are some excerpts of early history taken from *The Families of Furman*, compiled by Stuart J. Furman (March, 1987): Josias Furman, of Newtown, L. I., was the son of John Firman (1588–ca 1648) who emigrated to Massachusetts Bay Colony in 1630 with Governor Winthrop's settlers. He was one of the founding fathers of Watertown, Massachusetts, and his name appears on the monument near the Charles River dedicated to the founders. The name is spelled "Firmin" on the monument, whereas his name appears on page 71 of the Winthrop Fleet of 1630 as "Firman."

John Firmin was from Nayland, in County Suffolk, England, which is the eastern-most county of Britain. He was born in 1588, the son of Gyles (Giles) Firmin and Katherine Ive who were married in September 1577. Church records indicate that John Firmin was first married in 1614 at Ipswich to a Judith Bridge; however, she died soon after childbirth, and her burial occurred on February 21, 1617. The church records then show that on June 30, 1618, John Firmin, widower, was married to Susan Warick, widow. Baptismal records show that their two sons who survived to adulthood were Josias, baptized on April 22, 1621, and John (Jr.) who was baptized on July 14, 1626.

According to additional baptismal records, there were two daughters from John Firmin's first marriage, Elizabeth (baptized on April 26, 1615) and Judith (date not known). By his second marriage, in addition to the sons, Josias and John, Jr., there were daughters—Mary, baptized on June 30, 1619; Martha, baptized on May 30, 1624; and Catherine, baptized on December 14, 1628.

The father of John Firmin, Giles Firmin, died in the summer of 1597, and his widow, Katherine Ive Firmin, subsequently remarried to a John Munes in 1599.

It is believed that the father of Giles Firmin was an earlier John Firman who was married to an Agnes. He wrote his will in 1549 and in it named sons Thomas, Edmund, Robert, Mylheris, and Giles. Since he was probably at least middle-aged when he died, his time of birth may have been as early as 1490, which is the year some Furman family historians have given.

The name "Firmin" and all of its variations came from the old French language of the Normans, which was based in Latin. Our family name originates from the word *firminus* meaning "firm" or "strong," according to P. H. Reaney in his *Dictionary of British Surnames*, 1958, page 128. The name appears in the *Doomsday Book of 1086* as Farman and Farmanus. This great book lists all the landowners of Britain, the vast majority of whom were Normans from the forces of William the Conqueror, who seized control of Britain in 1066.

The Normans were descendants of the Vikings who conquered France and settled there during the ninth and tenth centuries. This being so, the earliest roots of our family lie somewhere in Scandinavia, the countries we know as Norway, Sweden and Denmark.

Our first American ancestor, John Firmin, therefore, came from a line of Firmins who lived in England for over 500 years prior to his voyage to America. Charles W. Bardsley states in his *Dictionary of English and Welsh Surnames*, 1901, page 289, "The great home of this name and all its varied forms (Firmin, Farman, Fairman, Fearman, Fayerman, Firman, Fireman) was Norfolk. From thence, it extended as Firmin into Essex. In these districts, the surname is still common."

Watertown, Massachusetts records indicate that John Firmin was deceased by or early in 1648. His two sons, Josias and John, Jr., moved from Massachusetts to Long Island along with other English settlers around 1652, and John Firmin, Jr. appears in Riker's Annals of Newtown as one of the original proprietors. In *The Evolution of the American Town: Newtown, New York, 1642–1775*, it is stated that Newtown was the first English village on western Long Island; the Dutch were there first and then the English gradually encroached. John Firmin, Jr. had only one son who died without issue. Therefore, our entire Furman family traces back through Josias Furman who lived the remainder of his life at Newtown, dying in 1709.

It was after the move to Long Island that the spelling of the surname changed to "Furman." It is speculated that this change may have occurred due to the Dutch language influence, or perhaps it was politically motivated, since Long Island was still a territory of the Dutch at that time.

Advancing to William and Rachel Woolverton Furman, they had five sons and two daughters, all born in New Jersey. The eldest son was Isaac Furman, Stuart Furman's fourth great grandfather, born about 1776 and died in 1845. Daniel Furman was born about 1782 and died in 1842.

William and Rachel Furman were Baptist and, after moving to Northumberland County, Pennsylvania, belonged to the Shamokin Baptist Church, today know as the Deibler Station Bible Church, erected in 1794, rebuilt in 1871, located between Snydertown and Elysburg. It is about eight miles from the Deibler Station Bible Church to the farm they bought along Chestnut Road. I questioned why they would spend several hours traveling by horse and buggy to this church if there was a closer church. However, it was the only Baptist Church in Shamokin Township in the 1790s and early 1800s. The Rev. John Woolverton, pastor for a number of years, was a cousin of Mrs. William Furman.

The county seat of Northumberland County is Sunbury. In the 1740s, Sunbury was an Indian town. By 1756, settlers had built Fort Augusta along the Susquehanna River. Fort Augusta served as the bulwark of the Pennsylvania frontier during three wars—the French and Indian War, Pontiac's War, and the American Revolution. Northumberland County was established March 27, 1772. The borough of Sunbury was laid out in 1772, was incorporated in 1797, and has aged gracefully. Farmland surrounds the city's north, south, and east sides, while the usually tranquil Susquehanna River flows to the city's west side.

Since my forebears moved to Northumberland County about three years before Sunbury was incorporated, 1797, here may be a good time to introduce the Ancestry of John Wesley Furman, my father.

John Wesley Furman (1876–1973) and Emma Elnora Eister (1881–1976)

Children

Andrew Furman (1905–); in 1934, married Mercy James (1914–1985); two children.
Mary Elizabeth Furman (1908–); in 1947, married Bartholomew Dewey James (1918–1985); no children.
Franklin Foster Furman (1911–); in 1936, married Hazel Jane Epler (1904–); four children.

James George Furman (1914–1974); in 1942, married Edna
Beck (1919–1984); two children.
Elnora Amelia Furman (1916–); in 1940, married Norman
Geise (1918–); four children.
William Webster Furman (1920–1976); in 1940, married Dora
Propst (1918–); four children.
Alice May Furman (1924–); in 1943, married K. James Kohl
(1920–); five children.

Parents

George Orlando Furman (1852–1928) and Hulda Jane Wilhour (1854–1931).

Grandparents

Samuel Furman (1810–1875) and Margaret Weeks (1814–1897).

Great Grandparents

Daniel Furman (1782–1842) and Hannah Moore who were
born in New Jersey and came to Northumberland in the 1790s
with their parents. They were married about 1804 and lived at
the family homestead in Irish Valley (on present Chestnut
Road). Daniel Furman farmed his entire life and drowned in the
Shamokin Creek in October 1842, at age sixty. Hannah Furman lived until about 1856–1858. The burial place isn't known
but must be in the vicinity of Irish Valley, perhaps at the Sum-
mit Baptist cemetery where some of the children are buried.
(It is interesting that two Furman brothers, Daniel and Isaac,
were married to two Moore sisters (Isaac was married to Catherine Moore), and that their sister, Deborah Furman, married
Samuel Moore, brother of Hannah and Catherine.

My father, J. W. Furman, had a desk made by Daniel Furman. He told us Daniel Furman was a squire. Since he died in
1842, the desk must be over 150 years old. It was passed on

to my son, Franklin, as he is the oldest male descendent with the Furman name. When he was diagnosed with cancer, the desk was given to his son, Franklin G. Furman.

Great Great Grandparents

William Furman (1751–1826) and Rachel Woolverton (1754–1819). They were born in New Jersey and were married in 1774. William was a soldier during the Revolutionary War. On April 28, 1797, they purchased 306 acres of Land in Shamokin Township. William served as a constable for some years and farmed. The last paragraph of page one gives detail of their burial place.

Third Great Grandparents

Samuel Furman and Mary Holcombe, both of whom were born about 1730 and died after 1783. They lived in Hunterdon County and Mansfield Township, Sussex County (now Warren County), New Jersey. Mary's Quaker father was a prominent citizen, and the house he built about 1724 for his family stands to this day at Lambertville, New Jersey. George Washington stayed there on two occasions during the Revolutionary War.

Fourth Great Grandparents

Samuel and wife Hannah (surname unknown). He was born about 1700 and probably lived on Long Island and came to New Jersey as a youth with his parents. He farmed in Hopewell Township and then, from the early 1750s, in Amwell Township, both then in Hunterdon County. Hannah Furman died prior to the move to Amwell, and Samuel remarried to Sara Stout. He died at an advanced age in December, 1794.

Fifth Great Grandparents

Samuel Furman and Elizabeth Roberts. He was born about 1660 at Newtown (now Elmhurst), Long Island, and moved to New Jersey with his brothers, Josias, Jr. and Jonathan, by 1710. Samuel Furman farmed at "Furman's Corner" which today is Marshall's Corner, Mercer County, where he died in 1732.

Samuel's brother, Josias, Jr., was the father of Josias Furman, III, who married Sara Wood. Their eldest son, Wood Furman (1712 to 1783) moved to South Carolina in 1775, and his son, Richard, became pastor of the First Baptist Church of Charleston and was the most prominent clergyman in the late eighteenth and early nineteenth century in South Carolina. This church was the oldest Baptist Church in South Carolina being founded in 1682. Furman University, founded at Edgefield, South Carolina, in 1825–1826, is named in honor of this illustrious Furman.

Samuel's brother, Josias, Jr., was also the father of Martha Furman who married Edward Hart in 1712. Their son, John Hart (1713–1779), was a prominent politician and speaker of the New Jersey legislature. As such, he was sent to Philadelphia and was one of the five signers of the Declaration of Independence from New Jersey.

Sixth Great Grandparents

Josias Furman and Alice (surname unknown). He was baptized on April 22, 1623, at Nayland, County Suffolk, England and came to America with his parents in 1630. He moved to Long Island with his brother, John, about 1652. He died at Newtown Long Island in 1709 and was buried in the cemetery of the Presbyterian Church.

For years, I have been asked if we were any relation to the people who founded Furman University. I always answered, "not that I know of." About 1988, I was delighted to learn that the brother of my sixth great grandfather, Samuel Furman, was Josias Furman, Jr., who was the grandfather of Wood Furman (1712–1783) who moved to High Hills, South

Carolina. His son, Richard Furman, is credited in the Furman University catalog on History (page 6) as being the driving force to founding the University. I quote, "Furman University is the senior college of the South Carolina Baptist Convention and one of the oldest colleges in the state. It originated as an expression of the national spirit and Evangelistic fervor of Richard Furman of Charleston, who helped found the convention in 1821, largely for the purpose of establishing such a school."

Richard Furman's ministry is described in the Historical Sketch of when he became minister of the First Baptist Church, Charleston. Richard Furman was a minster of extraordinary ability. From 1787 to 1825, he led the church, the association, and South Carolina Baptists in promoting education and missions. In 1814, he was named the first president of the Triennial Convention, the first national Baptist convention in America. In 1812, Furman organized the South Carolina Baptist Convention, the first state Baptist convention in America. It became the pattern for other state convention and the Southern Baptist Convention. Furman's stature has not been excelled in South Carolina since his death in 1825. He is buried near the southeast corner of the present church building.

My nephew, Kurt Kohl visited the First Baptist Church of Charleston when he was stationed at Charleston with the Navy and took a number of pictures. Below is a quote from a marker in a picture he gave to me:

SACRED TO THE MEMORY OF
THE REV. RICHARD FURMAN, D.D.
FOR MORE THAN HALF A CENTURY,
AN ABLE AND ELOQUENT PREACHER OF THE GOSPEL;
AND FOR THIRTY EIGHT YEARS,
THE USEFUL AND BELOVED PASTOR OF THIS CHURCH.
PURITY OF LIFE AND AN ACTIVE BENEVOLENCE,

DISTINGUISHED HIM AS A MAN;
PATRIOTISM AND PUBLIC SPIRIT AS A CITIZEN,
FIDELITY AND SYMPATHY AS A FRIEND;
TENDERNESS AND AFFECTION AS A RELATIVE.
IN MANNERS, HE WAS SIMPLE, UNASSUMING, DIGNIFIED;
IN DISPOSITION, MEEK, THOUGHTFUL, PHILANTHROPIC;
IN UNDERSTANDING, ENLIGHTENED, COMPREHENSIVE, VARIOUS.
AS A MINISTER OF THE GOSPEL,
PIOUS, PERSEVERING, CONSCIENTIOUS, DILIGENT, APOSTOLIC,
ACTUATED BY ARDENT ZEAL FOR THE WELFARE
OF HIS FELLOW MEN.
AND UNCOMPRISING JEALOUSY FOR THE HONOUR
OF HIS GOD,
"HE PREACHED JESUS AND HIM CRUCIFIED."
AS A PASTOR,
HE WAS THE GUIDE, THE FATHER OF HIS FLOCK.
HAVING SPENT HIS STRENGTH IN PROMOTING THE
MORTAL INTERESTS OF MAN WITH EMINENT SUCCESS,
HE DIED IN THE EVENING OF LIFE BELOVED AND VENERATED,
WITH A HOPE FULL OF IMMORTALITY.
AS A TRIBUTE OF RESPECT TO HIS MEMORY
HIS MOURNING CONGREGATION
HAVE CAUSED THIS MARBLE TO BE ERECTED.
OB'T 25 AUG 1825.

My first contact with Furman University was in 1980. On our way home from Florida in 1980, we were luncheon guests of Alester G. Furman, Jr. At that time, we did not know we were eighth or ninth cousins. He really treated us wonderfully. He apologized for not having us in his home, but his wife was sick and the servant was off. He was a typical wealthy southern gentleman. After lunch, he took us to his home which had large white pillars in front and was furnished with imported furniture. Alester G. Furman, Jr. had been chairman of the board when, in 1958, Furman University moved to a beautiful 750-acre campus five miles from Greenville. His family

gifted a replica of the tower of the Main Building on the original men's campus in Downtown Greenville.

I will be forever grateful for the afternoon he spent giving
a V. I. P. tour to us of the Furman campus. I asked him if they
had co-ed dorms. I will always remember his terse reply, "No,
and we will not have as long as I am living." In 1989, I wrote
a letter to him regarding visiting him again. I received an answer from his son, Alester G. Furman, III, saying his father had
passed away in December of 1980.

Another distinguished Furman relative we visited at Boone,
North Carolina, in January on our way to Florida, was Doctor
Richard Furman. I understand that he and his brother donated
the office space for Samaritan's Purse for a number of years.
While visiting them in 1986, we met a few minutes with Franklin Graham, son of Billy Graham. Franklin Graham is International Director of Samaritan's Purse.

Dr. Richard Furman wrote a book titled *Reaching Your
Full Potential*, which every Christian should read. Dr. Richard
Furman and his brother, Dr. Lowell Furman, practice surgery
in Boone and founded an organization called World Medical Missions. Soon after its conception, they persuaded Franklin Graham to become its president. This organization will
send out about 140 physicians this year to third world countries to assist in mission hospitals. I understand these doctors
donate their time and money for these trips. I enjoyed meeting Dr. Richard Furman's father who, I believe, was in his late
eighties.

As I mentioned before, I would like to give my sincere
thanks to Stuart Furman who spent many hours on the ge-
nealogies of the Furman family. Anyone wanting more information on your particular branch of the Furman family should
contact Stuart Furman, 15370 Gatehouse Terrace, Woodbridge, Virginia 22191.

History of the Puritans

I have prayed a lot as to how to present the truth in a concise manner. It is not the purpose of this book, nor is there sufficient space, to treat the Puritans in detail. However, since their principles were one of the main reasons why John Firmin left a comfortable home to brave the harsh winters and wild country of New England, it is worthy to find out just why he was a Puritan and for what they stood.

The name Puritan in itself describes being pure from the religious errors of the Church of England and of the Catholic Church. The name Puritan was first used during the late 1560s as a label for those Englishmen who urged that the English church proceed further in the rejection of practices and beliefs than it had done since the formal separation from Rome under Henry VIII. He had declared himself "the only supreme head on earth of the Church of England." Under his rule, people who did not conform to his edict were put to death.

Thirty years later, under Queen Elizabeth, the more ardent reformers who were still attempting to complete, as they saw it, the work of purifying the English church came to be designated and to call themselves Puritans.

In 1604, soon after he became king, James VI of Scotland was presented a petition by the Puritans when on his way to London, unsigned but expressing the wishes of about a thousand clergymen. A conference was called at Hampton Court. On the third day, the king and the bishops conferred by themselves and, after they had settled the matter, four Puritans were called in and told what they had decided. The king said he expected of them obedience and humility, and added, "If that is all they have to say, I shall make them conform themselves or I will harry them out of the land or else do worse."

Puritans, more and more, came to affirm that the Bible, and only the Bible, deserved to be followed. Most of the Puritans shared basically common beliefs about the Christian faith and its out-working in the world. Almost all were re-formed in theology. But they believed with Luther, as well with Calvin, that people were spiritually debilitated by original sin. All people were unwilling, and therefore unable, to meet the demands of God or enjoy His fellowship unless God Himself changed their heart of stone into a heart of flesh. They believed as well that God's gift of grace led to living faith in Christ. The distinctive contribution of the Puritans on the subject of human salvation was their emphasis on conversion. For them, becoming a genuine believer would mean repentance followed by the experience of liberating faith. With all the Protestant reformers, the Puritans also believed in the supreme authority of the Scripture.

Three hundred Puritan ministers, who had separated from the established church, were silenced, imprisoned, or exiled in 1604. But the more they were afflicted, the more they multiplied and grew. And now, the persecuted pastors and people began to think of emigrating. The Separatists went to Holland, Smyth to Amsterdam in 1606, and John Robinson with the Scrooby Church to Amsterdam and Leyden in 1608. Some the Puritans also sailed for Virginia. Many of those who immigrated to Holland later returned to England and then immigrated to the United States.

In 1628, a group of Puritans purchased controlling interest in the New England Company; in 1629, the company reorganized to emphasize colonization and de-emphasize commerce and obtained a new charter from the King. In 1630, more than 1,000 settlers embarked for Massachusetts Bay, including Governor John Winthrop and a dozen of the company directors. (This is the group that included John Firmin.) In the next ten years, 20,000 more would make that same journey.

Early historians of America, like Thomas Hutchinson who wrote in the mid-eighteenth century, honored the Puritans as courageous pioneers who had labored to construct a freer world in a difficult environment.

Although Hutchinson, as the last royal governor of Massachusetts, did not share their view, many in his day praised the Puritans for working toward the same kind of freedom from English tyranny that the patriots sought in the Revolutionary period.

The Puritans of New England were very strict in observing Sunday. Law books are full of fines for violating their idea of the Sabbath. Parents were held accountable for their children's actions.

There was a lot friction between the Puritans and the Quakers. It seems that their movements were incompatible. The Quakers found compulsory attendance at public worship where a hireling minister preached the written Word a form of legalism from which Christ set men free. Puritan laws were based on the Ten Commandments. Moral infidelity was severely punished. Even today, sometimes we are called puritanical when we stand for moral laws and principles. As America became more secular, public opinion turned against the Puritans.

All of this began to change in the late 1920s when a small group of scholars, mostly at Harvard, out of curiosity began to take another look at the Puritans. Their curiosity soon turned to respect. In 1930, Samuel Eliot Morison described the builders of the Bay Colony as a serious-minded religious individuals worthy of rewarding study. Perry Miller described the Puritan theology as sophisticated, tough-minded, and durable. Today, only the most uniformed would now repeat the error of the Progressives and think of the Puritans as insubstantial or contemptible. I agree with many Bible believing Christians that secular history has been very unkind to the Puritans.

John Winthrop

Winthrop was a Puritan leader and first Governor of Massachusetts, who was born in 1588. His father, Adam Winthrop, belonged to the newly-risen Suffolk gentry and owned the

Groton Estate. John attended one year at Trinity College, Cambridge, and also studied law at Gray's Inn and learned to manage his properties; by 1618, he succeeded his father as lord of Groton Manor. He was appointed justice of peace and, in 1627, secured a minor government place as attorney at the Court of Wards.

The only exceptional aspect of Winthrop's life was his Puritanism. Sometime in his youth, he underwent a shattering conversion experience which enlisted him in the service of the will of God. Even for that intensely religious age, Winthrop's zeal was notable; he poured his whole resources into scriptural study and prayer. His religion gave him a strong conviction of social responsibility. As Winthrop's latest biographer put it, he had to learn to do right in a world that does wrong.

In 1629, he was dissatisfied with the King and the Church. He gave moral support to some of his Suffolk friends who were prominent Puritans and who were imprisoned for their opposition to the King and the State Church.

On March 29, a diversified group of merchants, gentry, and clergy received a royal charter which incorporated them as the Massachusetts Bay Company. Their purpose was to convert and trade with the Indians and to explore other avenues of profit. In July 1629, John Winthrop decided to join them after it was decided that the colony in Massachusetts should be self-governing and not subordinated to the company in England.

In treatises circulated among fellow Puritans, John Winthrop stated bluntly some reasons why he wanted to emigrate.

> All other Churches of Europe are brought to desolation, and it cannot be, but the like Judgement is cominge upon us. . . . This lande growes wearye of her Inhabitantes, so as man which is the most pretious of all Creatures, is heere more vile and base, then the earth they treade upon. . . . The fountains of learninge and Religion are so corrupted. . . . that most Children even the best wittes and of fayrest hopes, are perverted cor-

rupted and utterly overthrowne by the multitude of evill examples and licentious government of those seminaryes.

Unquestionably, religion was the prime impetus for Winthrop to immigrate to America.

Winthrop's history in New England was largely that of the Massachusetts colony, of which he was twelve times chosen governor at annual elections. He gave all of his strength and fortune to the colonies. He was conservative and somewhat aristocratic, but just and magnanimous in his political guidance. He defended Massachusetts against threatened parliamentary interference on several occasions. The colony's early success was due largely to his wisdom and skill.

Chapter 21
Bible School—A Good Foundation
Written by: Dr. Sherrill Babb, President,
Philadelphia College of the Bible

Direction determines destination. Or to rephrase it, the way one starts on the journey of life usually determines the way that person will end life. Being born into a good family environment with loving, encouraging parents is vital to producing a mature, balanced, adult person. Along with a proper home setting goes the schooling or education that launches a young boy or girl in the right direction. As the Greek philosopher Plato said nearly two and a half centuries ago, "The direction in which education starts a man determines his future life."

Family and education played a significant role in molding the character, aspirations, and accomplishments of Foster Furman. He personally experienced the reality and promise of Proverbs 22:6: "Train up a child in the way he should go and, when he is old, he will not depart from it." His parents, John Wesley and Emma Eister Furman, motivated their son to live morally and ethically and to be pleasing unto the Lord. Their instruction in practical living was indelibly written in the fabric of his soul.

Public education did for Foster what it does for most occupants of the local school house—it provided the basics. The ability to read, write, speak, calculate, and think came from his exposure to early education.

A dramatic educational opportunity impacted Foster for the remainder of his life when, during the winter of 1934, he attended the Bible Institute of Pennsylvania. It was this small, little-known school that would provide him spiritual direction toward accomplishing God's will, the highest of all destinations.

The way in which Foster learned of the Bible Institute centers around the school's founding president, W. W. Rugh. After the turn of the century, Rugh, affectionately known as "Brother Rugh," traveled throughout the northeast, especially Pennsylvania, conducting Bible classes. The story is told that Rugh frequently was dependent upon the generosity of others to provide transportation to his Bible study sites. On one particular occasion, he arrived at the Philadelphia train station without a penny to purchase a ticket. A stranger at the station bought Rugh's ticket so that he would be able to visit the central Pennsylvania village of Northumberland, and as God's directing plans would have it, Rugh arrived in the hometown of the Furmans.

Foster grew spiritually under Rugh's Bible teaching. He also was introduced to the possibility of studying at the Bible Institute of Pennsylvania. This specialty school could afford him an in-depth study of God's Word. After graduating from Northumberland High School in 1928 at the age of 16, Foster naturally became a part of his father's business. There was simultaneously a supernatural pull in his life for spiritual growth. He recounts the calling of God in the Old Testament for Samuel. It was as though God was calling Foster to be a man of God in some fashion as He had called the young man Samuel to be a prophet for Israel. This calling to Foster caused him to hunger for the study of God through the Bible.

Being as spiritually sensitive as their son, John and Emma were in favor of Foster's desire to attend the Bible Institute.

The family business could wait for Foster's return; God's business of spiritual preparation was elevated to a higher priority.

It was a cold February night in 1934 in Northumberland when Foster left for his next educational adventure. It appeared to be even colder when he arrived in Philadelphia. For someone who had been to no cities other than Northumberland and Washington, D.C., traveling the several hundred miles to the city founded by William Penn was no easy assignment. His only comfort was that an aunt lived on the edge of Philadelphia. And then his fearfulness was compounded when his late night street car ride took an extraordinary amount of time to deliver the scholar-to-be at the Bible Institute. Unintentionally, he had been given the wrong number for the street address of his destination. That evening, Philadelphia appeared larger than reality. Rugh's school became a "needle in the haystack."

The work of the Institute was begun July 8, 1913, as an early catalog described, "because of a deep conviction that it was God's will to provide training, through the teaching of His Word, for Christian men and women, that they might become soulwinners in any place and service to which God might call them." This purpose or mission statement became profitable and prophetic for Foster Furman.

It was at the Institute that he would receive his foundational instruction in God's Word that would last a lifetime. Here he would develop his evangelistic zeal to communicate Jesus Christ as Saviour. Here he would be equipped to become a parent, churchman, businessman, and civic leader. According to Foster, the winter semester of 1934 at the Bible Institute was the greatest period in his life concerning his spiritual growth.

With today's high cost of college education and meager educational results, it is astounding to review the financial investment and ultimate outcomes from Foster's Institute experience.

The Bible Institute made no charge for tuition. An early handbook declared, "the Institute looks to God to provide training for those who attend its classes through the gifts of His people." Students were required to pay an enrollment fee of $10 per year. Room and board were provided at the cost of $6 a week, provided that the student did an assigned amount of domestic work, not exceeding one hour each day. If domestic work was not done, the cost was increased by $1.20 a week. Most students were able to work on campus for the required $6 room and board fee. For a while, Foster's work on campus was to clean bathrooms. On one occasion while he was engaged in this humbling task, the Dean of the Institute, Dr. Wade Gosnell, appeared on the scene and proclaimed to Foster in pointed but humorous fashion the words of Paul in Colossians 3:23: "Whatever you do, work at it with all your heart, as working for the Lord, not for men." Perhaps it can be said that one who diligently handles the unpleasant tasks of life is fit for more significant responsibilities. A required college course in facility sanitation may be one of the best ways to produce future leaders!

When Foster came to the Institute in 1934, there were only thirteen day-school students enrolled in his class. In addition, however, there were several hundred evening-school students who attended classes on a part-time basis. Facilities for the school were small but well maintained. Located at 1530 North 16th Street, the three-story Institute building was not impressive in terms of contemporary college campuses. However, it was the godly, spiritual faculty members and their instruction in and out of the classrooms that were of value to Foster and his classmates. They were taught from Matthew 6:19–21, "Do not store up for yourselves treasures on earth, where moth and rust destroy, and where thieves break in and steal. But store up for yourselves treasures in heaven, where moth and rust do not destroy, and where thieves do not break in and steal. For where your treasure is, there your heart will be also." Therefore, spiritual responsibilities and rewards took precedence over materialistic considerations. Their focus as students was upon Jesus Christ and God's Word where, as Colossians 2:3 declares, "in whom are hidden all the treasures of wisdom and knowledge."

During his 1934 winter term, Foster took fourteen courses for sixteen semester hours of academic work. In eleven of his courses he earned an A! In addition, he received two Bs and one C. The curriculum included classes in Essentials in Christian Belief, Introductory Bible Study, Child Study, Doctrine, Bible Introduction, Personal Evangelism, Elementary Gospel Music, Homiletics, World View of Missions, Life of Christ, Old Testament Synthesis, Old Testament Typology, Bible Ethics, and Department Specialization. Every course played an important role in molding Foster into becoming a man seeking to please God. It was this rigorous program of study, as he later said, that gave him an understanding of the Bible and made him an effective witness for Jesus Christ. But, there was more. The classes taught him how to raise his children with a spiritual dimension, how to conduct business based on biblical ethics, the priority of world missions, the essentials of preparing and delivering a Bible lesson, and an appreciation for good gospel music.

As the radiant spring flowers interrupted the bitterly cold Philadelphia winter, Foster's educational odyssey at the Bible Institute concluded. The family business had pressing need of his help. When he arrived back in Northumberland, Foster was well equipped for the challenges that were ahead. More significantly, he was God's man prepared for leadership in his family, church, business, and community.

Foster was not the only person in his family to attend the Bible Institute of Pennsylvania. Although he was the first to enroll at the Institute, his brothers Bill and James ventured to Brother Rugh's school. Sisters Elnora, Alice, and Mary likewise attended. The only child of John and Emma who did not enroll was Andrew, but his daughter Beverly attended in 1962.

The impact of the Bible Institute was so dramatic in Foster's own spiritual pilgrimage that he strongly urged his four children—Franklin, Joel, Jane, and Sara—to spend at least one year at the Institute. Not only did they follow in the educational footsteps of their father, but five of Foster's grandchildren have received or are currently receiving their training at Philadelphia College of the Bible, the name of the present-day institution. A remarkable statistic is that a total of twenty-four descendants of John and Emma Furman are alumni of the Bible Institute or Philadelphia College of the Bible. No other family associated with the institution can boast of this special heritage.

Foster's involvement with the Bible Institute now spans nearly 60 years. As a faithful alumnus, he has attended countless homecoming activities and special events. He has for many years served on the school's President's Advisory Council. During these six decades, he has seen the Institute merge with the Philadelphia School of the Bible to form the Philadelphia Bible Institute (1950), receive degree-granting status with the Commonwealth of Pennsylvania (1951), achieve accreditation with five agencies, and move to a new expanding campus with over 100 acres. From the small number of 13 students who attended the day school in 1934, Philadelphia College of the Bible currently enrolls annually over 1,000 degree students and hundreds of others in continuing education classes. Nearly 10,000 alumni now are scattered throughout every state in the Union and in 73 different nations. As God has blessed the life of Foster Furman, He has also blessed the school that impacted his life for time and eternity.

W. Sherrill Babb

Chapter 22
Missions and the Christian Businessman

Written by: Dr. Frank Severn, General Director,
SEND International

In the economy of God, when a person or family experiences the grace of God which brings salvation, all of life finds a new focus. A believer in Jesus Christ recognizes God's ultimate ownership of all of life. Therefore, all of life's activities need to be related to God's revealed will as declared in the Scripture.

Before ascending into heaven, the Lord Jesus left His people some very specific commandments which should give direction and focus to life. We call these the Great Commission. Jesus told His disciples that proclaiming the good news concerning forgiveness of sins found through faith in Christ is to be an essential part of Jesus' finished work.

"He told them, 'This is what is written: The Christ will suffer and rise from the dead on the third day, and repentance and forgiveness of sins will be preached in His name to all nations beginning at Jerusalem. You are witnesses of these things' " (Luke 24:46–48).

In the gospel of Mark, the Lord Jesus emphasized the scope of the Great Commission. The gospel is to be declared to "all creation." In the gospel of John, Jesus declared the method of getting the gospel to the ends of the earth. He said, "As the Father has sent me, I am sending you" (John 20:21). His method is for His people to carry the gospel to the ends of the earth. We are "to be there" with the message. We are to live and speak the message with the people to whom we are sent.

Perhaps the clearest command with the most specific methodology is found in Matthew 28:18–20:

> Then Jesus came to them and said, "All authority in heaven and on earth has been given to me. Therefore, go and make disciples of all nations, baptizing them in the name of the Father, and of the Son, and of the Holy Spirit, and teaching them to obey everything I have commanded you. And surely I am with you always, to the very end of the age."

The focus of Jesus' Great Commission to His people is "make disciples." Disciples are to be made among "all nations." Jesus declares that a disciple is one who has repented and believes in Jesus. He declares this through baptism which makes him a part of God's church in its local expression. A disciple is one who is a learner—being taught all that Jesus commands with the intent of obedience. That obedience is focused in being a disciple and making disciples. In other words, every believer should be actively involved in seeing that disciples are made among "all nations."

Jesus' last words recorded by Luke in Acts 1 command all believers to be witnesses "in Jerusalem, Judea, Samaria, and unto the uttermost part of the earth." This witnessing is to continue to the ends of the earth, to the end of the age.

It is obvious that every Christian will not be able to go to the ends of the earth; however, every Christian should be a witness where he is and should be concerned that the gospel be proclaimed and disciples made among all peoples.

As a Christian businessman, J. W. Furman and his family built their business with the intent of supporting gospel work around the world. This commitment was carried into corporate policy, as well as personal practice. As God prospered the business, a percentage was set aside for God's work around the world. Missionaries scattered around the world are proclaiming the gospel because businessmen and women like those of Furman Foods have understood their significant role in fulfilling Christ's commission to His church.

Missionaries and mission organizations like SEND International could not exist apart from dedicated Christian businessmen who give to their churches and who give personally to see the gospel reach the ends of the earth.

In our day, it is rare to see Christian corporations who are committed to excellence in the market place with the intent of making a profit for the glory of God.

The New Testament presents life as a stewardship of resources. All of our life is to be lived for the glory of God under the lordship of Jesus Christ. He gifts some to be gospel proclaimers and cross-cultural missionaries. He gifts others to use their financial and administrative skills to provide the resources to enable His church to carry out His commission. He asks all of us to be witnesses wherever we go.

Christian businessmen who obediently obey God's call in their lives are partners with the missionary in "making disciples." Each one is responsible to obey the "Lord of the harvest" in the sphere in which Christ calls and leads him. When all are obedient, there will be sufficient resources in both personnel and finances to get the gospel to the ends of the earth.

As I have personally observed the Furman family, specifically the Foster Furman family, I can testify to the impact on missions in at least three significant ways.

Prayer

Missionaries all over the world are faithfully prayed for daily. As Foster and Hazel have traveled to visit our fields, they have become prayer partners with many of our missionaries.

315

Prayer can go wherever God can go! There are no language nor cultural barriers in prayer! Prayer, along with the word of God, is our chief offensive weapon in spiritual warfare. It is critical for penetrating Satan's territory.

Christian businessmen, like Foster Furman, who believe and practice intercessory prayer, are front-line participants in the preaching of the gospel and making disciples among the nations.

Jesus said, "Ask the Lord of the harvest, therefore, to send out workers into his harvest field" (Matthew 9:38). It is one thing to pray generally for laborers, it is another to pray specifically that the laborers will come from your own family. When my wife (Jane Furman Severn) was young, she heard her dad (Foster Furman) praying. She heard him ask that his Lord would send at least one of his children to the mission field. God answered that prayer when Jane and I left for the Philippines in 1965.

Giving

J. W. Furman and his children, grandchildren, and great grandchildren have committed themselves to carrying on a family corporation which continues to give a portion of its profits to the Lord's work. They have individually and corporately demonstrated their commitment by allocating large sums to missions. Many missionaries and mission organizations have been greatly blessed by their generosity.

In God's economy, they who sow, water, and reap are all important, because it is God who gives the increase. Missions would not be possible without the faithful support of Christian businesspeople who are committed to faithful stewardship of the resources entrusted to them by God.

Sending/Going

In order for disciples to be made, there must be those who go (goers), those who help train and mobilize missionaries (mobilizers), and those who send (supporters). Christian businessmen are called to participate in all three areas. Some will be able to use their business skills to actually go and be part of a mission thrust in a cross-cultural situation. Our mission is grateful for treasurers and business managers who enable our mission to function in each area where God calls us. We can use retired successful businesspeople who can use their skills to enable us to function better.

Christian businessmen make significant contributions to mission boards. Missions is a complex ministry with great accountability and careful stewardship needed of the funds and personnel God sends our way. We are grateful for faithful, godly, Christian businesspeople who are part of our board of directors. In the stewardship of God's economy, the Lord has equipped them with wisdom and skills that enable mission organizations like SEND to be faithful stewards of God's resources.

J. W. Furman and those who have followed him have made significant contributions to cross-cultural missions by sending some of their own, supporting many missionaries and mission organizations with both dollars and prayer, and also contributing their skills to the expansion of the gospel around the world.

This is a demonstration of the dynamic partnership that God has designed between "secular" work and the work of the church. All of life is sacred, and when men or women understand and live out their belief, then every vocation becomes part of God's design to disciple the nations.

Christian businessmen and businesses like Furman Foods can be more than good businesses, they can also be a vital part of fulfilling Christ's mandate of "making disciples of the nations."

J. W. Furman lived and worked out a vision of establishing a business through great sacrifice. This business was seen as a part of God's great purpose and was dedicated to the glory of God. Business was to be conducted with honesty and integrity. Sunday was to be set apart for worship. Profits were to be used to enable the company to grow, but only after God was honored by a corporate tithe and personal giving. As God prospered the business, even more money could go to His work.

While lifestyle choices are personal, it can be observed that J. W. Furman passed a commitment on to his children to live as simply as possible so they could give to God's work and also ensure the continued growth of the company for the glory of God.

Untold thousands have been brought to saving faith in Jesus Christ because Christian businessmen like J. W. Furman and his family have faithfully fulfilled their calling.

Another aspect of the life and ministry of the Furman family which has made a significant contribution to missions is their witness in the marketplace. While the founder and officers of the business have not been missionaries, they have shared the gospel by word and deed with those they meet. This is a direct fulfillment of Jesus' command to be His witness in "Jerusalem."

The perseverance of J. W. Furman and his children has resulted in a significant impact on missions beginning at home and extending to the ends of the earth.

Chapter 23
A Young Lawyer's Encounter With Christian Businessmen
Written by: Attorney Robert Diehl

Over thirty years ago, I graduated from law school and returned to the Central Susquehanna Valley in Pennsylvania where I was born and raised. I returned to the area of my youth because of strong family ties and because I love the land and the people who live here. It was and is a great place to live and raise a family.

I was fortunate to have a grandfather, Michael Kivko, with whom I entered the practice of law. Michael was a wonderful man and an excellent lawyer who mentored me—not only in the law of man but also in the law of God—and taught me to honor and respect His creation, especially people.

As I matured in the law, I also was growing in my knowledge of God and of the Lord Jesus Christ. I must admit that, at times, especially with the younger generation, I found it difficult to discuss God and His purpose for life. I may have become discouraged, but it was at that time I came to know the Furman, Geise, and Kohl families.

Early in 1961, Michael and I undertook the representation of the Furman business interests, and we found them to be unique. Before each business meeting, they would read the

319

Holy Scripture and pray. They not only prayed for wisdom for the conduct of their business affairs, but also for the well being of their employees and they sought guidance to help them and to be fair to them. Each year at their annual meeting, they spend time determining how to return to God part of the blessing He has given to them.

This had a lasting impact on me, and I am forever grateful that God permitted me to become associated with such wonderful people early in my professional career. Not unlike other family businesses, there have been difficult situations and times, but in each of these situations, they have "agreed to disagree" and work for the betterment of the business and those involved and to honor God. To this day, I meet regularly with Foster Furman, who has been one of my spiritual fathers, for intercessory prayer, and I have a deep spiritual relationship with several other family members including David Geise, the present C.E.O. of the Furman businesses.

In 1966, Michael Kivko became President Judge of the Northumberland County Common Pleas Court. It was at this time that I formed a partnership with John Carpenter, a fellow Christian, with whom I continue to practice law to this day. John also has a strong Christian witness and has blessed my life in many ways.

My desire in the remaining years of my active legal life is to use my position as a lawyer to proclaim Jesus as Lord in all that I do in the field of law and to be a help to those that God would send my way. I have found that many people who come to me for my legal advice really need advice about life, and especially they need to know the provision God has made for them in the person of Jesus.

Being a Christian lawyer in a secular world continues to be a challenge. It has not gotten any easier because society seems to frown upon open discussion of spiritual things. Other than with fellow believers, it has become more difficult to involve people in talk about things spiritual. People seem to be preoccupied with "making it" in their business endeavors and personal exploits. As I reflect, this should not seem unusual since our society seems to be preoccupied with self and personal desire. It now permits abortion upon demand, espouses violence and hatred daily through the television media, and promotes life styles which are contrary to God's Word. It seems strange, but we now can distribute birth control devices in our public schools, but we can't distribute Bibles or utter a prayer to the Creator of the universe. The pendulum on moral decency in our American society has swung about as far left as it can go.

I pray for the ability and opportunity to continue to help people with legal and life problems. I need the Stick-to-it-iveness of J. W. Furman and his wonderful family as described in J. W.'s book, *STICK-TO-IT-IVENESS*. It worked and succeeded for them, and I hope it will for me. I'm sure it will if I continue to have the influence of the Furman, Geise, and Kohl families and other godly people.

Chapter 24
Stick-To-It-Iveness in the National Football League and Prison Ministry
Written by: Mr. Bill Glass, President,
Bill Glass Ministries

For twenty-two years, I played football—ten as an amateur and twelve as a pro—in junior high school, high school, college, and professional. During those years, I was primarily a defensive football player. Through the years, I studied thousands of films of games that I played in or of teams against whom we were going to play. I discovered that about 80 percent of all tackles are made by players that appear to be totally out of the play, but because of their bulldog tenacity, they got up off of the ground or regained their balance and made the tackle anyway.

Sports teach us how to get really clobbered and keep going. What a valuable strength to our lives when we know how to take blows from many directions and not allow it to destroy us. Christians should actually go one step further and be strengthened by the adversity. There are two things that it takes to be motivated: a pull of desire—you must want to win, and a push of discontent—you must want to prove something. It is the storms of life that produce this build-up of discontent that can actually motivate us to achieve our goals.

If I had to choose what ministry I would be involved in after my professional career, I couldn't have possibly picked anything to do that would have been so right as working with inmates in prison. It is no work for sissies. We are dealing with misfits who have suffered every imaginable setback. All of the athletic bumps and bruises were good training for my ministry.

It is so easy to get preoccupied with all of the problems that you can't see the solutions. People who work in prisons often become institutionalized. They are infected with the attitudes of convicts. The problems are systemic. The whole system is infected. It's not just the criminal justice system; it is a problem of the entire culture, starting from the earliest childhood. It is fair to say that, in 1972 when we started, and even more so today, prisons and the entire culture needs a whole new way of life. The prison problems are only the extreme of the free world. It is only the tip of the iceberg when compared to the sickness of the rest of society!

There Were Some Other Tough Times

The bombshell of my young life came when I overheard my parents talking about the fact that my father had been diagnosed as having Hodgkin's disease. At that time, this blood disorder was fatal. But he was the eternal optimist and had great faith that God would heal him. Besides, the medical world was close to finding a cure. If he could hang on long enough, there was great hope.

He lived for two pain-filled years and shrank from an athletic 205 pounds at age forty-three to a frail invalid of 140 pounds when he died at age forty-five. I was crushed, but my sorrow soon changed to determination. My dad left me with a powerful positive attitude which he had ingrained into me from birth. He also impressed me with his unconditional love. On many occasions, he'd say, "If you want to play sports, that's fine. I'll back you all the way. But if you don't, that's fine, too. You'll still be great in my book."

I always dreamed of being a famous football star. However, I was terribly clumsy and growing fast and really knew that it would be difficult for me to ever be any good. Even though my dad attempted to be positive about my sports potential, I could tell he thought I'd never make it. However, as my coordination improved and my dedication to sports increased, things started to fall into place. I never drank or smoked because I wanted to be a great athlete. This was before steroids and drugs. Being the football hero was the thing to do. I also wanted to prove to my dad, now watching from heaven, that I could do a good job in sports just like he and my brother. I was never a wild kid; in fact, I was a real square. But not so much because I was a Christian. It was more because I wanted to be a clean-living athlete. Also, I was clumsy because I was growing so fast, and I had acne, which all conspired to make me insecure. Worst of all, I missed my dad.

In my worst moments, I felt clumsy, awkward, ugly, and now I was fatherless. Dad had been so fearless and stable, but he was gone. My mother was lonely and fearful. I felt I had to be brave and strong for her sake and my baby sister (twelve years younger), but I wasn't always successful.

Later in my high school years, I had a dynamic conversion experience. This further intensified my distaste for street people. I now see there was a large dose of self-righteousness in my attitude during that first prison experience. I am sure that God was not pleased with my "holier than thou" arrogance. Be that as it may, in my first experience, I was totally turned off by prison life. That's why it was so amazing that God has led me so obviously into this prison ministry.

I would have never dreamed that in the next twenty years, we would conduct "Weekend of Champions" in over 800 prisons with around 6,000 counselors. We hung in there, and it has paid off in changed lives among the throw-aways of our society in prisons, much as it did on the gridiron.

Through the years, we had always conducted city-wide crusades, much like Billy Graham, on an interdenominational basis in relatively smaller cities and communities. I was in the middle of an area-wide campaign at the county fairground in Bloomsburg, Pennsylvania, when I first met Foster Furman. He was already in his late seventies, and I was amazed with his unbelievable enthusiasm. He wife appeared to be just as healthy and in gear as he was, but he was so excited about the possibility of our coming to his area for a city-wide crusade, he hardly allowed her in the conversation. I later got to know her better and realized that she shared his enthusiasm and commitment to Christ as well.

He was a real soul brother to me. He had gone through his share of knocks and bruises through the years and had been knocked off of his feet just as I had in pro football. However, he had a never say die attitude that was amazing. Rather than a man in advanced years, he acted much younger. He worked tirelessly to get the churches of all denominations to cooperate with the crusade. He talked endlessly to ministers and laymen about a city-wide in Lewisburg, Pennsylvania. For over two years, he hung on to his dream and prayed and worked. Finally, it become a reality July 15–22, 1990. Foster and the Central Susquehanna Valley Celebration with Bill Glass, Inc. were the keys to making it happen!

We also conducted a "Weekend of Champions" in the prisons in the area, and he worked with us equally as hard on the prison impact. He had already served through a local prison ministry in the Lewisburg Federal Pen for years and was able to open doors for us in all of the prison units in the area. The fact that Foster hung in there, in spite of difficulties in the city-wide and prison work, was certainly a source of great encouragement to me. This made me understand why he could help to build the great company of Furman Foods, Inc. that stands as a testament to his persistence, hard work, and determination. Foster is a man of great faith. You can see how Furman Foods could start in the kitchen of J. W. Furman and grow into one of the really great companies in that part of the country.

Conclusion
If I Could Live My Life Over Again

There are two things that I think I should have done—spend more time reading and studying the Word of God and more time telling others about my wonderful Saviour.

As I think of witnessing, I think of the undelivered letter. The story is of yesteryear, in the days of the pony express. A young couple were engaged to be married. Before they were married, they heard that, in the Midwest, if a person lived on a farm for five years and built a house, it would be given to them free of charge under the Homestead Act. They decided that John would go west and claim land, build a house on it, and come back and marry Jane, and they would move to the homestead. John thought it would take about a year. Jane waited about a year, and one day the letter came saying, "Jane, it took me longer than I expected, but if you still love me, I will come on the first stagecoach after receiving your answer." She dashed to her room and wrote to John, "Come as quick as you can; I have been waiting for this day." Since they were having torrential rain, she gave the letter to her brother to mail as he was going to town. Then she waited—one month, two months—at the end of the year, she died of a broken heart. In the meantime, John waited one month, two months, and at the end of a year, he left the homestead and went to sea. Years later, in an old coat of her brother, the undelivered letter, yellowed with age, was found. You say what a shame that the letter that would have made a young couple supremely happy was never delivered. Then my eyes fill with tears as I ask myself how many undelivered letters do I have that may have saved people from eternal damnation. My friend, how many undelivered messages do you have that tell people how to go to heaven?

For morning devotions, I read a chapter from the Bible and spend twenty to thirty minutes praying for our missionary friends around the world, for my family, for our government, and for our business. Then in the evening, the family read a chapter from the Bible and prayed together. Remember, the family that prays together stays together. But with shame, I admit I spend very little time in actual Bible study unless I am preparing to speak. I have never heard anyone say they wish they had spent less time reading the Bible.

Another thing I have never heard anyone say was they wished they had spent less time with their children and grandchildren. As I went on sales trips in the summer, I would often take my family with me. The children often complained that when I was on vacation, often I would arrange to see a customer or stop at some factory to learn how other canneries were operating. When my children were growing up, we had very few vacation days. Dear parent, today most people have a number of paid vacation days. If you use those vacation days for doing the things you like to do without regard for your family, you may have to visit a jail cell after it is too late to get to know your children.

As you climb the ladder to success, be sure it is not leaning against the wrong wall. Demands on a person starting their own business are very heavy. But what is success worth if, on your way to the top, you lose your children and perhaps even your wife. A few hours now with your family may save you years of regret.

I am sitting in our living room at the word processor looking out of the window at the homestead where I lived from age six to age twenty-four. Our house is on an incline about twenty feet higher than the homestead and about 300 yards north. Because of the elevation, I can see much of the factory and warehouses. Also, looking out our kitchen window, part of the factory to the east is only a few feet from our home. This view brings back many pleasant memories of Father, Mother, three brothers, and three sisters. Also, it reminds me of the blood, sweat, and tears as we grew from 360 glass jars in 1921 to 124 million cans in 1992.

During those seventy years, the size of the factory grew from a few square feet to 127,340 square feet, and warehouses grew to a total of thirteen warehouses for a total square footage of 269,718. Total area covered by the buildings is almost 400,000 square feet or a total of 9.1 acres. An additional forty-one acres are required for parking, a tomato yard to park tomato trailers, and the waste treatment plant. This adds up to a total area of about fifty acres for plant operations.

As these memories flood my mind, I am reminded of how much the Lord has blessed us. Hazel and I have lived in the same house for over fifty-seven years. We are especially thankful to the Lord for our four children.

Franklin F. Furman was born in 1938. He and Esther have three children. They live about a half of a mile from our home. Franklin was plant manager before he was disabled with cancer around 1978. Today, he can walk with two arm canes.

Jane Furman Severn was born in 1940. She lives in Detroit with her husband, Frank, who is General Director of SEND International. They have four children.

Joel R. Furman was born in 1944. He is sales manager for Furman Foods. He and his wife, Margaret, have four children. They live in Sunbury, R.D., about fifteen miles from our home.

Sara Furman Cilderman was born in 1948. She lives in Fairlawn, New Jersey, with her husband, Andy, who is a mechanical engineer. Sara is a nurse and is in charge of quality review at the hospital where she works. They have two children.

We thank the Lord that all of our children, as well as five of our grandchildren, are married in the Lord. Our five married grandchildren are Frank Furman, Tammy Furman Ross, Ruth Severn Hassan, Esther Severn Parson, and Daniel Severn.

Since Hazel broke her left hip in December 1992 and her right hip in January 1994, she will never get out of the nursing home. Tears come to my eyes as I wish we would have spent more time together, including more trips. I always dreamed that before our family scattered, we would take a trip to Yellowstone Park and to the west coast. However, time moved on, and it never happened.

We have had seven personal tragedies in our family in the last 13 months. I mention this to say that I personally believe everything that happens to a committed Christian is filtered through God's love, and it happens for our good and His glory. I do not understand it, nor can I explain it, but God's word tells us this.

I have found great comfort in 1 Corinthians 10:11–13:

> These things happened to them as examples and were written down as warnings for us, on whom the fulfillment of the ages has come. So, if you think you are standing firm, be careful that you don't fall! No temptation has seized you except what is common to man. And God is faithful; he will not let you be tempted beyond what you can bear. But when you are tempted, he will also provide a way out so that you can stand up under it.

I have also found comfort in Hebrews 4:14–16:

> Therefore, since we have a great high priest who has gone through the heavens, Jesus the Son of God, let us hold firmly to the faith we profess. For we do not have a high priest who is unable to sympathize with our weaknesses, but we have one who has been tempted in every way, just as we are—yet was without sin. Let us then approach the throne of grace with confidence, so that we may receive mercy and find grace to help us in our time of need.

At eighty-three, I believe this powerful poem captures my feelings. It was written by my friend, Robertson McQuilkin, President Emeritus of Columbia Bible College, Columbia, South Carolina:

Let Me Get Home Before Dark
It's sundown, Lord.
The shadows of my life stretch back
   into the dimness of the years long spent.
I fear not death, for that grim foe betrays himself at last,
   thrusting me forever into life:
Life with you, unsoiled and free.

But I do fear.
I fear the Dark Spectre may come too soon—
   or do I mean, too late?
That I should end before I finish or
   finish, but not well.
That I should stain your honor, shame your name,
   grieve your loving heart.
Few, they tell me, finish well . . .
Lord, let me get home before dark.

The darkness of a spirit
   grown mean and small, fruit shriveled on the vine,
   bitter to the taste of my companions,
   burden to be borne by those brave few who love me still.
No, Lord. Let the fruit grow lush and sweet,
   A joy to all who taste;
Spirit-sign of God at work,
   stronger, fuller, brighter at the end.
Lord, let me get home before dark.

The darkness of tattered gifts,
   rust-locked, half-spent, or ill-spent,
A life that once was used of God
   now set aside.
Grief for glories gone or

331

If I Could Live My Life Over Again

Fretting for a task God never gave.
Mourning in the hollow chambers of memory,
Gazing on the faded burners of victories long gone.
Cannot I run well unto the end?
Lord, let me get home before dark.

The outer me decays—
    I do not fret or ask reprieve.
The ebbing strength but weans me from mother earth
    and grows me up for heaven.
I do not cling to shadows cast by immortality.
I do not patch the scaffold lent to build the real, eternal me.
I do not clutch about me my cocoon,
    vainly struggling to hold hostage
    a free spirit pressing to be born.

But will I reach the gate
    in lingering pain, body distorted, grotesque?
Or will it be a mind
    wandering untethered among light phantasies or
    grim terrors?
Of your grace, Father, I humbly ask . . .
Let me get home before dark.
                —Robertson McQuilkin–1981
                Columbia Bible College

(Author's Note: All proceeds from the sale of this book will be donated to the Lord's work.)